La Lucha Continues

La Lucha **Continues**
Mujerista Theology

Ada María Isasi-Díaz

ORBIS BOOKS
Maryknoll, New York 10545

Founded in 1970, Orbis Books endeavors to publish works that enlighten the mind, nourish the spirit, and challenge the conscience. The publishing arm of the Maryknoll Fathers and Brothers, Orbis seeks to explore the global dimensions of the Christian faith and mission, to invite dialogue with diverse cultures and religious traditions, and to serve the cause of reconciliation and peace. The books published reflect the views of their authors and do not represent the official position of the Maryknoll Society. To learn more about Maryknoll and Orbis Books, please visit our website at www.maryknoll.org.

Library of Congress Cataloging-in-Publication Data

Isasi-Díaz, Ada María.
    La lucha continues : mujerista theology / Ada María Isasi-Díaz.
        p.   cm.
    Includes index.
    ISBN 1-57075-557-4 (pbk.)
    1. Mujerista theology.   I. Title.
    BT83.5831I83 2004
    230' .082—dc22

                                                           2004006505

For Nina

Contents

Preface

This book, *La Lucha Continues: Mujerista Theology*, the second volume of my essays, is in an attempt to present the theo-ethical elaborations that have occupied me for the last nine years. As was true in the first volume, *Mujerista Theology: A Theology for the Twenty-First Century*, my goal is to make women and men theologians, the churches, and society at large take note of the religious understandings and practices that are intrinsic elements of the struggles for survival and liberation of Hispanas/Latinas in the USA.

An ongoing difficult task for me is to find ways to straddle the academy and the world of grassroot Hispanas/Latinas. My work in the academy—teaching, research, writing—and my work with grassroot Hispanas/Latinas—participating in liturgies and meetings, asking questions about God and meeting everyday obstacles—are very much of one piece. For me it is not a matter of applying what I learn in one of these worlds to the other. I engage in both of them consciously from a liberation perspective. My goal has always been and continues to be to help bring about justice for Hispanas/Latinas, for our communities, and for all oppressed people.

Valuable to me beyond measure in my life and work are those people who have been willing to engage my theo-ethical work. In my earlier books there appear the names of those who have encouraged me, have challenged me, have talked to me and with me at length about their own theo-ethical understandings. Those lists have grown longer and longer and, nine years after the last one, I find it impossible to include a record here that would not tax the reader unduly. So, except for a few names that I simply cannot omit, this time around I am giving the readers a sense of who my dialogue partners are by naming categories of people.

Time and again I have said what I now repeat: first and foremost I thank the grassroot Hispanas/Latinas who continue to teach me so much about their religious beliefs. I pray that my gratitude shows in my attempts to be faithful to what they have shared with me. I am grateful to my colleagues at Drew University. Though often we complain about the lack of time we have to talk to each other about our work, I continue to learn much from them. I particularly want to thank Otto Maduro, my brother in the struggle at Drew, who conspires with me to open doors for Hispanic/Latina and Latino students, thus assuring our work a bright future. I am grateful to my students who have given me valuable theo-ethical insights. I am proud to have been a co-learner with them. Particularly I thank Michael Humphreys, my research assistant at Drew, and Nikki Coffey Tousley, my research assistant at University of Dayton where I was a visiting professor for a semester while I worked on this book. There are many women theologians, and a few men theologians, with whom I dialogue through their written work and in our gatherings at meetings and conferences. I am particularly grateful to the women who have participated with me in a project funded by The Sister Fund where we struggled to learn how to write in a way that will reach a wider public.

Another thank you that I must repeat here goes to my immediate family now numbering more than fifty. Their untiring personal support, believing in me even when they are not too sure they agree with me, is something I cannot do without. I want to include here Cristina García-Alfonso, a Cuban friend, a Ph.D. candidate in Hebrew Scriptures at Brite Divinity School, who, though not a blood relative, is family to me all the same. *Muchas gracias.*

Ann Pat Ware continues to edit all my work written in English and I am most grateful to her for the work she does and, more importantly, for being my friend. Thank you likewise to Susan Perry, senior editor of Orbis Books, for again saying yes to working with me, for welcoming this project and helping me bring it to completion.

Finally, my greatest debt of gratitude for the present work is to Nina Torres-Vidal, to whom I dedicate this book. She has been my main interlocutor for the past four years. Every idea elaborated here I have discussed with Nina, professor of Language and Hispanic Literatures at the Department of Humanities in the Universidad del Sagrado Corazón in San Juan, Puerto Rico. I have profited enormously from her inquisitiveness, insights, and her insistence on precision of thought and language. It has been an immense joy to learn with you, Nina, and for your help, playfulness, and love I am most grateful.

Acknowledgments

The following essays have been previously published, however in a somewhat different form than they appear here. All have been edited and the arguments in some have been extended or deepened.

"*La Lucha:* My Story" appeared in *Transforming the Faiths of Our Fathers: The Women Who Changed American Religion*, edited bu Ann Braude and published by Palgrave Macmillan in 2004.

"Spirituality of the Picket Line: A Reflection" appeared as "Mystical Experiences While Walking a Picket Line" in *The Way: Supplement, 2001* as "Participation in the Divine: With God on a Picket Line."

"Communion through Words: A Sermon" is an edited translation of "La Palabra: Comunicación como Comunión," which appeared in *El Camino a Emaús: Compartiendo el Ministerio de Jesús*, edited by Ada María Isasi-Díaz, Timoteo Matovina, and Nina Torres-Vidal and was published by Fortress Press in 2002.

"Creating a Liberating Culture: Hispanas/Latinas' Subversive Narratives" appeared as "Creating a Liberating Culture, Latinas' Subversive Narratives" in *Converging on Culture: Theologians in Dialogue with Cultural Analysis and Criticism*, edited by Delwin Brown et al. and published by Oxford University Press in 2001.

"Re-Conceptualizing Difference: A New *Mestizaje-Mulatez*" appeared with a similar title in *A Dream Unfinished: Theological Reflections on America from the Margins*, edited by Eleazar Fernandez and Fernando Segovia and published by Orbis Books in 2001.

"*Lo Cotidiano:* Everyday Struggles in Hispanas/Latinas' Lives" was published under the title "*Lo Cotidiano:* A Key Element of *Mujerista* Theology" in the *Journal of Hispanic/Latino Theology* 10:2 (August, 2002).

"In a Time Such as This: 9/11/01" appeared in *Strike Terror No More*, edited by Jon Bergquist and published by Chalice Press in 2002.

"La Habana: The City That Inhabits Me: A Multi-Site Understanding of Location" appeared in *Spirit in the Cities: Searching for Soul in the Urban Landscape*, edited by Kathryn Tanner (Minneapolis: Fortress Press, 2004).

"*Burlando al Opresor*: Mocking/Tricking the Oppressor: Hispanas/Latinas' Dreams and Hopes" appeared in *Theological Studies* 65:2 (June 2004)

A longer version of "Reconciliation: An Intrinsic Element of Justice" applied specifically to Cuba was published under the title "Reconciliation: A Religious, Social and Civic Virtue" in the *Journal of Hispanic/Latino Theology* 8:4 (May, 2001).

"*Identifícate con Nosotras:* A *Mujerista* Christological Understanding" appeared as "Christ in *Mujerista* Theology" in *Thinking of Christ: Proclamation, Explanation, Meaning*, edited by Tatha Wiley and published by Continuum in 2003.

Introduction

Why? Why continue to insist on the importance of the religious understandings and practices of grassroot Hispanas/Latinas? Why continue to use these understandings in the elaboration of *mujerista* theology? Why continue to see our theological elaborations as a praxis of liberation even when "liberation" has stopped being fashionable? Why? Because justice is a constitutive element of the Gospel message. Because without the participation of those who suffer injustice in the institutions, norms, and practices that affect our lives, justice will not be accomplished. And because the struggle for liberation is our way of contributing to the unfolding of the kin-dom[1] of God in our world—an essential mission for all Christians.

None of these ideas are new in *mujerista* theology. They are the same ones that have always motivated me and have framed my pastoral and theological work. However, at the beginning of the twenty-first century with the repeatedly announced but not as yet accomplished demise of liberation struggles, it seems important to re-state these understandings adamantly, stubbornly. In spite of rumblings that *mujerista* theology has accomplished little and should be put to rest for good, there is no doubt that it has contributed in a positive way to the lives of Hispanas/Latinas—and I can indeed provide names and addresses! In addition to the bettering of individual lives, *mujerista* theology also has contributed valuable insights to other liberation theologies and has brought to light, as well, new understandings about the divine derived from the religious beliefs and practices of Hispanas/Latinas. This theological enterprise, grounded in the perspective of Hispanas/Latinas in the USA but not valid and important exclusively for us, works to provide a platform for oppressed and marginalized Hispanas/Latinas. *Mujerista* theol-

1

ogy knows that their cries of protest and resistance can move us all to stand firm against injustice and work to bring about a world from which no one is excluded.

Mujerista theology works to contribute, in the name of Hispana/Latina communities and for the sake of all the poor and the oppressed, to the ethical norms that guide society and its future. Our hope has always been to help build open and flexible relationships among all persons and between persons and institutions. These new dialogic, non-competitive relationships provide a firm foundation to create the kind of society we want, one that promotes the welfare of all, with a particular focus on those who are most vulnerable.[2] Only on the basis of such a society can we hope for a truly democratic political regime with institutions and practices that enable the full participation of all its members, a society that leaves no one behind and that carefully guards against a few of its citizens flourishing at the expense of whole other sectors.

How does *mujerista* theology contribute to such a society, to this kind of *proyecto histórico* (historical project), to this utopian vision? First of all, in *mujerista* theology utopia does not function to define social structures but rather to indicate theo-ethical understandings, values, norms, and virtues based on the religious beliefs and practices of grassroot Hispanas/Latinas who struggle for liberation in the USA. Hispanas/Latinas' *proyecto histórico* does not offer details for a political, economic or social model but rather a vision of what should/could be that is "sufficiently concrete to provide a guide for action and to elicit a commitment."[3] The *proyecto histórico* to which we seek to contribute is one that challenges present systems considered by the rich and powerful as ultimate, fundamental, permanent. What we seek to do is to insist on alternatives, on possibilities that are open to the unimaginable. We dream of a world beyond the limitations of the present, beyond those restrictions named "true universals." *Mujerista* theology seeks to contribute to the elaboration of "reality-based universals" open to differences and diversity, seeking to include instead of excluding, reconciling instead of establishing hegemonic understandings that promote the privileges of the few at the expense of the many. The reality-based universals to which we seek to contribute are made up of "situated universals," which start with the concrete reality of *lo cotidiano* and not with abstract understandings of the truth or the application of true universals to a particular situation.[4]

Reality-based universals, situated universals give us a firm basis for action and concretize our *proyecto histórico*. Our *proyecto histórico*, based on our daily struggle to survive and to live fully, is an action, a practice of resistance. Our reality-based universals lead us to understand that instead of attempting to bring about large changes, what we must insist on are small structural changes, changes taking places at many levels and in many places, changes that will make a difference someday precisely because they take into consideration the personal, the specific, the local. We are bent on changes that set processes in motion and do not seek "true solutions" because these seem to ignore particularity, diversity and differences. Our struggles give priority to what is needed and useful, to effectiveness on a small scale, at the level of everyday reality. We give priority to creating relationship instead of insisting on changing bureaucratic set-ups that will continue to ignore the personal.[5] Likewise in our theological enterprise, we attempt to bring about fullness of life, committed as we are to hope for and to be open to the irruption of the divine in our everyday lives. *Mujerista* theology advocates and tries to live an on-going process of conversion that focuses on the need to bring radical change in those everyday, violent, and exploitative practices that oppress and marginalize us.

Mujerista theology seeks to contribute to a liberating *proyecto histórico* by providing insights and understandings regarding norms, values, virtues, and understandings of the divine that are life-giving instead of silencing the cries of the poor. However, we also focus on Hispanas/Latinas as subjects of our own history, as moral agents who have much to contribute and who want to participate actively in bringing about justice for all. At the beginning of the twenty-first century the struggle to survive as moral agents fashioning our own history is ferocious, for we battle understandings that displace persons from the heart of reality and make capitalism and militarism—the market and weapons—the center of reality. Living in a society that continues to promulgate the myth that anyone willing to work hard can "make it," Hispanas/Latinas have to be adamant about developing and sustaining dreams and hopes that are not acceptable as part of the present "American dream." To do this we have to take responsibility for bringing about change in our lives and in our communities. To be subjects of our own history means that we cannot wait for others to better our lives. Only those solutions achieved by the sweat of our brows, by the work of our hands, and with the convictions that our hopes and dreams give us are acceptable. Living in the richest and most powerful nation in the world makes us all the more prone to look for an individualistic way out of oppressive structures. The temptation to do all in our power to participate in privileged structures, even when it means acting at the expense of our own people, makes our struggle for liberation all the more difficult.

Mujerista theology insistence that grassroot Hispanas/Latinas are organic theologians perfectly capable of explaining their religious beliefs and the role these play in their daily struggles is a way of rescuing our thinking, imagination, and consciences from the hands of the dominant culture. Our religious beliefs and practices challenge the rationality of modernity that has so miserably failed the poor and the oppressed. They also challenge the non-rationality of post-modern thought that, though centered on the singularity of each person, proposes an individualism beneficial only to the rich and powerful. The non-rationality of individualism is countered by the acknowledgment of human sociality. It is the need for community and the recognition of common interests that moves us to true solidarity. It is precisely Hispanas/Latinas' commitment to family and community that makes hope flourish. However, to maintain the hope so essential to our *proyecto histórico*, we need to insist on a critical conscience not only about our reality but also about ourselves. "We are not subjects of a reality that is apart from ourselves, reality which is at the same time object of our actions. We are both cause and effect of such a world. . . . Therefore, there are no objective changes without a radical transformation of the political subject. There is no change of the political subject without action that radically transforms reality."[6] This is what *mujerista* theology embraces as its mission when it claims to be a liberative praxis: we seek to transform ourselves as Hispanas/Latinas by taking responsibility for our reality, by seeking to transform it so we can live fully.[7]

The essays in this book, then, are simply links in the elaboration of a *mujerista proyecto histórico* that seeks to transform oppressive reality by sustaining and enabling Hispanas/Latinas' struggle to survive and live fully at the beginning of the twenty-first century in the USA. Honoring our belief that we need to be accountable for our subjectivity, for our hermeneutics, and for demonstrating how our stories and practices intersect with other persons and with societal forces, the first part of this book has three essays that inform the reader about life-experiences that have influenced my worldview. I do not think my life-experiences and my worldview are exceptional or radically different from those of other Hispanas/Latinas. These beginning essays open the door not only to my world but to the world of many other Hispanas/Latinas and provide for the reader a different view into the reality that the rest of the book seeks to explicate.

The second part of the book consists of nine essays that articulate a variety of *mujerista* ethical-theological understandings pertinent to our vision for a just future. They draw from a variety of sources: theology, ethics, literature, philosophy, epistemology, sociology. In each there are methodological understandings that insist on the importance of process, on the fact that how we do what we do influences and even delineates in specific ways the content of our theo-ethical enterprise.

All of the essays are directed first and foremost to Hispanas/Latinas. They are an attempt to give back to Hispanas/Latinas and to our communities what I have heard and learned from them. By sharing with Hispanas/Latinas the information they have given me I seek to enunciate a liberating mystique that will enable us to face our daily struggles and provide us with a sense of community to sustain us in situations we are not capable of facing alone. This book is also directed to other oppressed and marginalized groups in gratitude for what we have learned from them and in the hope that our perspectives and understandings will benefit them in their struggles. In this sense *mujerista* theology is a praxis of solidarity with other communities of struggle, for we are convinced that unless we build common understandings and practices among those of us who are marginalized, our communities will continue to be denied access to what they need for fullness of life.

This book is also directed to the academy at large, to theologians and ethicists who are committed to base their truth-claims in a reality that excludes no one. It is our contention as *mujerista* theologians and ethicists that theology and ethics need "to transcend the possibility of methodological alienation" by always expanding their "interpretative horizons."[8] This means that all theo-ethical enterprise has to be in dialogue with as many other theo-ethical perspectives and understandings as possible and always acting with theoretical and methodological rigor. For us, from a liberation perspective, this dialogue has to privilege the voices of the poor and the oppressed. Further, this dialogue has to be a praxis in which theory and practice are inexorably linked. Theology, therefore, is not something we read, study or write but an enterprise: liberative doing, liberative action.

This book is an attempt as well to talk to the official church, that is, to church officials in charge of ecclesiastical structures and practices. It presents to them for their serious consideration the religious understandings and practices of Hispanas/Latinas that are part of the on-going revelation of God in our world today. Hispanas/Latinas, who constitute numerically a significant part of the Christian community in the USA, are indeed an important element of the people of God. Yet our religious beliefs and practices are not known and our communities receive little pastoral attention. It is our hope that the elaborations of *mujerista* theology will reach the clergy in our churches, enlightening them about what Hispanas/Latinas need and want from our churches, what we wish to contribute, and how we want to contribute it so we can indeed feel at home in our churches.

Finally, this book is addressed to society at large. *Mujerista* theology is grounded in Hispanas/Latinas' reality and it seeks to bring about radical change in society that will allow us to free ourselves of oppressive understandings and structures. We cannot overemphasize that *mujerista* theology is a liberation praxis from the perspective of Hispanas/Latinas but not exclusively for us. Our *proyecto histórico* is all-inclusive, seeking to transform society and its institutions, including the churches. The space in which *mujerista* theology seeks to play an effective role is that in which Hispanas/Latinas move: the USA society. Our task continues to be a theo-ethical one but because we believe that all history is history of salvation, our theo-ethical scenario is history too. In this effort we contribute a history from the past re-interpreted from the perspective of the vanquished, and a history of the future into which we project ourselves as responsible subjects, as Hispanas/Latinas not afraid to struggle for liberation, for fullness of life.

Notes

[1] The use of kin-dom instead kingdom or reign stems from the desire to use a metaphor that is much more relevant to our world today. From the perspective of *mujerista* theology, the point of reference for kin-dom of God is the concept of family and community that is central to Latina culture. There is also a need to move away from "kingdom" and "reign" because they are sexist and hierarchical metaphors.

[2] Though I do not endorse a functionalist approach to society in which social groups are understood as functioning harmoniously, neither do I want to use a dialectical model of society. This is one in which conflict is not only recognized where it exists—between the different social groups—but is also seen as a necessary element that needs to be purposefully exacerbated in order to be able to bring about change. Instead of a dialectical understanding of society I prefer to use a dialogical understanding of society in which differences—including contradictions—among social groups are recognized but which also recognizes the possibility of resolving contradictions by engaging in dialogue. Dialogue in my view moves social groups to understandings, positions, and situations that emerge from the sharing of different perspectives and from compromises that recognize the limitedness of all human enterprise. In a dialogic understanding of society and in a dialogic process, partial solutions are embraced that emerge from the historical reality in which we are involved, which privilege the understanding of the poor and the oppressed, and opt always to protect the most vulnerable. Instead of heightening contradictions, dialogic understandings and practices work towards reconciliation, an on-going process of inclusivity that moves us toward justice for all.

[3] José Míguez Bonino, *Toward a Christian Political Ethics* (Philadelphia: Fortress Press, 1983), 52.

⁴ See Yamandú Acosta, "Tareas de reconstrucción para la filosofía latinoamericana," *Pasos* 69 (enero-febrero, 1997); Hugo Assmann, "Teología de la liberación: mirando hacia el frente," *Pasos* 55 (septiembre-octubre, 1994); Mario C. Casalla, "El Cuarteto de Jerusalén," in *Márgenes de la Justicia* (Buenos Aires: Grupo Editor Altamira, 2000), 238 and 262 (footnote 11).

⁵ Veronika Bennholdt-Thomsen, "What Really Keeps Our Cities Alive, Money or Subsistence?" in *There Is an Alternative: Subsistence and Worldwide Resistance to Corporate Globalization*, ed. Veronika Bennholdt-Thomsen, Nicholas G. Faraclas, and Claudia von Werlhof (London: Zed Books, Ltd, 2001), 223–224.

⁶ Frei Betto, "Vigencia de las utopías en América latina (educación popular, pedagógica y política)," *Pasos* 55 (septiembre-octubre, 1994), 14.

⁷ See Fernando Torres Millán, "Educación popular y teología de la liberación: juntando caminos," *Pasos* 62 (noviembre-diciembre, 1995); Juan-José Tamayo-Acosta, "Sujeto, comunidad y utopía," *Pasos* 84 (julio-agosto, 1999); Isabel Rauber, "Perfiles de una nueva utopía," *Pasos* 72 (julio-agosto, 1997).

⁸ John O'Brien, *Theology and the Option for the Poor* (Collegeville, Minn.: Liturgical Press, 1992), 152–153.

Part I

THE PERSONAL IS POLITICAL

1

La Lucha

My Story

I was born a feminist Thanksgiving weekend 1975 at the first Women's Ordination Conference (WOC). I was at the time living in Rochester, New York, and had driven with a group of women to Detroit. A friend in charge of religious education for the diocese knew about the conference and insisted I should go. After nine months as a salesperson at Sears, I had recently started to work part time in an inner city parish while beginning my studies on a Master's in medieval history. I had no money to travel to Detroit, stay in a hotel and pay the conference registration fee. "Several of us are going by car so you can just come with us," answered Denise Mack. "And, you can stay in our room. Don't worry about it." Regarding the registration fee, she said she would talk with Lyn Sommers, another Rochester woman who was responsible for organizing small discussion groups for the conference. Lyn called me. "I need one more facilitator for the small groups," she said. If I could do that task, the conference fee would be waived. "Sign me on," I said, with a sense that there was no way of avoiding this conference.

Friday after Thanksgiving, hours before the sun rose, my brother-in-law drove me to the group's gathering point. We started the long drive to Detroit. Little did I know, as I sat in the back seat of the car on that cold November morning, that this conference would influence radically my worldview and give direction to my life for the rest of my days.

The sense of excitement and possibility that filled the hallways of the hotel where the conference participants gathered was incredible. The process that had been designed for the conference remains one of the best I have experienced. In the small groups in which we gathered after the plenary sessions the participants discussed the issues presented and began to organize themselves for action. Given what we had heard and what we were discussing, what did each of us want to do? Little by little the small groups dissolved as people moved to all sorts of caucuses being formed according to the interests of the conference participants. The small group I facilitated carried out this assignment conscientiously and after the second plenary session the group had dissolved. I was jobless, but not for long!

My conference name tag identified me as a facilitator and during one of the breaks, as I stood in a hallway drinking a cup of coffee, a tall imposing woman asked me in quite an abrupt manner, "Where is your group?" Learning that my group had already dissolved, she thrust papers and markers into my arms and said while rushing on, "Then come and help me." Marjorie Tuite, a nun well-known because of her work against racism, was facilitating a caucus formed to consider establishing an organization on the issue of women's ordination in the Catholic Church and she needed someone to take notes. I followed her without saying a word, fascinated by the energy she exuded. During the next hour I was to have the most intense lesson of my life in group dynamics.

Never losing sight of the task at hand, Marjorie allowed everyone to speak. Her no-nonsense attitude invited people to think before they spoke. The meeting moved along at an incredible pace. She was constantly summing up where we were as I did all I could to write down every step we took. When the meeting was over, she briefly checked what I had written, told me to whom to give the notes, and left the room to solve some problem that had come up with the dynamics of the conference. Later, at the last plenary session, the assembly was asked to consider the resolution from our caucus. I felt a certain awe when I heard read the words I had written.

My birth as a feminist took place at the ending ritual of the conference. When those who believed themselves called to ordination were asked to identify themselves, I knew I had to be honest and stand. However, a battle was raging within me. I felt caught between a sense of vocation—what I wanted to do with my life—and a sudden awareness of the intense struggle that lay ahead. I turned to Mary Walden, an Ursuline sister whom I had met fifteen years earlier only three days after arriving in the USA as a refugee from Cuba. In tears I said, "Mary, I do not want to stand. I am tired of battles." She smiled at me reassuringly. Then I felt myself rising to my feet, almost forced by the belief that I was called to be ordained. I was among the last ones to stand. When I looked around I found myself surrounded by a "cloud of witnesses." In this battle, at least I would not be alone. After a few seconds I sat down thinking, I have been born, baptized and confirmed in this new life all at once! As I left the assembly I signed a paper indicating my interest in working on the ordination of women in the Roman Catholic Church.

Back home working in an inner city parish and studying at the university kept me very busy. A few months went by. One day the phone rang and it was Rosalie Muschal-Reinhardt, a member of the task force that had organized that first Women's Ordination Conference. "You signed the list of those interested in forming an ongoing organization and I am calling because we are doing just that," she said. The first meeting was going to be at Rosary College (now Dominican College) outside Chicago, and once again I simply did not have money for an airline ticket. "We have vowed," said Rosalie with her characteristic passion, "we will not meet again without women of color participating." I was to save the date, she insisted, and she somehow would find the money to pay for my ticket. She did and I became involved as a volunteer for several years and eventually worked as paid staff for WOC. It was in the women's movement in the Catholic Church that I began to learn about gender oppression. The Catholic Church with its oppression of women turned me into a feminist!

In the 1960s I had been a missionary in Lima, Peru, and there the poor had taught me the real meaning of religion. They taught me that if religious beliefs are not the basis for the struggle for liberation, they can indeed become the "opium of the people." They taught me that God stands with the poor and that liberation and salvation are inseparable, that "poverty is a slap in God's face." In 1970 when I left the convent and came back to the USA, I had the sense that I was starting life anew. Those were difficult years, for, despite the love and support of my family, I simply did not feel at home in the USA and I did not know what to do with my life. I knew that leaving the convent did not absolve me from my vocation to ministry — re-defined by my experience in Peru as ministry with and for the poor. Every week I would read the *National Catholic Reporter*, a liberal Catholic newspaper, looking for clues as to how I could get involved in the church. As I read news of the church in the USA, nothing seemed important to me, nothing seemed to resonate with me. One day I stopped to read a small announcement that I had noticed ran every week. It talked about the Deaconess Movement: write, it said, and they would send a newsletter. After I saw it three or four times, I am not sure why I did it but I responded. Soon I received a homemade newsletter written by Mary B. Lynch, a Roman Catholic laywoman. Years later I learned she was the one who called together in Chicago a group of women who organized that first Women's Ordination Conference in Detroit. I found the newsletter interesting but it did not touch what then was at the heart of my personal struggle: looking for ways to get involved in stopping poverty and the exploitation of Latin America by the USA.

During 1976, the first year of my life as a feminist, I worked hard at educating myself. Though I knew next to nothing about feminism and gender analysis, I understood early on that I could apply the same processes and categories of analysis I had used to learn about poverty and its relationship to the Gospel message to the oppression of women. There was not much available to read, but I have always learned best from experience. I began to wear my new-found gender-analysis lens all the time! Soon a group of us started to meet locally to see what we could do to move the church in Rochester to deal with the issue of women's ordination. Local and national involvement provided me with a community of women with whom I could learn. Many of them were veterans of the social movements of the 1960s. In Lima I had been thoroughly involved in advocating for the poor with civil authorities and in church circles. As I heard other women draw from their experiences in previous social movements, I could parallel their moves and draw from my own experiences in Lima. During this process of learning I led with my heart: I kept in mind at all times the commitment I had made when I stood at the closing ritual of the Detroit conference for women's full participation in the church. Group reflection and reading began to provide me with the intellectual tools I needed to see the connections between poverty and sexism. My vision became clearer but my world became more complicated as the days went on. Soon I could sing with full conviction, "I wish my eyes had never been opened."

Much of the work we did in those early years of WOC fell into three categories. First of all we were hard at work creating an organization, trying desperately to expand our membership, to create an economic base for our work, and to set up procedures for communication and decision-making that followed feminist understandings of group process. As part of the WOC office team my job was to expand our membership and work with local WOC groups. Second, we also did all we could to keep the issue alive publicly. The fact is that both the secular and the religious press were kind to us in those early days of the movement. We worked hard to provide all the background they needed on the issue of women and the church and to accommodate their requests to the best of our ability. Many of the reporters we worked with let us know they were sympathetic to our cause and did all they could to keep our issue in the public eye. For example, when John Paul I died a few weeks after being elected pope, one of the main television networks decided that instead of rehashing the church's procedure for electing a pope they would look at issues facing the church. WOC was contacted and I was selected to be the one interviewed on a popular morning show, "Good Morning America." I learned much from this experience and was happy to have played a role in having our message reach millions. Soon surveys were saying that over 60 per cent of Roman Catholics wanted women to be ordained.

The third area of our work, which undoubtedly caused us the most frustration, was dealing with the Roman Catholic bishops. Some of them were convinced that women should be priests but they did little to move the issue within church structures. With the help of Bishop Charles Buswell we were able to pursue a two-year dialogue with the bishops' committee that dealt with women's issues. I was one of the WOC dialoguers during that process and learned much about church politics.

One night I was in the elevator with a bishop involved in the process. We considered him a friend and yet I sensed that he did not understand our arguments. As the door of the elevator closed I said to him, "Why do you not understand what we are saying?" With a pained expression he said to me, "Ada, don't you see that if I understood I could not remain a bishop in this church?" I wanted so much to ask him why he wanted to be a bishop if that meant compromising the truth. It was a crude awakening for me to realize that truth does not always carry the day, that knowing does not necessarily lead to action. The dialogue with the bishops taught me much about the insidiousness of power and the need for power to be re-conceptualized as a capacity to bring about justice instead of being a tool to control and dominate. I believe we need to understand that power belongs to the community, to those invested in the organization or institution in question and not solely to its leaders. Leaders must understand that they are only given the opportunity to exercise power by the community and for the good of the community and that, therefore, they have to be accountable to the community. Unless power is understood this way, it will continue to be used to oppress instead of to liberate. The re-conceptualization of power is a task that feminist theory, feminist theology, feminist sociology, and feminist organizations have not focused on sufficiently. Until we do, we will continue to undermine the work we do on behalf of justice for women.

I have never known how to proceed in life without seeing what I do as either a way of surviving (like washing dishes or working at Sears as a salesperson when I could find no other jobs) or as part of my vocation in life. I was not surprised, therefore, that I began to find work on the issue of women's ordination, which I soon saw as but one way of working against sexism, as part of my vocation. The experience of a woman involved in WOC in the early days helped me realize this. She called one day and said that she needed a break; she felt burned out. What she said impacted me greatly: the fact is that it scared me out of my wits! For weeks I chided myself for perhaps not taking the issue seriously enough, for I certainly did not feel anywhere near exhaustion. On the other hand, I did not want to become so drained that I had to step away from my commitment to the women's movement. I had gotten involved thinking that women would get ordained within a decade or so and then I could once again concentrate on working with the poor. But what if involvement in this issue left me psychologically spent?

One day, as I drove home from work in the middle of a snow-storm, three things became clear for me. First of all, I realized that sexism was a category of oppression and that it did not exist apart from poverty but compounded it and vice-versa. (Soon, together with Rosalie Muschal-Reinhardt and Marjorie Tuite we designed a visual to explain the interconnections of sexism, racism/ethnic prejudice, and classism.) Second, as I slowly inched ahead on slippery roads, I could hear my mother saying the words with which she always ended her letters to me: as long as God gives us the energy we need for the struggle, we will be all right. Mamá has always insisted we should not ask God to free us from struggling but rather we should thank God we have something to struggle for. What we need to do is ask God to give us *fuerzas para la lucha*, strength for the struggle. (Years later I would work on developing *la lucha* as a category of social analysis and as a theo-ethical category.) Third, the snow-covered windshield of my car became like a movie screen where I could see my next-door neighbor in Lima, a woman who lived in extreme poverty yet never lost her sense of dignity and purpose of life. I remember the steadiness of her struggle: day after day she dealt with the reality of the present and survived that day in order to be able to face the next. (That reflection has led me to develop the category of *lo cotidiano* as the main site for strug-gle, as the site that reveals oppression at the same time it illu-mines the preferred future.) What I realized that day I came to understand more and more as I discussed it with my women friends in Rochester. From that day forward I have never been scared of burning out, often singing to myself, "I ain't no ways tired. I've come too far from where I started from. Nobody told me the road would be easy." And, as to burning up, that is what life is all about, isn't it? For me life is about being passionate for justice! That is what fulfills me; that is what gives me energy and creativity.

In 1976, to celebrate the bi-centennial of the founding of the USA, the Catholic bishops organized a consultation process to define the main issues that the church needed to address in the years ahead. The process finished with a conference in Detroit. Initially Women's Ordination Conference was not invited but several of the leaders of the organization pressed for inclusion and eventually we were allowed to participate. Our work at this conference, called "Call to Action," was the first public action of WOC as an organization. We worked hard to be a positive presence at that meeting. For me personally, "Call to Action" was very important, for there I met Yolanda Tarango, a Chicana nun from El Paso, Texas. After the Catholic Bishops' Conference I asked her repeatedly to join WOC. Yolanda was not eager to do so, and little by little I learned the reason. At the end of the WOC conference the year before two women had read an important statement to the whole assembly. María Iglesias, a nun from New York City who was at the time national coordinator of LAS HERMANAS (a Hispanas/Latinas Catholic organization), and Shawn Copeland, then president of the National Black Sisters Conference, had spoken to the largely white women's assembly. Shawn had warned conference participants not to re-build the walls of Jericho to keep black and Hispanas/Latinas out once white women made it into the priesthood, "One of the other parts to the story of Joshua is that after the people took the city of Jericho, Yahweh said to them, 'Never build in this place again a city like this.' So if you go through the walls and you take the city, then don't build the same city again."[1]

With Yolanda's help, I began to analyze and study the issue of racism/ethnic prejudice in the women's movement. In the summer of 1978 Yolanda invited me to participate in the national meeting that brought together Hispanic priests and members of LAS HERMANAS. At that meeting I began to understand the complexities of the ethnic prejudice against Hispanics in the USA, its connection with racism, how ethnic prejudice is present in the women's movement, and the role it plays in oppressive structures. That meeting also made me realize that, given that the vast majority of Hispanas/Latinas in the USA are poor women, working for justice for women in the church could be an effective way of working for justice for women who are poor. I left that meeting with two firm convictions: I needed to listen to grassroot Hispanas/Latinas just as I had learned to listen to the poor in Lima. (Years later Yolanda and I developed a method for doing *mujerista* theology that starts with the voices of grassroot Hispanas/Latinas. Several key theological claims have arisen from this conviction: *mujerista* theology is a liberative praxis; grassroot Hispanas/Latinas are organic theologians for they are admirably capable of explaining their religious understandings and the role religion plays in their daily struggles; the lived-experience of grassroot Hispanas/Latinas is the source of *mujerista* theology.) Second, I needed to begin to bring to the table of WOC and other organizations in which I was participating the voices I was listening to: I needed to voice the perspectives and issues of Hispanas/Latinas.

Many of the women I worked with in WOC, almost exclusively white women, were committed to the struggle against racism. I believe many of them came to understand the particulars of the struggle of Hispanas/Latinas in this society. However, as I began to speak more and more as a Latina from that special perspective and as I attempted to link sexism to racial/ethnic prejudice, I began to become invisible in the movement. Jamie Phelps, an African-American nun active in WOC in those early days, offered me advice time and again. "Girl," she would say, "be careful. They will sideline you as soon as you become too vocal as a Hispanic." How right she was! After five years of being at home in the women's movement struggling for justice in the church, I began to feel alienated. Disagreements regarding priorities, styles of leadership, and strategies, as well as struggles for control of WOC together with my own personal shortcomings created a most difficult situation and I was asked to resign from my job with the organization in which I had been involved for seven years. Extremely distraught by what had happened I spent time analyzing the reasons for it and trying to learn from it. It seems to me that, though we had struggled to wield power in non-oppressive ways, when difficulties arose we fell back into the way we had been treated all of our lives in patriarchal structures: we turned disagreement into confrontation and we wielded power to control and dominate instead of to enable and facilitate. However, though wounded and disillusioned I was not about to turn my back on the struggle for justice for women. That had become part of my vocation in life, of who I am. I simply needed to find new avenues for involvement, new ways of contributing to the liberation of women.

Religion always has been a central part of my life. Religion, in particular Roman Catholicism, is a key element of Latina culture. It is not at all exceptional for me, therefore, to have become aware of gender discrimination through my involvement in the church. Nor is it remarkable that a church issue, the ordination of women to a renewed priestly ministry, provided for me the opportunity to struggle for justice for women. My awareness of how sexism operates in the Catholic Church and how it influences our religious understandings and practices has never created for me a crisis of faith. My religious beliefs, on the contrary, seem to grow stronger. The injustices I have suffered in the church, the many pitfalls it harbors, have led me to a deeper understanding of myself and my vocation in life. Since I was young I have always distanced the divine and my relationship with the divine enough from the church (and now from theology) so that what the church teaches and the way it acts do not scandalize me or disappoint me in any way that affects negatively my faith. At the same time, as a young missionary in Lima, I learned that the church has power and influence in society. Though in the USA the role of the church in society is different and though today that role is not what it was even as recently as the 1980s, I believe that churches still have a powerful moral influence in society. I believe churches have an obligation always to take a prophetic stance: they always have to be on the side of the poor, the oppressed, the exploited, the marginalized, the vulnerable. Furthermore, I believe that justice is a constitutive element of the Gospel message. The Gospel message is intrinsic to my worldview: it is an ongoing source of understanding; it is, most of the time, the backdrop against which I make judgments; it motivates me and sustains me.

While working at WOC I had begun to take courses in the Master of Divinity program at a seminary in Rochester, New York. As I tried to sort out what to do with my life after leaving

WOC, I knew that it would have to be related to the struggle for justice for women from the perspective of religion. I decided I would finish my theological degree and then return to what has always given me greatest joy: working with grassroot Hispanas/Latinas. I knew I had to look beyond Rochester. My willingness to look for new ways of being involved in the struggle for women's liberation in church and society and the commitment to diversity of women theologians like Carter Heyward led me to participate in the project that produced the book *God's Fierce Whimsy.* Then, thanks to the sisterly care of Beverly Harrison and Ardith Hayes, in the spring of 1983 I found temporary employment at Union Theological Seminary in New York, and that fall I started my studies there. Yolanda Tarango and I had been working on gathering the voices of grassroot Hispanas/Latinas for publication, and I intended to use my theological studies to finish this task. Our book, *Hispanic Women: Prophetic Voice in the Church,* was first published in 1988. *Mujerista* theology was born in the many conversations Yolanda Tarango and I had with groups of LAS HERMANAS all around the country. It emerged from the many struggles we had as Hispanas/Latinas with church officials to have our voices heard and taken into consideration. It came from the conviction that we had to speak for ourselves or we would continue to be invisible or, at best, Hispano/Latino men would speak for us.

But the elaboration of *mujerista* theology never would have happened without the community of which I was a part at Union Theological Seminary in the 1980s. Angela Bauer, Elizabeth Bounds, Pamela Brubaker, Katie G. Cannon, Chung Hyun Kyung, Marilyn Legge, Margie Mayman — how much I learned from all these women as we took courses together, spent time reading each other's work and commenting on it, and cried and laughed together! Then there are the women who used their contacts and influence to open roads for me personally and to insist on including *mujerista* theology as one of the theological voices of women that needs to be part of women-centered theologies. Among these women, and there are many, I particularly remember Rosemary Radford Ruether, who referred us to her editor at Harper & Row and helped us to get our first book published. Letty Russell made sure time and again at the American

Academy of Religion and elsewhere that *mujerista* theology was included. Marcia Riggs and Karen McCarthy Brown helped me become a professor at Drew University. For years when I could not find any other Latina at the annual conference of the American Academy of Religion, it was with Katie G. Cannon, Joan Martin, and other womanist theologians that I felt at home. Their struggles to have their own sessions at the AAR were the blueprint I followed to propose establishing a Latina/Latino theology session at the AAR.

Having decided to go on to study for a PhD and to work as an academician I still had to deal with the fact that it is the work I do with grassroot Hispanas/Latinas that is most life-giving to me. It is from them that I draw creativity and strength to continue to struggle for justice. Through the years I have learned the difficult task of straddling both worlds, the academy and the grassroot Latina community. These two areas of involvement have been my mainstay as I have worked to develop *mujerista* theology.

Also during these last twenty years I have been blessed with coming to know and become friends with women from many other parts of the world who under much more demanding circumstances than the ones we Hispanas/Latinas face here in the USA, insist at all times on justice for women. Aruna Gnanadason, Mercy Amba Oduyoye, Elizabeth Tapia, Mary John Mananzan, Ofelia Ortega, Elsa Tamez, Ivone Gebara, Tania Mara Sampaio— these and many other women have taught me that we cannot struggle for justice for women thinking only of our own communities. They have taught me that if we do, some women will benefit at the expense of others, a tragic development given the fact that no one is truly liberated unless we all are liberated. The dictum, "think globally, act locally," is one we need to continue taking to heart as we move ahead in the twenty-first century.

Together with the struggle for justice, friendships and relationships have been central in my life. As a *mujerista* I have come to understand how these two themes are intrinsically linked. Very important to me is the belief that we cannot sustain the struggle for justice for women without a deep sense of commitment to each other as women. There is no possibility of creating just structures in the academy, in the churches, and in society at large if just relationships and solidarity do not inform our lives on a daily basis. At least I can bear witness to how much we can accomplish when we come together as community. I can also bear witness to how destructive we are when we forget about each other or use each other and the movement for our own self-aggrandizement. For me, the struggle for justice for women is part of who I am; it is, therefore, a religious issue. My most profound religious experiences have happened in the midst of *la lucha*; and *la lucha* is what gives meaning and joy to my life. In *la lucha* I find God time and again. Yes, for me *la vida es la lucha:* we must struggle to create community if we are to contribute to making justice for women a reality in our lives and our world.

Notes

1. Anne Marie Gardiner, SSND, *Women and Catholic Priesthood: An Expanded Vision — Proceedings of the Detroit Ordination Conference* (New York: Paulist Press, 1976), 189.

2

The Spirituality of the Picket Line

A Reflection

The shining sun did not warm me.[1] My heavy coat, gloves and winter hat seemed to do little to protect me against the chilly wind. It was a winter day in Washington, D.C., in the early 1980s and I was one of about fifty persons walking a picket line outside the South African Embassy protesting apartheid. I remember that the sign I was carrying, not of my own making, said something about children in South Africa. As we circled around behind the police barrier, I kept thinking about the effectiveness of our action. Economic sanctions seemed to be taking a toll, but we did not really think that the end of apartheid was even a remote possibility.

Adamantly, I kept chanting and walking, chanting and walking, lowering my head to protect my face against the cutting air. Little by little I became aware of an immense peace washing over me. I felt myself to be where I was and in many other places at the same time. I felt I was being cared for by God, that the divine was with me and in me in a way different from my usual experience. This sense of the divine in me and I in the divine was a bodily one: I could feel, sense God, and I could wrap my arms around the divine. I was experiencing the divine in an unmediated way, unmediated by understanding or even faith. The intensity did not last long, and yet this sense of participating in the divine filled me in such a way that it remains with me today. The experience left me with an immense sense of joy beyond anything of my own willing.

Verbal descriptions and explanations do not convey adequately what I experienced. What happened to me that day is beyond human words. Traditionally such events are called "mystical experiences," moments in which one knows that what is happening is taking place in a realm other than the natural one, beyond the day in and day out reality. Finding no adequate way of describing what happened to me in that picket line, I did not talk about it for a long time. Also, having mystical experiences does not fit very well into the concept I have had of myself as an activist. A few years ago, however, when I heard a dear friend, a committed activist, say that she prays best with a picket sign in her hands, I smiled to myself remembering my experience in Washington. What she said helped me see that mystical experiences and struggling for justice do not exclude each other. I can indeed say, "I have mystical experiences with picket signs in my hands!"

Throughout my life I have harbored a deep desire to be "holy," a word I began to use when I was about seven years old and preparing for my First Holy Communion. Of course, what I mean by holy has varied as circumstances in my life have changed, as I have learned new concepts, and as I have grown to understand myself better. Initially I equated being holy with being good, and being good at age seven had to do with pleasing those who loved me. By the time I was thirteen I remember beginning to feel that holiness meant doing for others, always a source of great satisfaction for me. From very early on I wanted to help the poor, and I thought that was a necessary part of telling them about Jesus and his love for them.

Avidly I searched for ways of doing for others. Thinking back to my teenage years I see that though helping others extended beyond the religious field, it certainly included Jesus-talk. Besides, I did not think that what I wanted to do and what God wanted of me were that far apart. Even from my early years I did not think I had to give up what I wanted in order to follow what later I would call "my vocation," or "God's will" for me. Early in my life I began to understand that as a child of God, God guides me from within and God's call is incarnated in others, and I have held on to this belief for dear life!

Never being one to easily embrace what others say without thinking it through for myself, I have always resisted the usual talk about "spirituality," the category in which mysticism usually is placed, for it seems to exalt certain religious practices above others. People who follow devout practices and who are serene, reflective and quiet are perceived as being more holy than others. I experience this as an attempt to create an elite, a separate group to whom special grace is given. It reinforces the perception that some either have received such grace because they are better than the rest or that receiving grace makes them better than the rest. This is why I am not at ease with any "spirituality" that sets up some people as superior to others.[2] I have also resisted even the word "spirituality," for I believe it has been a key tool of dualistic understandings, of the false notion that the soul is a separate entity, or that one can counterpose body and spirit as if the human person could be split in two. My own mystical experience while walking the picket line confirmed a hunch that guided me from the age of seven when I was made fun of by my brothers and sisters for wanting to be holy! To be holy is to be fully immersed in the work for justice; to be holy is to embrace the fact that we are a gift from God to ourselves as well as to others. To be holy is to embrace God in such a way that we can be God's sacrament in the world. Spirituality, therefore, has to do with a reflective life, one in which we take time to be conscious of our motives and of the forces that move us or paralyze us. It has to do with consciously struggling to be our very best selves and helping others do the same. Such a life makes us turn to the radical immanence of God in each of us. True spirituality stops cold the trivialization of life so common today that spurns those who do not contribute to the accumulation of capital by the rich, turning them into "surplus people" who have no value in the grab for power of those who control societies.[3]

I have become even more apprehensive about using the word spirituality because, rightly or wrongly, today in the USA spirituality tends to be associated with "New Age."[4] New Age spirituality seems to be centered on spiritual practices that are not related to the "love your neighbor as yourself," one of the cornerstones of the Gospel message of Jesus. New Age, in my view, promotes practices unconnected with any social consciousness that would make one struggle "actively and deliberately and in very diverse situations against becoming habituated to death."[5] Not wanting to dismiss anything that might be worthwhile exploring, however, I repeatedly have asked practitioners of New Age spirituality what they see as implications of their practices. I remember years ago asking a friend in California how I might present New Age spiritual practices to Latina women in East Harlem who struggle to make ends meet. How could these practices help them in their daily struggle for survival? My friend looked at me squarely and said, "Well, maybe you are right; maybe this kind of spiritual practice has nothing to offer Latinas in East Harlem." Convinced that justice is an intrinsic element of the Gospel message, I asked her, "If these practices are not worthwhile for Latinas, are they really worthwhile for anyone else?"

Nothing is more accurate in conveying what Latinas' spirituality is all about than a *fiesta*, especially *fiestas* in honor of patron saints. An example of this are *fiestas* honoring Our Lady of Guadalupe. This is the name most commonly used in Mexico for Mary, the mother of Jesus. The fact that the parish where I worship in East Harlem has only a small number of parishioners from Mexico does not keep us from celebrating Guadalupe's feast on December 12 with splendor and gusto. On that day I try to get to church early to be with the other parishioners for as long as possible. My own faith is strengthened by the faith of the grassroot people who believe so strongly that the divine is with them and walks with them daily. This belief sustains their daily struggles for survival.

On that festive day the church is blanketed with roses of all colors. I watch the faces of women and men as they kneel, pray, and sing to Guadalupe. With great fervor we all sing, "*Ven con nosotros a caminar, Santa María, ven.*" (Come walk with us, Holy Mary, come.) She who is mother of God, fully human as we are, walks with us. She cares! I relish this kind of spirituality. Here are people considered to be of little or no importance by the powerful of this world who set the standard and who decide what is normative in society. The religious practices of these "minoritized" people enable them to resist the negative feelings society projects on them. Their expressions of deep love and admiration clearly proclaim that they consider themselves Mary's children. They are worthy children of this wondrous mother. It is clear to me as I watch the love and devotion of the people for Mary, Jesus, and the saints that reciprocity is the key to these relationships. While they believe that Jesus and his mother and the saints walk with them, more importantly they know that they in turn are loved and admired by Jesus and Guadalupe! They know how special they are to Jesus and Mary! Living in a society that does not value them, their conviction that Guadalupe and her divine son love them satisfies the need we all have to be precious for someone. Just as we are giving ourselves to Jesus and Mary, they are giving themselves to us without reserve. This is all that these grassroot folk need to know. This is what gives us strength to carry on in very difficult circumstances.[6]

True spirituality has to do with living a reflective life, knowing that we are guided by God from within, that we are loved and admired by God. This God who falls in love with us over and over again, as is true of all lovers, waits for us to reciprocate. Spirituality has to do with who we are and how we live, with one's personality, character, motives, dispositions, attitudes, intentions, and even with the way we perceive reality. Spirituality has to do with the persons we always are in the process of becoming. We become our true selves as we choose and act, being responsible by taking into consideration the effects that our actions have not only for ourselves but for the many persons with whom we are connected. Spirituality has to do with the fact that God influences our values and our choices because God is a concrete reality in our lives. We become who we are immersed in the divine. To recognize and live aware of how our lives do not happen apart from the divine — this is the true meaning of spirituality. Just as who we are and how we live are not apart from the divine neither are they apart from our relationship with each other. As Madeleine L'Engle's poem "Epiphany" says, we must unclench our fists, we must hold out our hands, we must take each others' hands. This is the way God is manifested in our world.[7] And if our human relationships manifest God, then our relationship with God depends on our love and care, our concern and struggles for each other. Human relationships are, for me, the road to God. They affect us deeply, calling us to be our best selves, or perhaps hurting us and deflecting us from what we know God wants of us. My own relationship with the divine finds expression in walking picket lines more than in kneeling; in seeking ways to be involved in the work of reconciliation more than in fasting and mortifying the flesh; in striving to be passionately involved with others more than in seeking to be detached from human love. What an aberration to think that detachment from others makes room for God! I believe my relationship with God demands being faithful to who I am and to what I believe rather than following prescriptions for holiness that insist on self-negation. Spirituality is measured by our ability and willingness to immerse ourselves in personal relationships and in struggles for justice. This is the only way we can transcend ourselves.[8]

The social aspect of spirituality was brought home to me in a very special way by a group of men — fathers, sons, brothers, cousins, grandfathers, husbands, and boyfriends — incarcerated by the state. I had the opportunity of spending an evening with them as part of a prison study program. Each of the men in the group spoke of the need to prepare himself to repair the damage he had done before he could return to his community. Each one realizes that they must all struggle to change the circumstances in which their communities live if they and their communities, their sons and daughters, their younger sisters and brothers, are to have a better future. These incarcerated men do not shrink from responsibility for whatever they have done, for they are keenly aware that they are social beings and that they will not change personally unless they can work to bring about radical change in their communities.

The importance of community in understanding spirituality is in constant conflict with the emphasis on individuality that suffuses our world, even suffusing the Christian religion and the religious expressions of Christians.[9] But it is precisely the understanding that spirituality is not an individual, private affair that will resuscitate Christianity, for it will highlight the centrality of the kin-dom of God in the Gospel message of Jesus: all of us are members of God's family. Spirituality is not my relationship with God exclusive of others. Spirituality is our dance with God, but we cannot dance with God alone. To dance with God we have to bring others.[10] True spirituality, a reflective life that helps us embrace the radical immanence of the divine in us, "enables community" and makes it possible for us "to get away from the privatization of joy, happiness, and oneness with God."[11] For our God is a God thoroughly involved with us as we are, humans who inhabit this world, suffused in materiality, struggling to go beyond the limitedness of our humanity to embrace the divinity in which we are called to participate.

Our dance with God,[12] our spirituality, is not something that follows a set path. It is not something that can be taught or learned. As all relationships, our relationship with God is unique, though it has some elements that resemble those of other relationships. But each relationship in our lives is different, wonderfully original, fascinatingly inimitable, distinctive, exceptional, irreplaceable. Traditionally, however, this has not kept those who write about spirituality from identifying and labeling three stages in the journey towards mystical experience: "purification," "illumination," and "union." Dorothee Soelle, following Matthew Fox, reworks these stages, calling them "being amazed," "letting go," and "resistance."[13] I believe that our spirituality, like mystical experiences, also goes through different stages that meld one into the others. I call these stages "falling in love," "nurturing the relationship with the divine," and "full participation in the kin-dom of God."[14]

Our spiritual journey starts with a "falling in love," indeed an amazing experience for us humans, one in which we touch the divine in us in a very special way because we transcend ourselves without renouncing who we are.[15] To fall in love is to connect with someone in a way that fills us with happiness and suffuses us with such joy that we want to run and tell everyone what is happening. To fall in love is to be in touch with oneself in a way that is unrepeatable. It is a coming home to oneself precisely because one has given oneself totally. Falling in love with God is somewhat different from falling in love with humans. First of all, we know the limitedness of our humanity and we know that despite the best intentions, we fail each other. But when it comes to God, we know God will not fail us. This inspires such a trust, it gives us such a firm ground for our lives, that we can indeed enjoy a freedom beyond measure. Furthermore, we know that the object of our love, God, will always love us more, and that God's love will call us and enable us to become our very best selves. Falling in love fills us with enthusiasm, with energy to do, be and become in ways that fulfill us in ways that surpass our wildest dreams. And when the one we fall in love with is God, the wonder of it all spurs us on in ways we can hardly imagine.

A second stage in the spiritual journey has to do with tending to the relationship and nurturing it. Love can pass away. Love can indeed die. The only way to keep love alive, to be faithful, is to fall in love again every day. That is what God does. That is what it means to say that God creates anew each day, blesses us each day, embraces us each day. And for us to fall in love with God again every day requires seeing God in more and more places, in new and different ways. We see the beloved no matter where we look; we think of the beloved no matter where we are or what we are doing. We take the beloved very seriously and in doing so we take ourselves seriously: we struggle to become our best selves. Keeping love alive means folding oneself into the life of the beloved without losing oneself or absorbing the beloved. There is a coupling of ways of understanding, of points of view, of interests, of commitments that do not reduce the two to one but rather amplify each one, bringing each to the simplicity of being that in the end allows one to embrace the other fully. I believe this reciprocal process also happens in our relationship with God. We affect God because God has wished it to be so. We affect God because God has involved us in bringing about the kin-dom of God. Yes, God could have done differently but the fact is that we are God's hands and feet. God has chosen not to be able to do or be in this world apart from what we do and who we are.

Finally, our relationship with God results in our belonging fully to the family of God. As a member of the kin-dom of God I am better able to emulate the divine. I come before God without pretense—naked. I will be recognized by God and others as a member of the divine family. I will be able to walk with my God, my beloved, because I do justice and love kindness (Micah 6: 8), because I am compassionate and merciful (Matthew 25: 31–46), because I love others as I love myself (Matthew 22: 39). To belong to the family of God means that we participate in the divine, that we are in touch with the divine in us.

One of the oldest prayers in the official liturgy of the Roman Catholic Church is the one the priest says when he adds a few drops of water to the chalice with the wine: "may we become participants in your divinity, you who became participant in our humanity." In my struggle to find an adequate way of seeing and expressing spirituality as an element of who I am and what I do instead of as mere religious practices, this prayer has always been important to me. This concept of participation in the divine is based on Peter 1:4, which mentions our being "sharers in the divine nature." This is a concept of great currency in the Eastern Christian tradition. Christians understand that sharing in the divine nature begins with being created in God's image and lasts to our final union with God. All aspects of our lives require that we be intentional about participating in the divine. This is why we can say that the moral and the spiritual life are intrinsically connected.[16] This view is not that different from Aquinas' concept of attaining the beatific vision or union with God. However, it seems to me that the notion of our being sharers in the divine invites us to an understanding of ourselves as intrinsically linked to God, to our own selves and to others in a way that attaining the beatific vision does not.

There are two important elements in this understanding of our participation in the divine. The first element, already mentioned, is that we are called to become the best selves we can be. Understanding ourselves as images of God requires deep respect for who we are and how we are, realizing that, as social beings, the essence of our humanity is linked to the humanity of others. In many ways, then, our lives are a search for self-fulfillment, a social self-fulfillment rather than an individualistic enterprise. Individualistic self-fulfillment is laced with selfishness, egoism and the aberrations of self-aggrandizement that make us become exploiters of others in so many different ways. But true self-fulfillment, which takes into consideration human sociality, is the recognition of the work of God in us. This is why the Gospel makes "love of self" the measure against which to judge our love of neighbor (Luke 10: 25–28). The love of self found in the Gospel is contrary to an individualistic love of self that searches for self-fulfillment at the expense of others. Indeed, individualistic self-fulfillment is rooted in the absence of true love.

The love of God for me is what urges and inspires me. It is what enables me and fills me with joy. God's love for me is what in religious-theological language we call "grace." Grace refers to my participation in the divine, my communing with the love God has for me, which makes me capable of loving others passionately. As a matter of fact, I believe that the love God has for me obliges me to love others passionately. There is nothing lukewarm about love. Though the language used by Scripture may not have the same appeal for everyone, undoubtedly this is what Revelation 3:15–16 refers to when it says that it is better not to be at all than to be lukewarm. Love is always passionate. True love always has to find ways of expressing itself tangibly. The love God has for me expresses itself passionately in the way it demands me to love others and to love in a very special way those who are poor and oppressed. This is why it is precisely in the midst of justice actions—like walking the picket line—that I feel and experience the love of God in such a special way.

A second element in understanding spirituality as participation in the divine is related to the first. God "had to" become human. If God is love, then God has to create others in order to fulfill the God-self, for there is no love without giving of one's self. Personal self-fulfillment has to do with embracing the love God has for each of us. This is what makes us of infinite value. The love of God makes it possible for each of us to live fruitful lives, lives in which we can become fully ourselves by contributing to the happiness of others and to justice and peace in our world at large. All true love requires the give and take of relationships and this is concretely what spirituality is: a give and take with God. When one loves, all one wants is to be with the beloved. Therefore, it is not surprising that when Jesus was about to finish sharing in this world our mortal life, he had to find ways of remaining concretely with us. Those of us from the Roman Catholic tradition believe that this is precisely what the Eucharist is: Jesus remaining with us in a very tangible way. Jesus loves us, wants to be with us, and, being God, he can "invent" giving himself in the Eucharist. Those of us who have loved and have had to depart from the beloved have experienced the urgency Jesus felt, the need he experienced to find a way of remaining with the beloved. The miracle of the Eucharist is the miracle of love.

The Eucharist, however, is not the only way Jesus remains with us. As Matthew 25 indicates, Jesus chooses to be present in the poor and the oppressed in a very tangible way. It is important to notice in Matthew 25 that the language of the parable directly identifies Jesus with the naked, the hungry, those who are sick, those who are in prison. The language is not analogical; there is no "it is as if it were." When we feed the hungry, we feed Jesus; when we clothe the naked, we clothe Jesus; when we visit those in prison, it is Jesus who is consoled.

The incarcerated men whom I visited for a few short hours understood this very clearly, most probably because they saw it from the underside. I share this experience because I can think of no better way to explain what I am trying to say here. I was with those men in prison that evening because, having read an article of mine about the kin-dom of God, they wanted to talk to me. When they said how grateful they were that I had taken time to be with them, I could only reply how much it meant to me that they trusted me and wished to dialogue with me. One of the men who described himself as a Haitian-New Yorker told me that in going to be with them that evening, "you have made a reality what you say in this article about kin-dom of God, for we are in prison and you are visiting us." I received that as the highest praise anyone has ever given me. How clearly this young man understood Matthew 25! This prison visit was a tangible expression of the love of God for them and for me. Visiting with them was a very concrete way for me to relate to God, to live out my relationship with God. Perceiving self-fulfillment as intrinsic to spirituality, that is, as a key element of participation in the divine, is based on believing that God truly is love. Just as God had to create us in order to fulfill the God-self, so personal self-fulfillment means embracing God's love for each of us. This love makes each of us infinitely valuable and able to live fruitful lives by contributing to the happiness of others and to justice and peace in our world at large. The love of God, like all true love, is reciprocal. This is what spirituality is, our relationship with God, a concrete relationship that becomes reality in our love for one another. Spirituality is our love for God that calls us to engage each other, to share ourselves with each other.

Notes

[1] This essay was originally written as a meditation or a reflection. In adapting it for this book I sought to keep as much as possible the original feel of the essay while adding more scholarly explanations. My interlocutor while I have done this work has been Dorothee Soelle, particularly her book *The Silent Cry: Mysticism and Resistance* (Minneapolis: Fortress Press, 2001). Dorothee was my teacher at Union Theological Seminary in New York City during the mid 1980s. I admired her greatly mainly for her unflinching commitment to struggles of liberation, for her tireless quest to live fully a life of justice, and for her unabashed respect for each and every one of her students. Dorothee died April 27, 2003, about a year after the essay on which this one is based was published. I humbly dedicate this to her.

[2] Soelle's intention in writing her book on mysticism was "to democratize mystical experience, that is, not to understand it as an elitist affair of a few selected people . . ." ibid., 11.

[3] See also ibid., 13.

[4] I do not consider the Goddess movement necessarily as part of the "New Age" movement. It is clear that believers in the Goddess are deeply involved in justice movements because for many of them what they believe leads them to a being and doing of which justice is an intrinsic element.

[5] Ibid., 4.

[6] I explore other theological implications of the relationship of the people with Guadalupe later in this book in the essay "*Identifícate con Nosotras:* A *Mujerista* Theological Understanding."

[7] Madeleine L'Engle, "Epiphany" in *The Weather of the Heart* (Wheaton, Ill.: Shaw, 1978), 9. Here is the whole poem:
Epiphany
Unclench your fists
Hold out your hands.
Take mine.
Let us hold each other.
This is his Glory
Manifest

[8] Ibid., 23.

[9] If it is the same in other religions I do not know.

[10] Soelle, 194.

[11] Ibid.

12   Soelle quotes New York anarchist Emma Goldman (1869–1940), "If I can't dance, I don't want to be in your revolution" (ibid., 200).

13   Ibid., 88–93.

14   The use of kin-dom instead kingdom or reign stems from the desire to use a metaphor that is much more relevant to our world today. From the perspective of *mujerista* theology, the point of reference for kin-dom of God is the concept of family and community that is central to Latina culture. There is also a need to move away from "kingdom" and "reign" that are sexist and hierarchical metaphors.

15   The steps of the journey of spirituality that I present here use some of Soelle's understandings.

16   Mark O'Keefe, *Becoming Good, Becoming Holy: On the Relationship of Christian Ethics and Spirituality* (New York: Paulist Press, 1995).

3

Communion through Words

A Sermon

"Give me your word; that's enough for me," we often hear and frequently say ourselves. Ah! The mystery of the human word! Words make possible explanations and since there is no way of explaining what one does not understand, we can say that words also reveal our thoughts. But even more, our words make us present. Our words carry who we are. They convey our honor, our dignity. When I say, "I give you my word," that is all you need to hear to know that I will stand by what I am saying and that I will carry it out.

These are good reasons for giving great importance to words. But the importance they have goes beyond this. As we weave together one word with another, as we describe what we are doing, what we see, what we think, what we desire, what we hope for, we create stories that make us present, not only to others, but also to ourselves. As we create/tell/construct our own stories we also enter into the process of understanding ourselves, of understanding better how we have lived. We come to realize that our experiences are not a string of individual and unrelated events but that they are our lives. They are events in our lives to which we give sense and meaning with the values and beliefs we hold. When we hear what we have to say we come to realize that

Based on a sermon preached in Spanish and English at St. Mary's Parish in Kodiak Island, Alaska.

what we have experienced, what we have gone through in life, has created certain patterns — ways of thinking, of facing life, ways in which we relate to others — patterns that in part are what define us, what identify each of us. When we hear ourselves talk about what we have done and how we have lived, we begin to discover a unifying thread, a vision of life, which even though we are hardly aware of it, has been developing since very early in our lives and has been guiding us.

But that is not enough. We need to go even further in our consideration of words. Words not only help us to understand and to express, words not only make it possible for us to know the meaning we have given our lives, words also make present, they make real that which they signify. Words call forth, make concrete, and turn into reality their meaning in such a way that it is very difficult and at times impossible to take back what has been said. Let us remember what happened with the blessing Isaac gave his son Jacob. The blessing should have been given to Esau but once he had given it to Jacob, Isaac could not take it back (Genesis 27: 1–40). We often have this experience with children. Once we tell them we are going to do something, they hold us to what we have said. It is as if children instinctively know that once we say something, because we have said it, it becomes real and there is no way we can undo the reality our words have created.

The Eucharist is the best example of the efficacy of words, the best example of the fact that what words express becomes reality. To repeat the words said by Jesus at the Last Supper makes Christ present on our altars. This sense of the efficacy of words in the celebrations of Christian communities continues today what the people of Israel believed: the word of God does not return to God without having accomplished what it declares (Isaiah 55: 10–11).

At times we think the long hours friends and lovers spend talking to each other, no matter what age they are, is an exaggeration. Deep down we know, however, that the long conversations are necessary not only in order to get to know each other. Their sharing begins to create a life together for them. The long hours those who love each other spend talking to one another creates their friendship, fashions their caring for each other, makes their love concrete. The more they verbalize what they feel, the more their caring for each other and their love grows, the deeper the roots of their love sink into the ground, the stronger their relationship becomes. The more they talk with each other about how they feel for each other, the more what they are telling each other becomes a reality.

It is difficult for us to believe that someone loves us if that person never tells us. We cannot think that someone is interested in us if they do not communicate that interest, if they do not tell us. We need words to confirm what we are seeing expressed perhaps in gestures, which really are nothing but a message that we say and hear with the other senses. This is why it is so common for lovers to beg for words: "Tell me you love me; say it; I need to hear it." It is as if we know intuitively that the more the expressions of love are concrete, the deeper the communication will be, and the deeper the communication, the nearer we will be to communion, to being with the other and in the other in such a way that without that relationship one is incomplete.

In order for a communion between persons to exist we not only need to articulate words. We also need someone to listen to the words, someone who will reverently and with great honesty receive our words. One cannot fully be without words. Likewise one cannot exist without someone receiving our words. This someone has to be someone specific, with first and last name, someone who is a real friend. So many times in life I have been silent, without being able to say a word. In the most radical sense I have been mute. I have not been able to communicate in an authentic way simply because I have not found anyone willing to listen, willing to embrace what I had to say. So many times I have been with Latinas to whom no one has ever paid attention, to whom no one has been willing to listen with care and tenderness. When I have asked these women to tell me about their lives, they have experienced grace-filled moments during which, through their own words, they have come to know themselves and to affirm their value and importance. In these conversations Latinas thread their experiences together enabling their stories to emerge. These stories have great meaning for them and for all those willing to listen to them.

The importance of words, of communication, is key to understanding the gospel story of the Transfiguration of Jesus (Matthew

17: 1–9; Mark 9: 2–10; Luke 9: 28–36). If we concentrate on what this event meant for Jesus we will see the great importance that sharing has for us and for our communities. If we pay attention to what the text says about words we will understand the reach and importance of this event for Jesus. We will see that in order to understand himself and his mission, Jesus had to talk about it. He had to put his thoughts into words and share them with his disciples, both men and women. If we read this text carefully we will see that for Jesus words shared meant deep communication, a communion.

In the texts that relate the event of the Transfiguration, there are three references to "words." First we have the words of the conversation Jesus has with Moses and Elijah. They talk about what is going to happen to Jesus in Jerusalem or, according to different versions or translations, they talk about what Jesus is going to be able to accomplish in Jerusalem (Luke 8:31). This text indicates that Jesus needed to talk about the risks he was taking, about the difficulties he was going to have to face. He needed to talk about them in order to be able to understand them and to be able to embrace what was going to happen to him. Given the reactions of the Jewish authorities to Jesus' insistence on justice, Jesus and his disciples were conscious that confrontations with the authorities would not only continue but would intensify and escalate. This is what Jesus wants to talk about, needs to talk about.

Several of the gospels tell us that shortly before the Transfiguration Jesus tried to talk with his disciples about what was going to happen to him in a not-too-distant future but the disciples did not want to engage in such a conversation. It is as if they were afraid that if they talked about it, well, then for sure it would happen. When the disciples do not allow him to talk, Jesus answers them with very strong words. He scolds them for not wanting to face what is going to happen (Matthew 16: 23 and Mark 8: 33). Jesus needed to share what he saw was approaching so he could understand it, so he could grasp how the events to come were part of his mission in life. The very harsh answer of Jesus to the disciples, "Get behind me, Satan," indicates how urgent it was for him to talk about those future events. Jesus seems to worry about not sharing with his disciples because, if he does not talk with them about what is going to happen to him, how could he have the strength to face it? How is he going to be able to embrace the events that will lead to his execution? How are the disciples going to be able to survive Jesus' demise?

Since the disciples did not allow Jesus to engage them in conversation, here come Moses and Elijah to the rescue! Thanks to his conversation with Moses, the leader of the people during the first great liberation of Israel, Jesus sees his life as a new Exodus, as a new liberation. In talking to Elijah, whom the people of Israel expected to return before the coming of the Messiah, Jesus begins to understand what is going to happen to him in view of his mission in life. That he will be jailed, tortured and executed is a direct outcome of his preaching about justice and love, of his confrontations with the religious and political authorities who oppressed his people. His imprisonment, torture and execution will become for his disciples—including us today—the Passion and Death of Christ, events with profound religious meaning. Jesus' conversation with Moses and Elijah helps him to understand this. It is with words and through words that Jesus gives his mission a liberative and salvific meaning.

The second time the text of the Transfiguration refers to words has to do with a theophany, a specific and concrete revelation of God. A voice is heard coming from the midst of the clouds, "This is my son, the Chosen One; listen to him" (Luke 9:35), or "This is my beloved Son," as the accounts of Matthew and Mark say, or, according to other translations, "This is my beloved Son whom I have chosen." Jesus had already heard these words at the beginning of his public life. When he was baptized by John these words confirmed for Jesus that his life had a purpose, that his mission was to preach and struggle to establish the kin-dom of God, and that it was his mission to make his disciples—including us today—members of the family of God. At the beginning of his public life, of his work to carry out his mission, to know that God loved him gave him the strength he needed to move ahead. The same thing happens now at the time of the Transfiguration. Faced with imminent danger Jesus needs to know that he is loved. Jesus needs to feel he is loved. It is not that he doubts God loves him. But Jesus, being fully human, needs to feel God's love, he needs to hear God say it. He needs to experience this love with his senses, in his flesh. He needs to hear it.

At times we think that what is needed for the struggle for justice and peace is unflinching commitment, and that is indeed so. But in order for our struggles for justice and peace to be effective we also need love and tenderness in our lives. This is precisely what we see in this event in the life of Jesus. The words from God that we hear during the Transfiguration give Jesus in a tangible way the assurance he needs by allowing him to know through his senses that God loves him, and that the love of God as much as his own commitment to justice and peace is what made his mission effective.

The last words we hear in the scene of the Transfiguration make it clear that in order for words to be understood, those who say them and those who hear them have to have similar experiences. Jesus asks the disciples that have been with him in the mountain not to talk about what has happened. He does this not to set up an elite group among the disciples, a group that knows more than the others. Jesus is concerned that because the rest of the disciples have not shared in the experience of the Transfiguration, they will not be able to understand what is said about it. It will be little by little, as they experience similar events, particularly the Resurrection, that the rest of the disciples will be able to understand what the Transfiguration was about and what it meant to Jesus.

Without shared experience or similar experiences, our words do not find resonance in others and return to us empty. When what we say does not echo in our friends, we are pained. We feel not understood, alone. We feel so alone when what we share falls into a vacuum. It is only through the love and care of friends that we can do away with the distance created by not having the same experiences. It is only through solidarity born out of our commitment to justice and peace that we can do away with the distance there is between us and those we do not know personally but with whom we are committed in our struggle to be part of the family of God.

The Transfiguration of Jesus teaches us that, as members of the community of his disciples, we have to put aside time to share, time to talk and to listen. It also teaches us that sharing through words is a communion. Sharing is necessary no matter what our role in the community is, whether we are ordained ministers or not, whether we always attend church or do so only occasionally. We have to start by talking to ourselves. I have to talk to myself to understand better who I am, who I am called to be, what my mission is in life. This type of conversation with oneself takes time and requires intense listening. This type of conversation requires silence because often the answers in these conversations with ourselves are buried deep within us whether it is because we have not wanted to hear them or simply because we have not paid attention. To hear them we have to learn to be still and to wait with patience for the answers to surface. It is vital for us to give ourselves the time we need for the answers to impact our lives, for the answers to fill us with hope and give us life, for them to help us decipher and understand the meaning of our lives.

Besides talking to ourselves we need to find for ourselves a Moses and an Elijah. We need to find somebody to talk with in an open and intimate way so we can come to know ourselves better. We have to find someone who cares about us so that person can gather what we say, just as one gathers the pieces of a broken mirror, and can help us put all the pieces of our words together so that, despite the nicks and cracks, we can become our best possible selves. We need a friend. We need an intimate friendship, one of the most beautiful and enriching relationships in life. Friendship, a profoundly mutual relationship in which we constantly give and receive! To have a friend is to have someone who is interested in me, someone I can trust, someone who will not abandon me no matter what, someone who can find in me that same interest, trust and fidelity. With the help of a real friend we can go deep within ourselves to understand and embrace the infinite tenderness of God. With the help of true friendship we will come to understand that God is more intimate to us than we are to ourselves, that God embraces us.

The Transfiguration teaches us the importance of shared experiences. It teaches us that without similar experiences the words that we hear and say cannot always communicate what we mean, that without similar experiences words cannot help us share ourselves. If there is no similarity of experiences, all we can do is capitalize on our desire to be in solidarity with others, which is possible only through a mutuality made possible by dialogue, by words. The dialogue that supplements the lack of similar experiences is possible because all persons have certain common interests and because the gospel's "love one another" constitutes an integral element of the greatest commandment: love God and love your neighbor as yourself. Following the teachings of Jesus we have to accept the fact that our neighbors are the women and men, girls and boys, who are oppressed, who are excluded, marginalized, exploited, abused. Yes, they have not been heard because nobody listens to them. We have to listen to them or we ourselves will eventually not be able to talk.

The Transfiguration of Jesus teaches us how much we need to form deep friendships. It teaches us that as human beings unless we deeply communicate who we are and what we believe we cannot live fully. Without communication we cannot be in communion with each other, we cannot be in communion with God. May the Transfiguration of Jesus help us realize that God is in our friends, all our loved ones, in the care and the love we have for others and they have for us. May the Transfiguration of Jesus help us to embrace the tenderness of our God who says to each of us, "I delight in you."

Part II

IN GOD'S IMAGE

Hispanas/Latinas and Our Struggles

4

Creating a Liberating Culture

Hispanas/Latinas' Subversive Narratives

Convinced of the liberative value of the religious understandings and practices of Hispanas/Latinas living in the USA, *mujerista* theology has repeatedly gathered their stories, stories that reveal their theological insights.[1] These are women who struggle for survival and *"un poquito de justicia"*—a little bit of justice.[2] It is precisely out of a sense of justice to Hispanas/Latinas whose voices—whose lives—are hardly ever taken into consideration by academics or by society at large, that we have not wavered in our commitment to provide a platform for them in *mujerista* theology. Our faithfulness to their stories, to their understandings and insights, and our ongoing commitment to privilege their preferred future is also grounded in a firm conviction that their vision of the future contributes to make the kin-dom of God a reality.[3] It is not that Hispanas/Latinas are morally superior. It is rather because they benefit so little from the present structures and arrangements, because they have so little to protect in the present, that they can really look for and see a radically different future, a liberating future.[4] We have included the voices of Hispanas/Latinas in our theological elaborations, in *mujerista* theology, because we believe in the ongoing revelation of the divine in the lives of the poor and the oppressed and because we believe that Hispanas/Latinas are admirably capable of knowing and explaining what they believe and the role those beliefs play in their lives.

Hispanas/Latinas' stories of survival seem so ordinary that few value them. Few are willing to listen to them and understand that for Hispanas/Latinas liberation-salvation is brought about and worked out in the ordinariness of *lo cotidiano*—the everyday reality.[5] Those of us who do *mujerista* theology have paid attention to Hispanas/Latinas' stories because, as Hispanas/Latinas ourselves, we perceive that those stories are a *tela*, a cloth, out of which our own beliefs and self-understandings are made. We have paid attention to those stories because we have heard and have been formed by similar stories told to us by our own *mamás, abuelitas, tías, madrinas, comadres.*[6] It is precisely in these stories that we have come to know the beliefs that are central to grassroot Hispanas/Latinas. As we have listened to the life stories of Hispanas/Latinas for over twenty years, the importance for us of these narratives has grown exponentially.

Besides learning about the different themes we have explored in the conversations we have had with Hispanas/Latinas — understandings of the divine, of sin and grace, of conscience, of embodiment and sexuality, and of morality—there are other reasons why creating a new narrative woven out of our lived-experience is important and valuable. First, a new narrative, a narrative in which we can see ourselves as moral agents, as subjects of our own history, is important in helping Hispanas/Latinas conceive our preferred future and work towards liberation. Our own narratives help us to imagine ourselves in a new way, to know ourselves in a new way, in a way different from the one in which the dominant group knows us. A new narrative helps us to "read" ourselves in a different way because it talks to us about what up to now we have not been able to see in ourselves or have ignored. Second, it has become clear to us what the writers of the gospel stories knew long ago: people do not live or die for a creed, for this or that doctrine or dogma. Large-scale changes such as those that make liberation possible, which necessitate changes of the heart as well as changes of the mind, are not really possible on the grounds of reason alone. People need a story. A story puts sinews and flesh on the dry bones of reason and creed. People need a story—a narrative—that sets before us situations and understandings "by means of which we learn to join the ethical aspect of human behavior to happiness and unhappiness, to fortune and misfortune."[7] Discovering the stories of Hispanas/Latinas, and elaborating a *mujerista* narrative is important because it motivates us to remain faithful to the struggle for justice.

Third, Hispanas/Latinas' narratives are an important way of making obvious to those who are willing to see and to understand precisely what it is that has challenged the hegemonic Western male center, what it is that has called into question the different forms of oppression such as ethnic prejudice, racism, classism, sexism, heterosexism, and others. It is not theories elaborated in the academy that call the *status quo* into question. It is the struggle of marginalized and oppressed peoples that challenges it. What has erupted and threatens to dislodge the subjugating aspects of the rationality of modernity are not theories and debates about postmodernity, but the insistence of subjugated people on being subjects of our own histories, on being central characters in our own narratives. Hispanas/Latinas' narratives weave into subversive stories their subjugated knowledge producing "epistemological earthquakes and psychic shocks"[8] that can become intrinsic elements of new canons, of canons that are multiple and remain open.

Fourth, as Hispanas/Latinas struggle to have political significance in the USA, to have a political voice, our own narratives make known our interests in order to have them included in the institutions of this nation that are truly democratic. Our narratives help us to understand our political views and claims as "appeals to justice," and not as "mere expressions of self-regarding interest."[9] Our narratives become an important bridge "between the mute experience of being wronged and political arguments about justice."[10] Hispanas/Latinas' narratives maximize "the social knowledge available" to society at large, including the churches, and provide the information needed by local and national leaders "to make just and wise decisions."[11] Our narratives, then, are not only valuable for us and our communities but they also are important for society at large, particularly given the fact that Hispanas/Latinas' and Latinos constitute the largest racial/ethnic marginalized and minoritized group in the USA. Sharing our stories will not legitimize our claims but, in our attempt to have Hispanas/Latinas understandings be part of what is normative in society at large, our stories often serve as the only means for those in positions of authority and power "to gain some understanding of experiences, needs, projects, problems, and pleasures of people in the society differently situated from themselves. . . ."[12] Furthermore, telling our stories helps us to enter into the process of public debate, which eventually leads to the elaboration of ruling principles for society. But those who participate with us in discussions must accept the premises operative in our arguments. Narratives in these situations can serve to explain to non-Hispanas/Latinas "what practices, places, or symbols mean" to us "and why they are valuable. Values, unlike norms, often cannot be justified through arguments. But neither are they arbitrary. Their basis often emerges from the situated narrative of persons or groups. Through narrative the outsiders [in this case non-Hispanas/Latinas] may come to understand why the insiders value what they have and why they have the priorities they have."[13]

Hispanas/Latinas' stories weaved into a *mujerista* narrative, with liberation-salvation as its goal, are indeed central to our theological enterprise. These stories and the narratives that emerge from them are entrenched in *lo cotidiano*, the day-to-day reality that grounds the lived-experience of Hispanas/Latinas.

Lived-Experience

It has been our contention from the very beginning that *mujerista* theology has to do with explaining what Hispanas/Latinas in the USA believe, beliefs that ground and motivate our struggles and that are lived out in *lo cotidiano*. We base this on a very old dictum that conceives theology as "faith seeking understanding."[14] We are also motivated to focus on Hispanas/Latinas' beliefs by what is referred to in the Roman Catholic tradition as the *sensus fidelium*, that is, the ongoing revelation of God that happens in the midst of and through the community of faith.[15] Based on these traditional understandings and the conviction that religious beliefs are integral to Hispanas/Latinas' experiences, *mujerista* theology claims the lived-experience of Hispanas/Latinas as the source of our theological elaborations. In other words, it is in the lived-experiences of the everyday life — of *lo cotidiano* — that we relate to God, that we come to know who God is and what God is like.

Second, the focus on the lived-experience of Hispanas/Latinas is what leads us to claim that *mujerista* theology is not simply critical reflection on praxis, but is a liberative praxis in and of itself.[16] We understand reflection and action to be inseparable, both integral elements of praxis. Praxis is reflective action that, as such, requires analysis, planning, decisions — all of this guided by one's goal of liberation. In reality, there is no human activity which does not include the intellect: what we do cannot be separated from what we know. In *mujerista* theology we insist that "rational thinking cannot advance except through the dynamic interplay of thought and action within the process of inquiry itself. . . . We can grasp the world only by interacting with it. Action, choice, decision, contribute something indispensable to the mind's conquest of truth. We must interact with the realities we think about in order to create the experimental situations that will validate or invalidate our hypotheses about them."[17]

Lived-experience, then, is a process of interaction between thinking and action. Our actions concretize our experiences and make us present to the world since they are our evaluative response to it. Furthermore, our interacting with the world is the way we create ourselves, the way we become and express who we are. We cannot "act" ourselves into being apart from thinking; and we cannot "think" ourselves into being apart from action.[18] This intrinsic link between thinking and acting indicate that we emerge as subjects from our bodies, with our bodies, and through our bodies. Our bodies are what anchor us in our world constituted by "interacting physical forces of different degrees of consciousness and complexity. . . ."[19] Of all of these forces, "communities of persons . . . constitute the most significant and sustaining forces in the human environment."[20]

The centrality of the body in lived-experience acknowledges the materiality of our persons. Materiality makes it more difficult for the dominant group to ignore or silence marginalized groups. Whether the dominant culture likes it or not, the materiality of Hispanas/Latinas — our corporality, our bodies — affect this society in which we live. Our bodies, in this sense, not only are essential to us but they also are essential to society, if only because society needs the work produced by our bodies. It is precisely the exploitation of our physical labor that enriches the dominant group and provides for them the material base for their control and power. This is why one of the themes explored by *mujerista* theologians in our conversations with grassroot Hispanas/Latinas has been corporality, embodiment, and sexuality. These conversations, to which we refer repeatedly in this chapter, indicate there is a subversion of the patriarchal understandings of corporality and embodiment operating in the lives of Hispanas/Latinas, in our lived-experiences.

The construction of the person through lived-experience is a key reason for making it the source of *mujerista* theology. But, as a liberative praxis, *mujerista* theology does not understand lived-experience from a liberal, individualistic perspective that ignores the role of gender and ethnicitiy in Hispanas/Latinas' lives. If we did this, we would have to blame ourselves for the oppression we suffer. We do not claim that the lived-experience of all Hispanas/Latinas is the same. Instead of sameness we talk about "shared experience." Shared experience points to the fact that in talking about Hispanas/Latinas' lived-experiences we are not claiming a common identity, or common attributes for Hispanas/Latinas, or common situations or experiences. The shared experience we have as Hispanas/Latinas does not define us but rather points to our common cultural matrix.[21] Since part of this cultural matrix is the marginality/oppression in which we live, shared experience also refers to the way we experience the world because of how others conceive us. It points to the way in which our material environment of oppression and marginality conditions us. Each of us is our own person and acts in our own way. But we do so within certain limits and constraints set, to a great degree, by the racist/ethnic prejudice and sexism operative in the USA. Understanding Hispanas/Latinas' lived-experiences as shared experience, then, takes into consideration the social, political, and economic context of our daily lives, which does not determine or define us but certainly influences very directly our world-view. It is the background against which our lives unfold.[22] Shared experience refers to the way Hispanas/Latinas face reality: it refers to the similar elements present, because of our shared cultural matrix, in our way of understanding ourselves and the situations in which we are involved, in the decisions we take and how we take them, and in our way of acting.

It is important to point out that *mujerista* theology is about struggling against oppression, one of the key elements of the cultural matrix of most Hispanas/Latinas. There are Hispanas/Latinas who have the same countries of origin as we have, who speak Spanish, and who maintain in their homes Latino customs, but who do not identify or throw their lot in with the Latino community in the USA. They insist that they do not suffer discrimination. They espouse a liberal individualistic stance and, by identifying with and accommodating to the dominant culture, they have managed to deal with the ethnic prejudice and sexism in the USA in a way that satisfies them. They certainly do not have a shared experience with the vast majority of Hispanas/Latinas in the USA. And they are not the Hispanas/Latinas whose lived-experience is the source of *mujerista* theology.[23]

Focusing on the struggle against oppression helps Hispanas/Latinas to see ourselves as a group without having to claim that Hispanas/Latinas have some specific inherent attribute. To claim such would reduce Hispanas/Latinas to biological attributes and it would erroneously attempt to find essential social attributes in Hispanas/Latinas' actual lives.[24] On the other hand if we fail to see ourselves as a group, it would not be possible "to conceptualize oppression as a systematic, structured institutional process"[25] and to organize ourselves effectively against it.

In the understandings about Hispanas/Latinas' lived-experiences and shared experience used in *mujerista* theology we have struggled to stay away from any sense of inherent attributes while finding a way to be and to conceptualize ourselves as a group. We see Hispanas/Latinas' lived-experiences and shared experience as the key to this balance since they indicate that daily practices, and habits — *lo cotidiano* — which do not happen apart from reflection, are ways of articulating Hispanas/Latinas' subjectivity. Being Hispanas/Latinas, then, is not "a point to start from in the sense of being a given but it is, instead, a posit or construct, formalizable in a non-arbitrary way through a matrix of habits, practices, and discourses,"[26] by us about ourselves and about us by others. Being Hispanas/Latinas signals "an interpretation of our history within a particular discursive constellation, a history in which we are both subjects of and subjected to social construction."[27] This means that our subjectivity as Hispanas/Latinas is a fluid understanding since it is based on concrete lived-experiences and not on any kind of universal attribute. Our historical realities, our lived and shared experiences, central to our identity as Hispanas/Latinas, provide us with a powerful motivation for our struggles for justice and liberation.[28]

One last point needs to be mentioned about the lived-experiences of Hispanas/Latinas. Lived-experiences are not disconnected events. They are distinct events that form a continuum, a coherent picture, created by the person reflecting on how these events are connected and often lead one to the other. Lived-experiences are woven into narratives that make obvious the interaction between thought and action and the way the persons emerges from *lo cotidiano*. It is to narrative and the role it has come to play in *mujerista* theology that we now turn.

Life-Stories, Narratives

A narrative is a tool used to organize lived-experiences into meaningful episodes. "Narrative displays the goals and intentions of human actors; it makes individuals, cultures, societies, and historical epochs comprehensible as wholes; it humanizes time; and it allows us to contemplate the effects of our actions and to alter the directions of our lives."[29] Narratives allow us to link the distinct events of our lives by making us note that something is but a part of something else and that it is the cause and/or the effect of something else. Personal narratives, then, are stories of one's life that make it possible for the person to give meaning to her life and to interpret it within its historical and cultural context.

We always have been aware of how eager grassroots Hispanas/Latinas are to share and to interpret for others who are willing to listen to them what they have experienced. We have noticed repeatedly how when we gather to reflect theologically on issues of importance to our communities, usually during a weekend, the women use those opportunities to give shape to their lives: while on Friday they present their stories as isolated events, by Saturday afternoon they are elaborating them much more fully by explaining the meaning for them of their experience. Furthermore, as the weekend progresses, the women begin to place the happenings that they share in their context, making more and more explicit the conditions under which they have lived, the conditions that either helped them or kept them from doing what they wanted.

The women have not only revealed to us the facts of their lives; they have not only allowed us to come to know their world. As we have studied what they have shared in these reflection weekends we have come to see that these women have constructed a narrative: they have "invented" an image of their lives by creating characters out of those they have interacted with throughout their lives, creating a character for themselves, and becoming protagonists of their own stories. What connects their different lived-experiences seems to be not a theme or a linear time concept of their lives, but the character they have created for themselves, which allows one to see how they understand themselves.[30] The characters they create for themselves are ones that lead to or emerge from their present self-understanding. The characters of themselves they create are very influential in determining what they communicate during the sharing, what their goals in life are, and how they face *lo cotidiano*.[31]

In their narratives, Hispanas/Latinas share their understandings of how their gender impinges on their lived-experiences, on who they have been, and on who they have become. They explain cogently through their stories how prejudices about women and the systems based on them affect their lives. Their narratives indeed show how they have been conscious of having to adapt, to pretend, in order to survive and how, in other circumstances, they have been unwilling to do so because they did not want to betray who they were/are. In their narratives each of these Hispanas/Latinas makes obvious her heroic attempts to respond to her situation in a positive way and to create a person that can confront the conditions of her life. These attempts are not a misrepresentation, nor are they trivial conceits. They are the self-expression of a woman who is doing what we all do: struggling to make sense of events that are beyond our control and to establish a place for ourselves in terms of the things that are within her control, and doing so not only through our actions but also through our representation of those actions via language.[32]

The narratives woven by these Hispanas/Latinas seem to us to be subversive in nature because they unveil what has been suppressed or ignored by society and by the academy: how Hispanas/Latinas temporarily adapt and pretend, or do not think or feel or act the way they are "supposed to." Hispanas/Latinas' narratives are subversive, then, because they are "counterstories— narratives of resistance and insubordination that allow communities of choice to challenge and revise the paradigm stories of the 'found' [dominant] communities in which they are embedded."[33] These narratives are "sources of counterhegemonic insight" because they expose how the understandings of the dominant ideology are not universal, because they reveal lives that defy or contradict the "rules,"[34] and because they uncover quiet but effective forms of resistance. The effectiveness of these narratives may not be immediate: Hispanas/Latinas have not been very successful in challenging the dominant community in any extensive way. But these subversive narratives begin to break the hegemonic discourse by insisting that Hispanas/Latinas' lived-experiences and the narratives woven with them are legitimate sources of knowledge, vehicles used to pass on from generation to generation understandings that make it possible for Hispanas/Latinas to live with a modicum of self-definition. The narratives that we have been privy to are full of instances of counterhegemonic insight that help Hispanas/Latinas to re-define themselves and, in doing so, they begin to re-define the social institutions of society.

Here is an account of a conversation during one of the reflection weekends that exemplifies what we understand by subversive narrative. It is a topic with which we think many women will resonate. While discussing the first sexual experience she had had, one of the women said that at times she pretends to experience orgasm for the sake of her husband, so he will not feel bad, "*el pobre*"—the poor man—she said to punctuate the reason why she does it. Other women joined the discussion, most of them tacitly or implicitly indicating that they had done likewise. There was only one who strongly indicated that she had not pretended and would not pretend in this regard.

At first this narrative might appear to indicate how women are oppressed by men. But as the conversation developed, we could see the subversiveness of the way Hispanas/Latinas thought and acted. None of the women thought they were obliged to pretend having an orgasm. Their reasons for doing it or not doing it clearly show that they are aware of what they need to do to be able to live in situations they could not or did not want to leave. The ones who pretended did so to gain the good will of their husbands, or out of pity, or *"para que me deje en paz"* — so he will leave me alone. None did it out of a conviction that they were obliged as women to make their husbands believe their sexual performance was adequate. For sure they did not blame themselves for not having an orgasm. They pretended for their own sake as did those who would not pretend. From this perspective one can re-evaluate the perception that women who pretend to have orgasms are afraid of or controlled by their male partners. Instead, does it not show that Hispanas/Latinas claim the truth of their lives, that they act to protect themselves, they act for their own sake, and do not see themselves as failures because they do not have orgasms, even if they are aware of other versions of what the sexual performance of women should be? The narrative that emerged on this issue from the stories these Hispanas/Latinas shared with us shows that they are critical of "officially condoned untruths" because they consider them an injustice.[35]

The validity of Hispanas/Latinas' narratives is "not dependent on the approval of the established regimes of thought."[36] A *mujerista* narrative is made up of knowledge that the dominant group has "disqualified as inadequate to their task or insufficiently elaborated," and which it considers to be "beneath the required level of cognition or scientificity."[37] In reality, however, we believe that what a *mujerista* narrative shows is the deficiency of any of "the centralizing powers which are linked to the institution and functioning of an organized scientific discourse within a society. . . ."[38] It also questions the methods used in setting such a discourse and, in questioning the methods used, it also questions the contents.[39]

The narratives of these Hispanas/Latinas are subversive because they show that the image they have of themselves is different from the one that the dominant culture has of them. Body size and weight of Hispanas/Latinas is a good example of this sort of "independent thinking." At one of the reflection weekends, one of the facilitators shared feelings about her struggle to keep a positive self-image in spite of her big size. The women in the group immediately reacted in what could be considered a very pastoral way and repeatedly affirmed her by saying she looked wonderful. "*No estás tan gorda*"—you are not so fat—they repeatedly told her. Of particular importance was the comment made by one of the women who insisted that the facilitator should not have a negative view of herself because "*en nuestra cultura*"—in our culture—her body size would not be considered negatively.[40]

The ability of these grassroot Hispanas/Latinas to see the differences between how big women are seen in Latino and Euro-American culture reveals how conscious they are of the meaning of their experiences and of the social conditions in which those experiences take place. It is precisely from the coming together of their lived-experiences and the social conditions in which they live that Hispanas/Latinas draw their sense of reality.[41] Hispanas/Latinas' narratives reveal aspects of the human condition that are true not only for us. These revelations indeed can aid other women who are not Hispanas/Latinas if only they are willing to recognize that we are mirrors for them. If they can recognize that, they will be open to Hispanas/Latinas and our world and they will be able to lay aside prejudices and to embrace differences.[42]

Social Context

What role does social context play in Hispanas/Latinas' narratives? Social context is formed by the coming together of social understandings and values, including even what we would consider negative values like sexism, ethnic prejudice/racism, classism. As "speaking subjects" Hispanas/Latinas bring within us our race, class and gender—all of them elements of the social context. Within this context societal structures and institutions figure prominently and, for Hispanas/Latinas, we would need to include the churches in a special way. But "context is not a script. Rather, it is a dynamic process through which the individual simultaneously shapes and is shaped by her environment."[43]

A sense of place and world, of social context, is embedded in the particular language these women use.[44] The narratives of Hispanas/Latinas point to the different elements that are interwoven in their social context. Perhaps the most obvious is the interpersonal one. Hispanas/Latinas' lives are shaped, and maybe even made possible, by the way they mediate between themselves and others, by their relationships with others.[45]

> This reliance may well be a function of women's relative powerlessness, their lack of access to more formal and institutional routes to influence, and as such a survival strategy shared with other relatively powerless groups. While it must be acknowledged . . . that the relationships which contextualize the lives of the women in question are forged, negotiated, and experienced within the framework of larger social-structural forces and factors, the significance of such relationships is **seldom revealed** in the analysis of social structure per se, nor can they be explained through a focus at that level. It is in looking directly at women's lives that relationships come to assume contextual importance and interpretative power.[46]

The interpersonal relationships of Hispanas/Latinas are a key element of our social context, for we come from a culture that continues to function in a very personalized fashion. By this we mean that Hispanas/Latinas' culture has not been bureaucratized: the way we prefer to operate and the way we try to operate is not according to rules and regulations but rather according to relationships, knowing someone who can help you or who knows someone else who will find a way of assisting you. In a way this makes us see the interconnection that exists between the personal and the political, a connection that has been so important in the development of feminist consciousness in the USA. In Latina culture the individualism of the USA culture is considered something negative for any given person as well as for her/his family/community. This individualism, it seems to us, helps to sustain the false separation between the personal and the political that has so effectively kept women and so-called women's issues out of the political sphere. For Hispanas/Latinas individualism is the antithesis of a true sense of community without which we could not survive as a marginalized group and without which we could not conceptualize liberation and struggle for it. Understanding ourselves always within an interpersonal context, then, helps us to grasp the power dynamics that exist in society. It does matter who you know; it is not a matter solely of how good you are at what you do or how hard you work. The importance we give to the interpersonal helps us to see that central to societal structures are networks of people who vouch for each other, who help each other, and who do all they can to keep the benefits of society in the hands of those who belong to "their kind." This helps to demythologize political and bureaucratic structures, making clear that their procedures are not so different from those that are present at the personal level. This indicates the need to insist that everything that happens at the political level affects the personal, and that the personal is also political. The differences between the two are more at the level of scale and accumulation of causes and effects. Therefore, insisting on the importance of the personal and interpersonal in *lo cotidiano* is indeed an effective way of bringing about structural change.

A second element to consider when analyzing context is the way in which the socio-economic-political situation of Hispanas/Latinas' lives intersect with the dominant culture in which we live, and with the Latino culture and ideology that frames and informs our daily living. In the narratives of Hispanas/Latinas it is noticeable how they are able to juggle two cultural-ideological frameworks. What becomes obvious is that Hispanas/Latinas' lives and understandings of ourselves point to what is called "situational ethnicity" in which "cultural change and ethnic persistence occur simultaneously."[47] To understand how Hispanas/Latinas deal with the cultural-ideological frameworks in our lives it is best to consider a "multidimensional model of cultural change and persistence . . . [that takes into consideration] the study of the interrelationships of cultural, social and structural factors in historical perspective. . . ."[48] This means that for Hispanas/Latinas "the acceptance of new cultural traits and the loss of traditional cultural traits varies from trait to trait," some traditional traits being retained, some new traits being adopted.[49] In other words, what Hispanas/Latinas do is pick and choose from each culture whatever can be beneficial, depending among other things, on which of the two "worlds" in which we live we in any given situation. It is precisely this picking and choosing that gives birth to "new cultural and social patterns created by migrants and ethnic minorities in the new society,"[50] which we Hispanas/Latinas call *mestizaje* and *mulatez.*

Mestizaje and *mulatez* constitute our most immediate context; they refer to Hispanas/Latinas' condition as racially and culturally mixed people; our condition of people from other cultures living in the USA; our condition of people living between different worlds.[51] *Mestizaje* and *mulatez* for Hispanas/Latinas are not a given but a conscious choice made obvious by how we move in and out of Latino and Anglo-American culture according to need and desire.

A third element of context to consider here, one usually not included by sociologists but which we believe is extremely important, is the expectations and understandings that Hispanas/Latinas have of themselves, of their lives, and of the telling of their life-stories.[52] These expectations will lead them to choose from which point of view to tell their stories so they can construct meaning for themselves as they see best and take a stance, publicly or privately as they see fit. By expectations and understandings here we do not refer only to those the person had when she did or experienced something or when she has reflected on it in the past. We also mean, as indicated above, the reasons Hispanas/Latinas have for participating in gatherings organized so they can reflect on their lives, the way they view themselves when sharing their stories, how they perceive their narratives will be used, what they believe their stories have to contribute, and how they think sharing their stories will benefit them.[53]

Two examples make this point clear. Cuquita participated in a reflection group that gathered to discuss issues of embodiment and sexuality. She is a sixty-year-old woman born and raised in

Mexico who has no home of her own. She works as a maid, lives in the homes where she works, and only has one room in the house of one of her children where she keeps "*mis cosas*" — my stuff. Her full name is María del Refugio Quevedo; Cuquita is her nickname. We are using her name because she wanted us to. Why? When she was young she fell in love with a man who had been to Texas and had returned to their village. He was in love with her but he was financially better off than she was. Cuquita says that "*no fue lo suficiente hombre*"— he was not man enough — to go against his parents' wishes and marry Cuquita. She eventually left the village and married another man, but she never has forgotten the man who had traveled to Texas with whom she has always been in love. She keeps hoping she will find him. At the end of our time together when we were explaining to the participants that if we were to quote them directly we would use a pseudonym, Cuquita told us in unequivocal terms that we were to use her true name. "Maybe my love will read this book and he will come for me."

Since this was at least one of the reasons why Cuquita shared her story with us — her desire to be found by the man she loves — this has to be taken into consideration in analyzing her interpretation of herself and her life. Throughout she presented herself as someone who always has been and is sexually passionate. In no way do we believe that she invented this. Nothing of what Cuquita said led us to believe this was not true. But we do think that her self-portrayal in this regard is linked to her desire to find the man she has always loved. How conscious she is of this desire is not possible to tell, but we believe that her expressed wish to use this opportunity to find him indicates that wanting him to find her is actively operative in the way she portrayed herself.

Another example concerns one of the only two Hispanas/ Latinas who said they were not comfortable with recording the sessions but would tolerate it. One woman, Rosario, came to see the importance of this project not only for herself but for Hispanas/Latinas in general and, in spite of her initial reticence, she would lean into the microphone to be sure that what she was saying would be adequately recorded. Is it unreasonable to believe that what she shared was in part shaped by her desire to help other Hispanas/Latinas? We would venture to say that this most probably led her to a deeper reflection and analysis of her experiences. Wanting to help others by telling her story probably also gave her an added sense of confidence in herself and her ability to relate her experiences in a meaningful way.

Conclusion

Our purpose as *mujerista* theologians is not only to provide opportunities for personal growth for each of the women that participated in the reflection weekends — opportunities to review their stories, evaluate them, and be intentional about future actions — but also to help create a subversive, community narrative, a *mujerista* narrative, that will make public the hidden traditions and values of Hispanas/Latinas. Our purpose is not to create a grand narrative but rather a contextual narrative that is tied to and that grows out of Hispanas/Latinas' lived-experience in the USA at the beginning of the 21st century. Our purpose is not just to help the participants in the reflection weekends to evoke the past for the sake of the past; our purpose was to provide an opportunity for them to interpret their experiences so they can value them and thus make it possible to learn from their past in order to look confidently into the future. Our hope is that a *mujerista* narrative that gathers and weaves together Hispanas/Latinas' stories can be instrumental in creating a "cosmos of meaning" that enables new consciousness and creativity.[54] It is our belief that by helping to form a collective identity a *mujerista* narrative will contribute to form a vision of a just future for Hispanas/Latinas and our communities, and motivate all of us to action.[55] It is our belief that a *mujerista* narrative can bring together Hispanas/Latinas who have shared experiences, for "whether in touch with each other or not, the collective story . . . provides a sociological community, the linking of separate individuals into a shared consciousness."[56]

Our goal is to make known Hispanas/Latinas' narratives so that our beliefs and understandings can contribute to giving theological meaning to and transforming social institutions, including the churches.[57] We are convinced that Hispanas/Latinas' narratives gathered and recognized as a primary source for *mujerista* theology, make explicit the modes of thought and subjectivity of Hispanas/Latinas and offer a specific historical analysis that "explains the working of power on behalf of specific interests"[58] that do not include Hispanas/Latinas, as well as revealing opportunities for resistance against such exclusion. The *mujerista* narratives point to the fact that "subjectivity and consciousness, as socially produced in language, . . . [are] a site of struggle and potential change." Hispanas/Latinas' narratives indeed suggest that meanings are social constructs and that language is not an abstract system, but is always socially and historically located in discourses. Discourses represent political interests and in consequence are constantly vying for status and power. The site for this battle for power is the subjectivity of the individual and it is a battle in which the individual is an active but not sovereign protagonist.[59]

At present Hispanas/Latinas' narratives are not powerful discourses in society, for they do not have firm institutional basis. We trust, though, that because of the important role of Hispanas/Latinas in our culture and because of the rapid growth of our communities in the USA, a *mujerista* narrative will begin to challenge understandings, practices, and forms of subjectivity that at present are staunchly supported by society even though they are oppressive. We continue to gather and circulate Hispanas/Latinas' narratives because we are convinced of their value and because we know that they will never have a social impact unless they are widely known and valued.

Notes

[1] The religious understandings and practices of Latinas in their own words can be found in Ada María Isasi-Díaz and Yolanda Tarango, *Hispanic Women: Prophetic Voice in the Church* (Minneapolis: Fortress Press, 1992) and in Ada María Isasi-Díaz, *En La Lucha—In the Struggle: Elaborating a Mujerista Theology*, 2nd ed. (Minneapolis: Fortress Press, 2003).

[2] See article by this name in Ada María Isasi-Díaz, *Mujerista Theology: A Theology for the Twenty-First Century* (Maryknoll, N.Y.: Orbis Books, 1996).

[3] We do not use "kingdom," for it is a sexist and classist term. Furthermore, it is a term foreign to the reality we live at the close of the

twentieth century. Kin-dom brings to mind the whole concept of family, which is important in Latina culture.

⁴ José Míguez Bonino, "Nuevas tendencias en teología," *Pasos* 9 (1987), 22.

⁵ For a full explanation of *lo cotidiano* see Chapter 6 in this book, "*Lo Cotidiano: Everyday Struggles in Hispanas/Latinas' Lives.*"

⁶ Mothers, grandmothers, aunts, godmothers; *comadres* refers to the relationship of godmothers and mothers. We use Spanish here because English, being our second language, cannot convey the meaning for us of these relationships.

⁷ Paul Ricoeur, *A Ricoeur Reader: Reflection and Imagination* (Hertfordshire, England: Harvester Wheatsheaf, 1991), 428.

⁸ This is a phrase that I heard from Elizabeth Minnick at a conference.

⁹ Iris Marion Young, *Inclusion and Democracy* (New York: Oxford University Press, 2000), 115.

¹⁰ Ibid., 72.

¹¹ Ibid. Young deals exclusively with secular society. I have included church in this understanding, given the importance of the latter one for Hispanas/Latinas.

¹² Ibid., 74.

¹³ Ibid., 75.

¹⁴ This is a phrase that captures a key methodological understanding of Anselm of Canterbury who lived at the end of the eleventh and into the twelfth century. "The purpose of Anselm's work is not therefore to attain unto faith through reason, but 'in order to rejoice in the understanding and contemplation of that which they believe, and also in order to be always prepared in as much as possible, to answer all who may ask for the reason of hope that is in all of us.'" This quote from Anselm's work, *Cur Deus Homo* (Why God Became Man), 1.1, cited in Justo González, *A History of Christian Thought: From Augustine to the Eve of the Reformation*, vol. II, 2nd ed. (Nashville: Abingdon Press, 1987), 159.

¹⁵ In the hierarchical Roman Catholic tradition this understanding should be seen as a way of resisting attempts to make the pope and the bishops the exclusive conduit for the revelation of God. This traditional belief was reaffirmed in the Second Vatican Council. "Dogmatic Constitution on the Church," in Walter M. Abbott, S.J., ed., *The Documents of Vatican II* (New York: The American Press, 1966), 29–30.

¹⁶ Our understanding here is different from that of Gustavo Gutiérrez. See Gustavo Gutiérrez, *The Theology of Liberation*, rev. ed., trans. Sister Caridad Inda and John Eagleson (Maryknoll, N.Y.: Orbis Books, 1988), xxviii, 5–12.

[17] Donald L. Gelpi, S.J., *The Turn to Experience in Contemporary Theology* (New York: Paulist Press, 1994), 33. We are grateful to Dr. Robert Lassalle-Klein at the Jesuit School of Theology, Berkeley, whose unpublished article "Making Sense of the UCA Model for Christian Education: Thought on Practical Foundations for Theology in the Americas" has guided us in our study of Peirce's understanding of the intrinsic connection between thought and action, which is based on his understanding of how the rational mind works. See Charles Sanders Peirce, *Collected Papers*, Vol. 5, ed. Charles Hartshorne and Paul Weiss (Cambridge: Harvard University Press, 1935), 266–282.

[18] This is why we believe together with Gramsci that the lived-experience of *lo cotidiano* is a key element in the political struggle over meaning. One of the greatest mistakes of the theologies of and struggles for liberation: that they have concentrated on societal structural elements to the point of ignoring the lived-experience of *lo cotidiano*. We believe this is why the structural changes have not happened or, if they have taken place, have not been maintained.

[19] Gelpi, 126–136. We have replaced "self" with "subject" because "self" for us has tinges of Cartesian understandings that ignore the body and its social context as integral to the person. "Subject," on the other hand, emphasizes moral agency.

[20] Ibid.

[21] We have claimed that there are at least five key elements that form this common matrix or ethnicity for Hispanas/Latinas: *mestizaje-mulatez*, the struggle for survival, marginality as a socio-economic reality within the USA, the Spanish language, popular religion, and our *proyecto histórico* (what we hope for as Latinas living in the USA). See Isasi-Díaz, *En La Lucha*, Chapters 1 and 2. For a full elaboration of *mestizaje-mulatez* see Chapter 5 in this volume, "Re-Conceptualizing Difference: A New *Mestizaje-Mulatez*."

[22] See Iris Marion Young, "Gender as Seriality: Thinking about Women as a Social Collective," in *Social Postmodernism: Beyond Identity Politics*, ed. Linda Nicholson et al. (Cambridge: Cambridge University Press, 1995), 187–215.

[23] It is not our intention in any way to demean these women. We simply want to point out that individualistic solutions to oppression do not do away with oppression or prove that oppression does not exist.

[24] Young, 208.

[25] Ibid., 192.

[26] Linda Alcoff, "Cultural Feminism Versus Post-Structuralism: The Identity Crisis in Feminist Theory," in *Feminist Theory in Practice and Process*, ed. Micheline R. Malson, Jean F. O'Barr, Sarah Westphal-Wihl and Mary Wyer (Chicago: University of Chicago Press, 1989), 321.

27 Ibid.

28 Ibid., 318–326.

29 Laurel Richardson, "Narrative and Sociology," *Journal of Contemporary Ethnography* (April, 1990): 117.

30 This might be why the questions we pose in the reflection groups are not answered directly, though it might have to do also with the fact that the majority of the women who participated in the reflection weekends have limited schooling. We think this leads them to relate much more to the "oral" than to the "written" world. As Walter J. Ong explains, the world of orality is closer to life than the written world, which means that it is organized around relationships more than around discrete events that can be lined up in a sequential manner. See Walter J. Ong, *Orality and Literacy: The Technologizing of the Word* (New York: Methuen, 1981), particularly Chapter 3.

31 Daphne Patai, *Brazilian Women Speak* (New Brunswick, N.J.: Rutgers University Press, 1988), 1–35.

32 Ibid., 33. We replaced "self" with "person" for the same reason we replaced above "self" with "subject." See explanation above, note 19.

33 Hilde Lindemann Nelson, "Resistance and Insubordination," *Hypatia* 10:2 (1995): 24.

34 The Personal Narratives Group, *Interpreting Women's Lives: Feminist Theory and Personal Narratives* (Bloomington: Indiana University Press, 1989), 7.

35 Ibid.

36 Michel Foucault, *Power/Knowledge*, ed. Cohn Gordon, trans. Cohn Gordon et al. (New York: Pantheon Books, 1980), 81.

37 Ibid, 82.

38 Ibid.

39 In this we disagree with Foucault, who sees subversive knowledges as not being primarily opposed to the prevalent methods and content but to how they are used. See Foucault, 84.

40 See Christy Haubegger, "I'm Not Fat, I'm Latina," in *Reconstructing Gender: A Multicultural Anthology*, ed. Estelle Disch (Mountain View, Calif.: Mayfield Publishing Co., 1997), 175–176.

41 Ibid., 14.

42 Maria Lugones, "On the Logic of Pluralist Feminism," in *Feminist Ethics*, ed. Claudia Card (Lawrence: University of Kansas Press, 1991), 41–42.

43 Ibid., 14.

44 Tey Diana Rabolledo, "The Politics of Poetics: Or, What Am I, a Critic, Doing in This Text Anyhow?" in *Making Face, Making Soul— Haciendo Caras: Creative and Critical Perspective of Women of Color* , ed. Gloria Anzaldúa (San Francisco: Aunt Lute, 1990), 351.

[45] The elaboration of the first three elements is based on those (more than three) identified in *Interpreting Women's Lives*, 20–23. We gained further insight into these first three elements from Ricoeur, *A Ricoeur Reader*, 425–437.

[46] *Interpreting Women's Lives*, 20. Emphasis added.

[47] Susan E. Keefe and Amado Padilla, *Chicano Ethnicity* (Albuquerque: University of New Mexico Press, 1987), 191.

[48] Ibid., 195.

[49] Ibid., 15.

[50] Ibid., 18.

[51] Isasi-Díaz, *Mujerista Theology*, 64–66.

[52] Ibid., 22–23.

[53] Marjorie Mbilinyi, "'I'D HAVE BEEN A MAN': Politics and the Labor Process in Producing Personal Narratives," in *Interpreting Women's Lives*, 204–227.

[54] David T. Abalos, *Strategies of Transformation Toward a Multicultural Society* (Westport, Conn.: Praeger, 1996), 7–19. Abalos's work gives great importance to stories though he relies on literary fiction and uses as his lens, almost exclusively, the theory of transformation developed by Manfred Halpern.

[55] Ibid., 30. Our educational/research project was not set up to organize the women for action. Several of the groups wanted to find ways to keep meeting, and at least three of the groups are ongoing groups that we hope will factor this experience into their future projects.

[56] Richardson, 128. See also Nelson, 23–40. Richardson talks about "same experience" instead of the expression we use, "shared experience."

[57] This is what Michel Foucault called a discursive field. We are indebted here to the presentation of his ideas made by Chris Weedon, *Feminist Practice and Poststructuralist Theory* (Cambridge, Mass.: Blackwell Publishers, 1987), 35–42, 107–135.

[58] Ibid., 41.

[59] Ibid. We are not saying that it is only in language that subjectivity and consciousness are socially produced.

5

Re-Conceptualizing Difference

A New *Mestizaje-Mulatez*

Difference plays a significant role in all we are and all we do. Without any doubt whatsoever this is the key issue we have to deal with in this century, for it affects all. Any worldview that wants to remain vital needs to take difference into consideration. All societal institutions, every community and every person, all without exception have to examine what they understand by difference, what role that understanding plays both in self-conception as well as in relationships, and what part difference has in plans and strategies, in the everyday course of life.

Those of us who come from marginalized communities are positioned in a most advantageous way to re-conceptualize the meaning of difference, to deal with it in a constructive manner, to choose to embrace difference as a necessary ethical action, if our world is to move beyond the prejudices and divisions that exploit and maim, that thwart and constrain, that limit possibilities and threaten the very survival of the human race. It is not that we in marginalized communities are morally better or intellectually more capable than those of the dominant group who consider themselves normative and decide who is "different." Rather, it is because we are the ones that are labeled "different," because we suffer in our own flesh the negative understanding that such a label carries, because we have nothing to gain in this regard from the present situation. This is why marginalized people are the ones best situated to imagine another way of understanding and dealing with difference than the present one.

The importance of difference for Hispanas/Latinas and Latinos is made obvious by the insistence in Hispanic/Latino theology, including *mujerista* theology, on recognizing the importance of *mestizaje-mulatez*, a concept which originally referred to the mingling of Amerindian and African blood with European blood, but which now also includes the present-day mixtures of people from Latin American and the Caribbean both among ourselves and with people of other ethnic/racial and cultural background here in the USA. *Mestizaje-mulatez* also refers to the mingling of cultures, to the creation of a new culture that embraces elements from the African, Amerindian and Spanish culture. In our theological endeavors, *mestizaje-mulatez* is our *locus theologicus*, the place from which we do theology precisely because it is intrinsic to who we are. It situates us as a community in the USA society. *Mestizaje-mulatez* is so important to us that we understand it as an ethical option central not only to the Latina[1] community's identity but to everyone's sense of self.[2] Furthermore, we believe that it is precisely the importance *mestizaje-mulatez* has for us Hispanas/Latinas that is something we can and should contribute to the conversation with other marginalized communities in the USA. The reason for this is that in *mestizaje-mulatez* we find a way out of the excluding and oppositional understanding of difference so prejudicial to our own community and to all marginalized people.

Embracing Difference: An Urgent Need

I begin with a number of salient facts that are caused by the present understanding of differences and which are at the root of oppression and marginalization.

- We start the new millennium with barely 200 mega-transnational corporations controlling no less than one fourth of the economic activity of the whole planet. This in many ways is why the richest fifth of the world population receives 82.7 percent of the resources of our planet, the second richest fifth receives 11.7 percent, the fifth in the middle receives 2.3 percent, the fourth fifth receives 1.9 percent and the poorest fifth receives 1.4 percent of the total world income.[3]

- One hundred and eighty million children the world over are malnourished. Fourteen million children die every year before they reach the age of five.[4]
- The richest countries with about 25 percent of the world population consume 70 percent of the world's energy, 75 percent of its metals, 85 percent of its wood, and 60 percent of its food.[5] All the trees of the world would disappear in two years if the whole world were to use the amount of paper that is used in the USA, where only six percent of the world population lives.[6]
- Women do 67 of each 100 hours of work done in the world but control only 9.4 percent of the world's income. Of the estimated 1.3 billion people living in poverty, more than 70 percent are female. The number of rural women living in absolute poverty rose nearly 50 percent in the last 20 years. "Increasingly poverty has a woman's face."[7] Only four percent of the women are in positions where decisions are made. Though women constitute half the electorate, we hold only 10 percent of the seats in the world's parliaments and six percent in national cabinets.[8] Women are 66 percent of the illiterate people of the world.[9]

This view from the underside of the world is obvious to those who are willing to hear the cries of the poor and the oppressed. The unwillingness or perhaps (perhaps?!) the incapacity to see the misery of such a large percentage of the human race is grounded, I believe, in the refusal to recognize that these vast numbers of suffering humanity are our sisters and brothers, people to whom and for whom we are responsible. There are two main reasons for not accepting that the poor and the oppressed are our responsibility. First, we suspect or know that their misery is directly related to the privileges and goods that so few enjoy and will do anything to protect. At the root of such selfishness lies prejudice. Of course, since those who do not know about or listen to the interests of the poor are prejudiced, they rationalize their actions by thinking that there are valid reasons for what they do or do not do. Prevalent reasons are as follows: they have worked hard for what they have; they have paid good money for it; they have sacrificed themselves so their children can have a better life (more material goods). Prejudices are grounded in the belief, at times unstated and unexamined, that those who are different from the dominant group are inferior. This is a second reason why we do not recognize our responsibility for the poor and the oppressed: we believe their inferiority absolves us from responsibility. We have convinced ourselves that it is their inferiority and not our prejudice that is the reason for oppression and poverty.

Situations of apartheid based on a prejudicial understanding of difference are being created all over the world: an ever-smaller group of people control resources and decision-making processes, effectively setting up separate spheres for relating, acting, being and living. At the same time, because of quick communications, comparatively easy world-traveling, and the almost instantaneous accessibility to worldwide information, it is impossible to think that one can escape dealing with differences. A quick glance shows the role difference plays in our world. Religious difference is intrinsic to the conflicts in Eastern Europe that are supported by an ideology of genocide. Religious difference upholds the conflict between Palestinians and Jews as well as the conflicts within countries that include Moslems of different persuasions. What is decided by and happens to people different from us on the other side of the globe affects us in many ways. This is made obvious not only by the economic world where markets are so tied and interrelated, but also by such phenomena as acid rain, which does not stay inside a given country's borders, global warming and the deterioration of the ozone layer. It is also what is obviously at stake with the AIDS epidemic, which ignores all differences. Such realities affect all, regardless of differences.

The present understanding of difference "defines it as absolute otherness, mutual exclusion, categorical opposition."[10] Such an understanding leads to a conceptualizion of those who are different as outsiders, with those belonging to the dominant group having the power to decide what is normative (themselves) and what is deviant (others). As long as this continues to be the prevalent understanding, there is no possibility of having just personal relationships, or of creating just societal structures that will not benefit some groups at the expense of others. As long as this is the prevalent understanding of difference, we will always be oppressing those who are outside our group, threatening both them and ourselves with destruction.

Mestizaje-Mulatez in USA Hispanic/ Latina Theology

In our Hispanic/Latina communities a similar understanding of difference prevails. Our marginality, however, makes us question it in ways that the dominant group does not. The re-conceptualization of difference, therefore, follows our need to survive within a dominant culture. Hispanas/Latinas and Latinos have learned that, when we face the dominant group, we have to think in another way about difference. Although sexism, racism, and other prejudices indeed are operative in Hispanic/Latina communities, the need to present a united front makes it imperative for us to overcome them. Yet the way we think about difference at present makes this impossible.

The insistence in Hispanic/Latina theology, including *mujerista* theology, on seeing and using *mestizaje-mulatez* as a positive element and proposing it as an ethical choice is indicative of our preoccupation with understanding and dealing with difference. Virgilio Elizondo, whose work established *mestizaje* as a key element of Hispanic/Latina theology, speaks of it as "the birth of a new people from two preexistent peoples."[11] In the first instance, he argues, *mestizaje* "de facto . . . [came] about through military conquest, colonization, religious imposition. This certainly was the case in the Spanish-Indian *mestizaje*."[12] Elizondo also points to a second *mestizaje*, going on at present here in the USA between Mexican people and other peoples.[13] For Elizondo, therefore, *mestizaje* generates a new people, a new ethnic group, with cultural as well as biological characteristics. He considers acculturation as an accommodation to the dominant group that makes one leave behind one's own culture. Elizondo sees "group inclusion/exclusion" — that is, the social distance among groups that sets up the superior/inferior relationship and the need to eliminate anyone who attempts to destroy these barriers — as "anthropological law[s] of human nature." But Elizondo is not willing to accept these "laws" as immutable. His work is an attempt to show that Mexican-Americans can live out a radical understanding of *mestizaje* that would relativize these laws and bring richness to all. For Elizondo, the Christian faith plays a central role in what *mestizaje* is, means, and signifies.[14] Athough Elizondo speaks about "*la raza*" (the race), he does not make direct reference to José Vasconcelos, the Mexican philosopher who proposed the concept of "the cosmic race." It is in the work of Andrés Guerrero that we find "*la raza*" directly linked to *mestizaje*.[15] Guerrero claims that Vasconcelos' concept "stressed the inclusivity of the four races," and seems to use this concept as a way of grounding and perhaps even amplifying the idea of *mestizaje*. Guerrero proposes "*la raza*" as a symbol of *mestizaje*, of hope, of unity, of new creation, and of liberation. It is important to notice that this way of using "*la raza*" is how Guerrero elaborates what the Mexican-American community whom he interviewed told him.

When others of us Hispanas/Latinas and Latinos who are not Mexican-Americans started contributing to the elaboration of Hispanic/Latina theology including *mujerista* theology, we appropriated *mestizaje* and expanded its meaning. In the first book I co-authored with Yolanda Tarango, published a year after Guerrero's, we started by specifying that we were talking about Hispanics, particularly about the three most numerous groups of Hispanics — Mexican-Americans, Puerto Ricans, and Cubans.[16] Using *mestizaje* as a way of explaining *la raza*, we talk about the three-pronged *mestizaje* of Hispanic women that includes race, culture and history. In a second book, *En La Lucha — In The Struggle*, I expanded on the understanding of *mestizaje* from a *mujerista* perspective, working to develop what Elizondo had called the second *mestizaje*, the one occurring here and now among Hispanics. In the last chapter of *En La Lucha* I began to elaborate a non-exclusionary and non-oppositional perspective of differences and concluded by proposing embracing *mestizaje* as an ethical choice, as a *mujerista* truth-praxis: a denunciation of the racism/ethnic prejudice of this country that, together with the poverty it generates, constitutes a key element in the oppression of Hispanics in the USA.[17]

In *mujerista* theology we have proposed understanding popular religion as a form of *mestizaje* in itself, as well as a key factor of *mestizaje* at large. We recognize that African and Amerindian religious understandings and practices are intrinsic elements of both popular religion and of *mestizaje*. Our intention has been to broaden *mestizaje* to include African cultural, historical and biological elements. However, given the racism in the USA and in our countries or communities of origin, we have come to realize that in *mujerista* theology we need to name specifically the heritage we have received from Africa. Following the lead of Fernando Segovia we started to add *mulatez*, which refers to the mixing of the white and black races, to *mestizaje* instead of subsuming our African heritage under the latter term.[18]

Roberto Goizueta's work in 1995 pushed the understanding of *mestizaje* further. Working to develop a sense of praxis that is non-instrumental, Goizueta turns to Vasconcelos to find an understanding of human action as essentially aesthetic. In Vasconcelos' thought it is the special pathos of beauty that is the unifying principle of intellectual, moral and aesthetic forms of action. Goizueta indicates that Vasconcelos' "special pathos of beauty" means "empathic fusion," of which

> Latin American people are the progeny . . . which occurred historically between the Spanish culture and people, on the one hand, and indigenous and African cultures and people on the other. It was precisely through its openness to these "other" races and cultures and its willingness to intermix and interrelate with them, that Spain gave birth to the Latin American mestizo people, *la raza cósmica*.[19]

For Vasconcelos the *mestizo* community goes beyond a homogeneous community. Goizueta sees this as a key to the reason why the *mestizo* community "does not impose unity, but achieves it through empathic love. In so doing, the mestizo community affirms the identity of other persons as particular, unique, and different subjects (i.e., historical agents in their own right) who, as subjects, can be known only through love."[20] This calls for an understanding of difference that does not focus on opposition and exclusion but rather can make "emphatic fusion" possible without destroying the specificity of historical, moral agents. This new understanding of difference will make it possible to create a way of relating that leaves behind the prejudicial understanding of difference that exists at present.[21] I am convinced that a change in the notion of difference will yield a kind of moral subject for whom goodness is relational, for whom love and justice are inseparable, and find expression in effective solidarity. For *mujeristas*, this is precisely what *mestizaje-mulatez* points to and should mean; this is precisely what the moral option of justice-seeking people should make.

Difference — Relational Rather Than Exclusionary

In *mujerista* theology we have been working to re-conceptualize our understanding of difference because we believe that the way difference is thought about today is the basis for all prejudices and hate crimes. Difference is seen as what separates us from others, as what makes each of us unique. The preciousness of every human person and her intrinsic importance as a human being has been linked to her uniqueness, to whatever she is, has, or does that is different from others. Following these understandings, attempts to relate to others, to be a community, or to work in coalition have depended mainly on emphasizing what different peoples or groups have in common. This means that, following the logic of this schema, one has to leave behind and to ignore what makes one precious and important in order to be able to relate to others individually or communally.

The other conclusion one may draw from this way of understanding difference is that what needs to be done to do away with the prejudices generated by the present understanding of difference is to eliminate differences. This understanding is the operative one in assimilation theories, which, regardless of some claims to the opposite, is still the controlling worldview in the USA. Assimilation leads to three negative consequences. First, ignoring differences means forcing those who are different into the mainstream. It means that the dominant group defines the standards used in society, and that those who are not like them have to abide by what has been set as the norm. Those of the dominant group do not recognize the norm they have set as "culturally and experientially specific," but rather hold on to it as the ideal of a common humanity that poses as universal and neutral, in which all can participate without regard to race, gender, religion, or sexuality.[22] This is the second negative result of assimilation: "It allows the privileged group to ignore their own group specificity."[23] This leads the dominant group to claim neutrality and to regard not itself but the groups that are different as having particularity, as marked with a specificity that leads to consider them as "other."

Perhaps the third consequence is the most insidious one. Assimilation often makes those who are different internalize the negative understandings the dominant group has of them. Assimilation demands those who are different to fit, to be like the dominant group, leading to "the self-loathing and double consciousness characteristic of oppression. . . . When participation is taken to imply assimilation, the oppressed person is caught in an irresolvable dilemma: to participate means to accept and adopt an identity one is not, and to try to participate means to be reminded by oneself and others of the identity one is."[24]

In order to survive as a marginalized group within a dominant culture, Hispanas/Latinas and Latinos have developed, mostly unconsciously, great flexibility shifting from "the mainstream construction of life" to our own construction of life where we feel at home.[25] Our own construction of life is a hybrid reality, a *mestizo/mulato* reality which we create from elements of Latina culture and elements of the dominant culture that we import as we need them.[26] This flexibility, this traveling between worlds, is a "skillful, creative, rich, enriching and, given certain circumstances, . . . a loving way of being and living."[27] However, ethnic prejudice and racism turn this world-traveling into a negative experience, making it compulsory for marginalized people but absolving the dominant group from any responsibility to engage in it. The lack of knowledge and appreciation of marginalized cultures makes this world-traveling mostly a one-way affair, because Hispanas/Latinas and Latinos are not allowed to bring into the dominant construction of the world elements from our own culture. It is also a one-way traveling because the few people of the dominant group that travel to our world insist on changing it by acting in our world the way they act in theirs.

Such lack of ability for world-traveling and such insistence on assimilation on the part of the dominant group are the result of identifying people and things by highlighting difference instead of similarity. Identifying similarity and difference seems to be part of the way people "describe and sort out their perceptions of the world."[28] However, accepting that boundaries created by differences are needed "to make sense of perceptions, experiences, identities, and human obligations"[29] does not necessarily have to lead to assigning consequences to difference or to position ourselves in relation to them. In other words, most of the time the way we understand and deal with difference includes making moral judgments about it, "automatically" deciding that, because people are different they are either better or worse, never just different. Society has insisted on capitalizing on "categories of difference that manifest social prejudice and misunderstanding,"[30] and has ignored ongoing relationships among people that are based on similarities. Society understands boundaries as what keeps us out or away from each other instead of highlighting that "the whole concept of a boundary depends on relationships: relationships between the two sides drawn by the boundary, and relationships among the people who recognize and affirm the boundary."[31] Since boundaries do not exist outside connections among people, this means that, in order to bring about a paradigm shift in our understanding of difference, we need to emphasize how difference is related to relationships rather than to distinctions.

The moral judgment made about differences, especially the judgment of the dominant groups, results in prejudice and discrimination. The basis for the negative moral judgment—and, therefore, for prejudice and discrimination—rests upon five unstated assumptions. First, "we often assume that 'differences' are intrinsic, rather that viewing them as expressions of comparisons between people on the basis of particular traits."[32] Since we are all different from others in many different ways what is at stake is the selection of particular traits as the ones that are vested with negative or positive importance. Second, we assume that when we consider and judge others we do not have prejudices as our point of reference. The unstated point of reference of the dominant group, prejudice, "promotes the interests of some but not others; it can remain unstated because those who do not fit have less power to select the norm than those who fit comfortably within the one that prevails."[33] A third unstated assumption is that persons doing the judging do not have a perspective, as if one could be truly free from a perspective or one could see from someone else's point of view. Fourth, the dominant group assumes the luxury of thinking they do not have to take other points of view into consideration, that the perspectives of those being judged are irrelevant or have already been taken into consideration. Fifth, there is an assumption that the existing social and economic arrangements of society are "natural and neutral" and that, therefore, the differences in the way people are treated and the way they live is a matter of their own personal choice. These unstated assumptions lead to understanding difference as intrinsic to human persons:

> If difference is intrinsic, then it will crop up whether noticed or ignored. If difference is knowable by reference to an unstated norm, then the norm itself remains hidden from evaluation. If an observer such as a judge can see difference without a perspective, then those who "are different" have no chance to challenge the assignment of difference or its consequences. And if the status quo is natural, good, and chosen, then efforts to alter its differential burdens on people will inevitably seem unnatural, undesirable, and coercive. Noticing difference and ignoring it both recreate difference; both can threaten such goals as neutrality, equality and freedom.[34]

How do we change unstated assumptions that are considered natural and that, if noticed, are considered neutral? The only way is to turn to experience. Hispanas/Latinas and Latinos often notice that there are gaps between our experience and prevailing presuppositions. We know that often we ourselves or people we know do not fit in the slots society (the dominant group) assigns us. Our experience often makes us realize that we deal with people we consider "different" but who matter to us differently from the way we treat those whom we do not know or who do not matter to us. This leads us to understand how relationship is essential to the way we conceptualize difference: we may see persons as not similar to us, but in one case it matters and in the other one it does not. This does not mean that dissimilar characteristics disappear but rather that, in the case of the persons with whom we have a relationship, these characteristics are not considered determining traits nor looked upon as signaling exclusion and opposition.

Relationships make it possible to understand that differences are relative. Relationships make it possible for us to share the point of view of those whom an essentialist understanding of differences may have classified as deviant or at least as "other." The goal here is not to replace our perspective with that of another but rather to embrace the partiality of all human perspectives and to admit the point of view of others as a corrective lens to our own. We see that the present understanding of difference depends on a comparison between people with reference to a human-made norm that need not remain the way it is. It is a norm that must be challenged.

Relationships make it possible to realize that once differences stop being unfamiliar they are no longer frightening. Not being afraid opens the door for understanding that our point of view and experience of reality are as different to others as theirs are to us and that the concept we have of difference is a conceptual simplification that serves our interests, that reflects where we stand.[35]

As social beings we are called to relate to all those around us, and this we can do in a nondiscriminatory way only if we emphasize what connects us, if we understand the injuries produced by exclusion and isolation. Decentralizing ourselves would help us to be cognizant of what connects us, and to do this we must stop making ourselves the point of reference. We must stop having what has been called "boomerang perception."[36] The best way to explain what this means is by an example. Think of the well-meaning, committed to justice, Euro-American mother who sends her daughter to school the first day. When the little girl comes home and tells her that she has a Hispanic classmate, the mother, not wanting her daughter to be racist, reassures her by telling her that there is nothing to worry about, that the little Hispanic girl is just like she is. It is very difficult to imagine that such a mother in today's society would tell her daughter, "Do not worry, you are just like that Hispanic girl." The mother's comment reasserts the centrality and normativity of the dominant race and culture. Ultimately boomerang perception indicates that those of the dominant group do not consider the difference important, something worthwhile exploring for oneself. If it were important, the dominant group would see those of us who are different as mirrors who show them as no other mirror can. We, of course, are not the only mirror that they have or should use, but we do show those of the dominant group one of the people they are.[37]

Overcoming boomerang perception is directly connected to the ability to travel between worlds. I want to insist that this is not a matter of a tourist-like visit in which we look at life but do not enter into it. Traveling between worlds means entering the world of other people in such a way that not only do we learn how they see us but that we come to understand better how they construct themselves in their own world and the role we play in that construction. It is important here to understand that we all inhabit many different "worlds"—worlds that are never complete but only under construction—and that therefore we are always sorting out what to include and what to exclude. Additionally, because our social context is not, most of the time, completely of our own choosing, we may not understand or accept the prevalent construction of our world or how that world constructs us.[38]

This idea of traveling to different worlds relates to the need there is to "unlock subjectivity, such that self functions as a fluid, internally diversifying, and temporally open-ended process rather than a product of an autonomous essence."[39] This kind of social ontology necessitates the fluidity created and promoted by world-traveling, which yields mutuality—a key element of solidarity.[40] This world-traveling points to better possibilities for coalition-building, which in return opens doors for more effective world-traveling. Working in coalition with other marginalized groups once we redefine difference in a non-oppositional and non-exclusionary way leads to coalition-building beyond a very specific issue; it leads to understand coalition-building as an effective way to bring about radical change in society.

World-traveling helps one to understand coalitions not merely in an instrumental fashion because in the process of coalition-building one learns to look at the "other" from within his or her world and how the "other" understands us. If coalitions were to organize this or that strategy across interest groups, they would then become much more effective, not only bringing about a limited intended goal but also possibly contributing to radical societal change. When we look at coalition building in this fashion we move from pragmatic action to building that strong sense of solidarity needed both within and among marginalized groups.

Solidarity among Hispanas/Latinas and Latinos and between our community and other marginalized groups and justice-seeking people is not a matter of agreeing with, supporting, liking, or being inspired by a cause. Though all these might be part of solidarity, solidarity itself goes beyond all of them. Solidarity has to do with understanding the interconnections that exist among us. Solidarity is the union of kindred persons "arising from the common responsibilities and interests . . . ; community of interests, feelings, purposes, or action; social cohesion."[41] Solidarity then is grounded in "common responsibilities and interests," which necessarily arouse shared feelings and lead to joint action. This solidarity is not possible without mutuality, which is established through dialogue—world-traveling—and requires conscientization.

Conscientization is a process through which one becomes aware, with no more than a moment of insight, that there is something suspicious about one's condition. Almost anything can create the spark that moves people "from a 'naive awareness,' which does not deal with problems, gives too much value to the past, tends to accept mythical explanations, and tends toward debate, to a 'critical awareness,' which delves into problems, is open to new ideas, replaces magical explanations with real causes, and tends to dialogue."[42] Conscientization enables us to understand the real causes of oppression and the need to engage with others in changing a situation. The process of conscientization is not something that happens once and for all but rather it is a permanent personal effort to situate oneself in time and space, to exercise one's creative potential, and to assume one's responsibilities.[43] Conscientization is always a praxis, not just an intellectual understanding apart from action.[44]

A New *Mestizaje-Mulatez* and the Struggle for Justice

Unfortunately, even within marginalized groups the prevailing understanding of difference as exclusive and oppositional is operative. None of the marginalized groups in the USA have the power to impose their understanding of "other," and yet we reproduce it. It seems to be impossible not to fall under the spell of the preponderant characteristics and perspectives of the dominant group. Part of this problem derives from the fact that a negative understanding of differences is also operative in our countries of origin. *Mestizaje-mulatez* is not seen always as a positive element in our societies back home. However, it is my contention that the view the dominant culture has of us, Hispanas/Latinas and Latinos in the USA, has helped us to recognize the value of diversity and to embrace it as something precious.[45] I am not denying that the way the dominant culture homogenizes us under the label Hispanic is prejudicial to us. Nonetheless, such homogenization has also been instrumental in our coming to recognize ourselves as a community, at least vis-à-vis the rest of society. I am not denying or minimizing the injurious effects for us of the erasure and displacement we suffer when we are blanketed as one under the label of "Hispanics." Nevertheless, this oppressive mechanism has forced us to come together in ways that we would not do otherwise, to deal with each other across class, sex, and race as we have not done in our countries of origin. The labeling and marginalization of Hispanas/Latinas and Latinos make it difficult for us to have a positive sense of self and often lead us to internalize the negative understanding of us on the part of the dominant culture.[46] However, the need to present a united front to oppressive forces and groups makes us come together, create and sustain liberative strategies and understand ourselves as a community with certain shared characteristics and goals. This is what creating a new *mestizaje-mulatez* is about.

This new *mestizaje-mulatez*, which in *mujerista* theology we consider not only our *locus theologicus* but also a moral choice we need to make and effectively sustain, is not "an ethnic identity that Spanish-speaking people bring with them when they arrive but something they create in response to the conditions here in this country."[47] In many ways it is a result of the need to fight against discrimination, but it is also a result of the seeds planted in our countries of origin regarding the races that have come together in those lands. Notice, for example, to support claims of identity and greatness for their countries and to identify themselves with the people politicians in México and Perú refer to the Aztecs and Incas. This entails a certain ambivalent embracing of *mestizaje* even as laws and policies continue to oppress indigenous peoples.[48] The new *mestizaje-mulatez* being created here is at the base of what is called the Hispanic/Latina community, a community that needs an identity as a whole is order to create solidarity and fight injustice.

The cohesiveness that allows us to see ourselves as a community revolves around five elements: the Spanish language; popular religion; social-cultural-psychological survival; economic oppression; and our vision of the future.[49] These elements are the building blocks of *mestizaje-mulatez*. The last one—our vision of the future—is most important, because it takes note of the fact that the reason for *mestizaje-mulatez*, for mutuality, for solidarity among Hispanas/Latinas and Latinos, is not to make us good but to allow us to struggle for justice for our community. As a matter of fact, commitment to *mestizaje-mulatez* is what makes it possible for us to maintain the revolutionary momentum of the struggle for liberation. We are convinced that the liberation of Hispanas/Latinas and Latinos cannot be at the expense of any other marginalized group. *Mestizaje-mulatez* allows us to hope for our own liberation but it also makes clear that to this end we need to be in solidarity with other marginalized groups.

Solidarity is made possible by mutuality and world-traveling, by intersubjectivity and by an understanding of difference that is relational and determined to include rather than exclude. Solidarity and mutuality in *mujerista* theology are key elements of the struggle for justice. An important element of justice that has been ignored is directly related to mutuality: justice as right relationships. "Justice" throughout the Hebrew Scriptures refers to "righteousness" (*tzedeka* in Hebrew), not so much in the sense righteousness is used today but in the sense of right relationships.[50] Justice is not "a behavior in accordance with an ethical, legal, psychological, religious, or spiritual norm. It is not a conduct which is dictated by either human or divine nature, no matter how undefiled. It is not about actions appropriate to the attainment of a specific goal."[51] Rather, righteousness in the Hebrew Scriptures refers to the fulfillment of the demands of a relationship with others, with the divine and—today we need to add—with the rest of creation.

The Hebrew concept of righteousness is a relational one. The person does not exist outside the community. Each of us is set within a multitude of relationships: with parents; siblings; neighbors; friends; work mates; bosses; people who sell to us; people who work for us; people who govern society; priests or ministers; people whom we do not know personally but whom we depend upon like garbage collectors; mail deliverers; migrant workers who pick the fruit and vegetables we eat; factory workers in this country and abroad; researchers; scientists; and doctors on whose work we depend for keeping us healthy and prolonging our lives; the poor and oppressed, particularly those for whom we have to take responsibility, because their condition is caused by our high standards of living.

Righteousness also has to do with our relationship with nature, a relationship that we have ignored for so long that we need to rediscover and attend to it in a very special way. We are related to the rain forests in Brazil that are being destroyed daily at an incredible rate, to the dwindling world oil reserves, to all the animals species that are part of the biosphere in which we exist but which we continue to extinguish, to the atmosphere that our greed damages in so many different ways every day. Righteousness has to do with a right relationship with the divine, a relationship that happens within history, a relationship that God has chosen to have in and through the way we relate to all of creation.

In the Hebrew Scriptures not only are those who fulfill the demands of a relationship called righteous but also those who have had their rights taken away from them within such a relationship. Those who have been deprived of what was rightfully theirs, those who are in need, those who are oppressed or afflicted are righteous and must have their legal rights restored. Psalm 146[52] talks about this very clearly:

Happy are those whose help is the God of Jacob, . . .
who keeps faith forever;
    who executes justice for the oppressed;
    who gives food to the hungry.
The Lord sets the prisoners free;
    the Lord opens the eyes of the blind;
the Lord lifts up those who are bowed down;
    the Lord loves the righteous.
The Lord watches over the strangers;
    he upholds the orphan and the widow. (Psalm 146:5–9)

This is taken up and forcibly repeated in Matthew 25 where we are told specifically that we must restore our broken relationships if we want to enter the reign of God: we must feed the hungry, give drink to the thirsty, welcome the stranger, clothe the naked, visit the sick and those in prison.

The Role of Theology in Re-Conceptualizing Difference

As we move into the twenty-first century we are faced in the USA with the fact that in about twenty years there will be no racial/ethnic majority. Therefore, unless we want to help develop and sustain a system of apartheid, unless we want to feed the present system which makes oppression possible, we must change radically our understanding of difference. We must establish a strong solidarity among marginalized groups based on the struggle for liberation, on the restructuring of society so justice for all can flourish. Restructuring society needs not only a change of structures but also a radical change in culture. Changes in structures forced on society that are not complemented with changes in culture do not last.[53] Theology also has an important role to play in changing culture, of which it is integral part.

In *mujerista* theology culture embraces whatever we fabricate to deal with our world: customs, understandings, practices, artifacts that have been developed by our ancestors and continue to be created by us today to contribute effectively to our own lives and to the society in which we live. Cultures share many common elements, but what establishes the distinctiveness (not uniqueness) of each is the way in which such common elements "are used, how they are handled and transformed. The distinctiveness of cultural identity is therefore not a product of isolation; it is not a matter of a culture being simply self-generated, pure and unmixed; it is not a matter of 'us' vs. 'them.' Cultural identity becomes, instead, a hybrid, relational affair, something that lives between as much as within cultures."[54]

Given this understanding of culture, theology then is to be viewed as part of culture. It is a cultural activity because humans produce it, because it is a human activity. Theology is particularly related to that aspect of culture that deals with the worldview of a people, with the lens through which a people views life, works with it and finds meaning in it. As Kathryn Tanner puts it,

> Theology is a particular version of this search for meaning, for a pattern of fundamental categories that will, as cultures do, orient, guide, and order human life. The adequacy of theology can therefore be judged by how well it performs these general cultural tasks. Does it, for example, help people successfully navigate their world and cope effectively with life's vicissitudes?[55]

The theologies of marginalized groups help us find our world in the many worlds we have to travel to survive. At the same time it has to critique the dominant culture that limits our choices, that keeps us from contributing to society, that uses us instead of enabling us. Hispanic/Latina theology including *mujerista* theology uses *mestizaje-mulatez* as our *locus theologicus* precisely because it identifies our culture. Insofar then as *mestizaje-mulatez* refers to our culture it critiques the dominant culture against which we have to struggle to survive. *Mujerista* theology offers our relational understanding of difference as a contribution to a deeper understanding of *mestizaje-mulatez* in Hispanic/Latina theology and to the elaboration of a liberating culture, of a justice seeking culture, of an embracing culture that allows and enables fullness of life for all.

Notes

[1] All nouns in the Spanish language have grammatical gender and so do their modifying adjectives. *Comunidad*, community in Spanish, is feminine and so are the adjectives that modify it, in this case, *Latina*. This gives me the opportunity of using the feminine form *Latina* as a way of breaking through the traditional use of the masculine form to refer to a group of many women and only one man. Throughout this article, then, my use of *Latina* should be read to refer to both men and women from the *Latina* community.

2 Ada María Isasi-Díaz, *En La Lucha — In the Struggle: Elaborating a Mujerista Theology*, 2d ed. (Minneapolis, Minn.: Fortress Press, 2003), Chapter 6.

3 *United Nations Development Report* 1992 (New York and Oxford: Oxford University Press, 1992), 34.

4 Ibid., 14.

5 Ibid., 35.

6 Pedro Casaldáliga, "El Pregón del jubileo," *Presencia Ecuménica* (Caracas) 46 (January–March 1998): 23.

7 *United Nations Development Report 1995* (New York and Oxford: Oxford University Press, 1995), 36.

8 Ibid., 41.

9 Casaldáliga, "Pregón del jubileo," 23.

10 Iris Marion Young, *Justice and the Politics of Difference* (Princeton, N.J.: Princeton University Press, 1990), 169.

11 Virgilio Elizondo, *Galilean Journey* (Maryknoll, N.Y.: Orbis Books 1983), 10.

12 Ibid.

13 Ibid., 13–16.

14 Ibid., 16–18.

15 It is not my intention here to critique or endorse the use of Vasconcelos's concept of *la raza cósmica*, which some claim has strong undertones of racism. I do think that Guerrero uses it as a springboard and does not necessarily claim to embrace all that Vasconcelos meant by it. In this regard it is important to notice that Elizondo's use of *la raza* without mentioning Vasconcelos, as well as the popular use of this word/concept, seems to indicate that it has a meaning and a relevance among the people that goes far beyond Vasconcelos's elaborations. See Andrés Guerrero, *A Chicano Theology* (Maryknoll, N.Y.: Orbis Books, 1987), 118–137.

16 Ada María Isasi-Díaz and Yolanda Tarango, *Hispanic Women: Prophetic Voice in the Church* (San Francisco: Harper and Row, 1988; reprint, Minneapolis, Minn.: Fortress Press, 1993), xi.

17 Isasi-Díaz, *En La Lucha*, Chapter 6.

18 We heard Fernando Segovia use *mulatez* before he put it in writing. Orlando Espín and other Cuban and Puerto Rican theologians also use *mulatez*. See Fernando Segovia, "In the World But Not of It," in *Hispanic/Latino Theology: Challenge and Promise*, ed. Ada María Isasi-Díaz and Fernando Segovia (Minneapolis, Minn.: Fortress Press, 1996), 196.

19 Roberto S. Goizueta, *Caminemos con Jesús* (Maryknoll, N.Y.: Orbis Books, 1995), 97–98.

20 Ibid., 98.

[21] See Audre Lorde, "Age, Race, Class, and Sex," in *Sister Outsider* (Trumansburg, N.Y.: The Crossing Press, 1984), 114–23.

[22] Iris Marion Young, *Justice and the Politics of Difference*, 164.

[23] Ibid., 165.

[24] Ibid.

[25] María Lugones, "Playfulness, 'World'-Traveling, and Loving Perception," in *Making Face, Making Soul—Haciendo Caras: Creative and Critical Perspectives by Women of Color*, ed. Gloria Anzaldúa (San Francisco: Aunt Lute, 1990), 390.

[26] Of course, in being imported within a mainly Latina frame of reference, the elements of the dominant culture undergo certain modifications. For example, Latinas may be on time for meetings but our meetings still have to start with time for personal relationships instead of diving right into business.

[27] Lugones, "Playfulness, 'World-Traveling,' and Loving Perception," 390.

[28] Martha Minow, *Making All the Difference* (Ithaca, N.Y.: Cornell University, 1990), 4. The elaboration of the meaning of differences that follows is based on Minow's work and is also influenced by the work of María Lugones and Iris Marion Young.

[29] Ibid., 7.

[30] Ibid., 9.

[31] Ibid., 10.

[32] Ibid., 51.

[33] Ibid.

[34] Ibid., 74.

[35] Ibid., 379.

[36] Elizabeth V. Spelman, *Inessential Woman: Problems of Exclusion in Feminist Thought* (Boston: Beacon Press, 1988), 12.

[37] María C. Lugones, "On the Logic of Pluralist Feminism," in *Feminist Ethics*, ed. Claudia Card (Lawrence: University of Kansas Press), 41–42.

[38] Lugones, "Playfulness, 'World-Traveling,' and Loving Perception," 394–396.

[39] Catherine Keller, "Seeking and Sucking: On Relation and Essence in Feminist Theology," in Rebecca S. Chopp and Sheila Greeve Davaney, eds., *Horizons in Feminist Theology: Identity, Tradition, and Norms* (Minneapolis, Minn.: Fortress Press, 1997), 55.

[40] This idea of "world-traveling" moves away from static notions of subjectivity while still insisting on subjectivity since we do not lose ourselves as we cross worlds. Furthermore, this idea of traveling to other worlds to change ourselves involves a kind of reciprocity between the

worlds we relate to and our own agency as well as to the need to be open to those worlds and their construction of us as intrinsic to our own agency. This has ontological implications but our emphasis here is on unlocking subjectivity through world-traveling more as a strategy to change the way we conceptualize difference. I am grateful to Darla Jean Fjeld, a Ph.D. graduate from Drew University for her helpful analysis of Lugones's concepts ("Gender and Divine Transcendence: Preface for a Philosophy of Religion," [Ph.D. dissertation, 1998]).

[41] *The Random House Dictionary of the English Language*, 2nd unabridged ed. (New York: Random, 1987).

[42] Gustavo Gutiérrez, *A Theology of Liberation* (Maryknoll, N.Y.: Orbis Books, 1988), 92.

[43] Ibid., 92.

[44] Paulo Freire, *Pedagogy of the Oppressed* (New York: Seabury Press, 1973), 3.

[45] I first introduced this idea in *En La Lucha*, 192–193.

[46] Suzanne Oboler, "The Politics of Labeling: Latino/a Cultural Identities of Self and Other," *Latin American Perspective* 19:4 (Fall, 1992), issue 74: 18–36.

[47] Geoffrey Fox, *Hispanic Nation: Culture, Politics, and the Construction of Identity* (Tucson: The University of Arizona Press, 1996), 239.

[48] Once I was watching the Republican convention on television with a Euro-American friend and after about an hour of references to the USA as the best country in the world, the most powerful country in the world, I could not take it any more and began to rage against the self-aggrandizement of this country. My friend looked confused and explained that politicians always have to extol this country and the only way to do that was by claiming to be the best. Did not politicians everywhere do that? When I answered that was not the case, she asked how politicians in other nations extolled their countries. I explained that in most countries they did by reference to some sort of "glorious past," including their indigenous cultures. I remember her look of astonishment as I insisted that being better than others, that being unique and the most powerful was not the only way or necessarily the best way for politicians to instill pride about this country.

[49] Isasi-Díaz, *En La Lucha*, Chapters 1 and 2.

[50] *Tzedeka* is paired off with *mispath* that is more closely related to legal rights.

[51] Elizabeth R. Achtemeier, "Righteousness in the OT," in *The Interpreter's Dictionary of the Bible*, 4 vols. (Nashville, Tenn.: Abingdon Press, 1962), 4:80.

[52] Translation of Psalm 146 adapted in order to eliminate sexist language.

[53] In no way am I opposed to structural changes as those brought about by changes in laws. But we cannot think that because structural changes have happened they will be permanent. For radical change to happen the structural change has to go hand in hand with cultural changes, with changes in the values and priorities of society.

[54] Kathryn Tanner, *Theories of Culture: A New Agenda for Theology* (Minneapolis, Minn.: Fortress Press, 1997), 57–58.

[55] Ibid., 58.

6

Lo Cotidiano

Everyday Struggles
in Hispanas/Latinas' Lives

The women around the world who have birthed women-centered liberation theologies have done so against immense odds. Absolutely nothing has deterred us, however, for what guides and inspires us are the lives of our mothers, sisters, daughters, women lovers, friends. Very many of their lives, like very many of ours, are illumined by the struggle to survive and flourish in spite of many obstacles. To elaborate our women-centered theologies we have had to invent different ways of listening to each other, of understanding knowledge and religion and their functions. Audre Lorde taught us early on that unless we created new methods for doing theology we would not effectively dismantle the traditional ways of theology that have excluded women and our religious understandings and practices.[1] Much less could we develop our theologies using the same theories, criteria, and sources that men theologians have used. This is why we have developed new methods and theories. We have gone even farther and have re-conceptualized theories, understanding them as "contingent hypotheses, constructed not found, that need to be tested and continually revised."[2]

This constructive task led us to recognize the faith of the people as the source of our theologies, not an abstract faith but the faith that sustains grassroot people in their daily living. Indeed, women-centered liberation theologies consider of great importance the lived-experiences of women, of the most oppressed women in our communities who struggle to survive and flourish constantly. In *mujerista* theology we have developed a method that provides opportunities for and enables grassroot Hispanas/Latinas to speak about themselves and their religious understandings and practices. We have also created ways to bring their voices to "official" theological arenas and we have insisted that Hispanas/Latinas must be heard and that their lived-experience must be taken into consideration.

The work we *mujerista* theologians have done with grassroot Hispanas/Latinas has taught us that the horizon of Hispanas/ Latinas lived-experience is, first and foremost, the "everyday," *lo cotidiano*. We have come to see the importance of *lo cotidiano* of Hispanas/Latinas in such a way that we believe it has to be at the heart of *mujerista* theology and, we contend, *lo cotidiano* is of importance to all liberation theologies and struggles. Without clear knowledge of what *lo cotidiano* is and how it functions, we will continue maybe to refer to it but we will not give it the full importance it has for theology and all liberative praxis.

The Importance of *Lo Cotidiano*

The elaborations about the meaning, function and importance of *lo cotidiano* presented here clarify the presuppositions that ground our claims regarding Hispanas/Latinas' lived-experiences as the source of *mujerista* theology. They help us to better understand the issues at stake in such a claim and connect it to other theological and theoretical proposals having to do with "source," "story," "narrative," and "discourse."

More important than all of this, however, is the need for our theological endeavors to contribute effectively to women's liberation. This is a central criterion of *mujerista* theology and our exploration of *lo cotidiano* has been instigated by this requirement, an obligation imposed on us by the dangers women suffer all around the world. Thus what motivates us is the necessity to contribute effectively to the liberation of women.

What do we have to contribute effectively to the liberation of Hispanas/Latinas and of women all around the world? There is no doubt that we have to be committed to radical structural change while at the same time attending to particular situations, even if only in a temporary way. Yet, as one looks back over the last four decades one sees little change in structures of oppression. Although some changes have taken place, most of them are without lasting effect. Today we have slid back when it comes to issues of ethnic prejudice/racism and sexism. Struggles regarding economic oppression have not made significant headway either. As a matter of fact, the gap between those of us who have and those who do not have is broader than ever.

The main reasons structural changes have not come about or lasted derives from the fact that structural change has not been seen as integrally related to *lo cotidiano*. To correct this, I insist, it is time we listen to Hispanas/Latinas and other grassroot women around the world and, drawing from their wisdom, conceptualize structural change in a different way from the way it has been understood in the past. This does not mean ceasing to work on changing family structures, work-related structures, the economic structures of our societies, political structures, church structures. No. However, following the insights of grassroot women, structural change must be rooted in *lo cotidiano*. Unless the changes we struggle to bring about impact the organization and function of *lo cotidiano*, structural change will not happen and if it happens, it will not last. We want to be clear that it is not a matter of either/or. We certainly must continue to organize, to bring about changes in the way politicians are chosen, how multinational corporations operate, how the churches control what is considered orthodox. Those changes, however, cannot be conceived or brought about apart from the question, "What change will this bring to the everyday lives of poor and oppressed women?"[3] Maybe it is time to give up grandiose plans for sweeping changes and to realize that even if those changes were accomplished they would not last unless they brought about change at the level of *lo cotidiano*.[4]

The few structural changes that have happened seem not to have affected much the everyday lives of grassroot people. They have not reached what is immediate to people; they have not solved the problems of the here and now. These few structural changes "did not warm tenderly dreamed hopes, did not inter-change favors, did not open spaces for the gratuitous, for the spontaneous, for fantasy; they did not calm hatred, desire, vengeance, nor the frequent desire to end one's life."[5]

The struggles for structural change as they have been carried out since the 1960s have not done "battle against the absurd incremental gains of the forces that destroy life, which under-mine *lo cotidiano* in many ways."[6] The main reason proposals for structural changes have not taken *lo cotidiano* into consideration, I believe, is because we have not stopped to see its importance, to grasp its meaning. The task at hand, then, is to offer some markers for remedying our faulty understanding of *lo cotidiano*.

The Meaning of *Lo Cotidiano*

Lo cotidiano is a complex concept not easily defined. This does not mean that it is something imprecise or that it refers to any-thing and everything. Due to the complexity of *lo cotidiano* it is better to describe rather than define it so as to point out its many elements and characteristics. *Lo cotidiano* constitutes the imme-diate space of our lives, the first horizon in which we have our experiences, experiences that in turn are constitutive elements of our reality. *Lo cotidiano* is where we first meet and relate to the material world that is made up not only of physical realities but also is made up of how we relate to that reality (culture), and how we understand and evaluate that reality and our relation-ship with it (history). *Lo cotidiano* is necessarily enmeshed in material life and is a key element of the structuring of social rela-tions and its limits. *Lo cotidiano* situates us in our experiences. It has to do with the practices and beliefs that we have inherited, with our habitual judgments, including the tactics we use to deal with the everyday. However, by *lo cotidiano* we do not refer to the a-critical reproduction or repetition of all that we have been taught or to which we have become habituated. On the contrary, we understand by *lo cotidiano* that which is reproduced or repeated consciously by the majority of people in the world as part of their struggles for survival and liberation. This is why this conscienticized *cotidiano* carries with it subversive elements that can help us to question the reality in which we live.[7]

Lo cotidiano has much to do with the experiences we have lived, with experiences that have been analyzed and integrated into our understandings and behaviors. It is what makes the world of each and every one specific, and, therefore, it is in *lo cotidiano* and starting with *lo cotidiano* that we live the multiple relations that constitute our humanity. It is the sphere in which our struggle for life is most immediate, most vigorous, most vibrant.

Lo cotidiano is what we face everyday; it includes also how we face it. In no way should *lo cotidiano* be seen as belonging mostly to the private world. *Lo cotidiano* is in contact on a regular basis with social systems; it impacts their structures and mechanisms. *Lo cotidiano* refers to the way we talk and to the impact of class, gender, poverty and work on our routines and expectations; it has to do with relations within families and among friends and neighbors in a community. It extends to our experience with authority and to our central religious beliefs and celebrations.[8]

Lo cotidiano is intrinsically linked with what we usually call common sense,[9] and, therefore, we tend to see it as something "natural." When we talk here about "natural" we are not referring to the philosophical naturalism that limits reality only to what the human mind can conceptualize but to the obviousness that the expression "of course" indicates. This sense of "naturalness" of *lo cotidiano* points to the way it is concrete and specific, permeated by the material world.[10]

In *lo cotidiano* there is much "practical-ness" involved not in the pragmatic sense but in the "folk-philosophical sense of sagacity" that has to do with being prudent and levelheaded. Attention to *lo cotidiano* makes it possible for grassroot people not to be caught in situations they cannot effectively deal with or, if they can't avoid being caught, *lo cotidiano* alerts them so they are at least not surprised. Much of this folk-wisdom comes from the instincts of grassroot Hispanas/Latinas sharpened by their daily struggle for survival.[11]

Anyone who has worked with grassroot people knows about the "unmethodical-ness" of *lo cotidiano*, the ad hoc-ness of *lo cotidiano*.[12] This leads to what outsiders might consider inconsistency in the lives of Hispanas/Latinas, but in reality it has to do with the need to react immediately to what happens for, if not, most probably one is in danger. This "unmethodical-ness" is needed to deal with the unpredictability of Hispanas/Latinas' lives and of all those who have no power to control or change what happens to them, who can at best cope with what happens or survive in spite of it. All those who work with grassroot people marvel at the way they use every possible minute and how they manage to bring something out of nothing. Grassroot Hispanas/Latinas have a great capacity to pay attention to and to deal with a multitude of things at the same time.[13] They do not have the luxury of dealing with problems one at a time because the majority of situations they face cannot wait for attention. Not to deal with them at once can be disastrous. Grassroot Hispanas/Latinas have the ability to see the connections that exist among things, elements, and people who are very different. They would dull this ability if they were more methodical and dealt with things in a deductive and systematic way. Many consider the Latina way disorderly, but in reality it is a way that indicates the importance of the intuitive and of being totally present to details. It is precisely details that constitute the core of reality, of life. It is important always to remember that the lives of grassroot people bring them daily face to face with a reality of vital importance, that has to do with their own well-being and that of those for whom they are responsible. They cannot take that well-being for granted. They have to procure it day after day.

Lo cotidiano refers to the simple world, a world where one has to take care of what is scattered along the surface minute by minute. The urgency of *lo cotidiano* often makes it necessary for one to leave the causes or reasons for later, a "later" that often does not come because the urgency of the present never diminishes. This does not mean that Hispanas/Latinas are not conscious of the reasons or causes of *lo cotidiano*, of the struggles they carry on to deal with it. Concretely, dealing with that reality scattered along the surface means figuring out how to feed the family today, how to pay for the oil or gas they need to heat their homes today, how to get money to buy the medicine their children need today. When we say that *lo cotidiano* has to do with the simple reality of life we refer to those immediate necessities, to the crises that grassroot people have to face daily, and to the wisdom they show when, in some way or other, they survive.

Lo Cotidiano, Reality and Knowing

The importance of *lo cotidiano* does not consist only in what it is, but also in how one can or should use it. Our analysis of reality and of the process of knowing does not separate praxis from reflection but, proceeding from a perspective of liberation, it privileges the poor and the oppressed. It recognizes them as "organic intellectuals," to use Gramsci's term, admirably capable of understanding and explaining their experiences and beliefs.

This analysis of reality has as its goal not a mere comprehension of the meaning of reality but an apprehending and facing up to reality.[14] The starting point, from a liberation perspective, is the experience of grassroot people. Those experiences, which deal with the substance and the form of *lo cotidiano,* are used in *mujerista* theology to construct a Latina narrative that helps us to understand better who we are as Hispanas/Latinas and to explore the hermeneutical and epistemological threads that give continuity to our lives.

Taking seriously the descriptive function of *lo cotidiano* makes it possible for new narratives to emerge, narratives created by the poor and oppressed who take charge of reality.[15] In these narratives they find themselves and see themselves as moral subjects who exercise their right and power of self-definition. It is only when we are self-defining that we become historical subjects capable of conceiving future realities beyond the present. For the poor and the oppressed a new narrative, having continuity with the present but different from the "normative" one, is an important element of the process of conscientization. New narratives help us to see and to value parts of ourselves that we have ignored or that we do not know well, and they help us to know ourselves differently from the way oppressors define us. New narratives break the hegemony established mainly by men from the western and northern hemispheres, a hegemony that has contributed much to produce and maintain prejudices and oppressive structures, such as ethnic prejudice and racism, sexism and compulsive heterosexism, classism and material poverty.

The importance that *lo cotidiano* has in the narratives of grassroot Hispanas/Latinas helps us to recognize that people do not live or die for a creed or a belief. They need narratives that arise from their reality, that not only convince but motivate. That is to say, the descriptions of reality that are based on and fed by *lo cotidiano* have the capacity to move hearts in a way that laws, authoritarian dictates, and arbitrary exigencies do not have. There is a need for narratives that echo our reality, for it is through them that we learn to know ourselves, our lives and their moral aspects, and the relation that exists between the morality of human behavior and happiness or unhappiness.[16]

The importance of *lo cotidiano* is not limited to its descriptive function but also concerns what grassroot people think about themselves and what they do, the discourses they construct, and the roles and norms that society imposes on them. *Lo cotidiano* has hermeneutical importance because it is marked by subjectivity and because we cannot but see it and understand it except from a singular perspective. *Lo cotidiano* is the lens through which we apprehend reality. This means that hermeneutics refers not only to the meaning reality has for us but goes well beyond the perspective we have about what happens, how we live, who we are. Hermeneutics deals with context, with the use of power and determining who the ones are who mold the shape of daily life. Hermeneutics has to do as much with promised results as with actual results, which these grassroot people cannot control. The hermeneutical function of *lo cotidiano* makes visible the day-to-day oppression of grassroot Hispanas/Latinas because it not only points out clearly discriminatory practices but it also unmasks those who benefit from them.[17]

This way of understanding the hermeneutical importance of *lo cotidiano* highlights the multiple intentions present, the way oppressive discourses and practices are reenforced while liberating ones are obstructed. The hermeneutical function of *lo cotidiano* makes one understand the materiality of communications, the connection that exists between discourse and action. It enables one to see the importance of the motivations for a given praxis. Hermeneutics explains the role in *lo cotidiano* of values, presumptions, "facts," "truths," strategies, setting, material means and intentions. This is why we cannot apprehend reality and face it without taking seriously the hermeneutical function of *lo cotidiano*.

Once one has grasped these descriptive and hermeneutical functions it is not hard to deduce the epistemological importance of *lo cotidiano*. This means that when we speak about *lo cotidiano* of grassroot people, we refer not only to their capacity to know but also the characteristics of their way of knowing. Since knowing has to do with apprehending and facing up to reality, epistemology has to deal with efforts to understand and express the how and why of life and of human beings. *Lo cotidiano* is not only the starting point for apprehending and facing up to reality but it also plays a key role in this whole process. This is why we cannot ignore it or relegate it to some unimportant dimension. The emphasis on *lo cotidiano* makes it possible for one to understand knowledge as a fragmentary, partisan, conjectural, and provisional reconstruction of reality.[18]

Knowledge is fragmentary. What we will know tomorrow is not the same as what we know today but it will stand in relation to what we know today. What we know is what we have found through our experiences, through the experiences of our communities of struggle. Even this must be checked against our own reality. What we know is always partisan; it is always influenced by our own values, prejudices, loyalties, emotions, traditions, dreams, and future projects.[19] Our knowing is conjectural because to know is not to copy or reflect reality but rather to interpret in a creative way those relations, structures, and processes that are elements of what is called reality. And, finally, *lo cotidiano* makes it clear that knowledge is provisional, for it indicates in and of itself how transitory our world and we ourselves are.[20]

What interests us about *lo cotidiano* and what we have been referring to is not a matter of just "another" perspective. *Lo cotidiano* indicates that the poor and the oppressed understand and face reality in a different way from that of the powerful and privileged. The epistemological function of *lo cotidiano* indicates that the struggles of the poor and the oppressed taking place in the underside of history constitutes the place, the moment—the horizon—of grassroot people's knowledge of reality. There is a triple dimension to knowing reality: becoming aware/getting to know reality, taking responsibility for reality, and transforming reality (*hacerse cargo de la realidad, cargar con la realidad, encargarse de la realidad*).[21]

"Becoming aware/getting to know reality" means being in the midst of reality, and not merely facing an idea about it. It implies being among things through their material and active mediations. The descriptive function of *lo cotidiano* emerges from this aspect of knowing reality. At the same time, the descriptions, stories, narratives about the experiences of grassroot Hispanas/Latinas' *cotidiano* enable them to grasp reality. Telling their stories helps Hispanas/Latinas to know and understand the reality that surrounds them instead of merely facing an idea about it or the meaning of things as other have purported them to be.

The second dimension, taking responsibility for doing something about reality, refers to the ethical character of reality. Human beings cannot evade real commitments but have to take upon themselves reality and what it demands. The hermeneutical function of *lo cotidiano* is closely related to this ethical dimension, which is why we have included as part of it values, truths and intentions. It is worthwhile repeating that one cannot know reality without examining the perspective from which we understand it, and one cannot understand that perspective without analyzing whose it is and whom it benefits.

The third dimension, transforming reality, refers to the fact that one of the characteristics of knowing is to become involved in what we know. We cannot talk about knowledge if we are not ready to take on what we consider to be real. The epistemological function of *lo cotidiano* concerns this precisely. *Lo cotidiano* is the principal horizon of the poor and the oppressed who, in order to survive, have to struggle to transform reality. It is the poor and the oppressed, mainly made up of women, who know reality in a unique way because they transform it when they manage to survive by somehow providing shelter, food, clothing, medicine for themselves and their families.

The *Via Negativa:* What *Lo Cotidiano* Is Not

What we have claimed about *lo cotidiano* carries much weight in struggles for liberation, which has to do with the creation and upkeep of structures that human beings need in order to develop to our fullest human potential. However, we must insist that *lo cotidiano*, even the conscienticized *cotidiano*, is not the criterion we use to evaluate and decide what is unjust or just, what is oppressive or liberating. In other words, being part of daily life does not mean that a given praxis or value is necessarily a criterion in *mujerista* theology. It is only if *lo cotidiano* contributes to justice, to liberation, to the struggle for fullness of life for grassroot Hispanas/Latinas, that it can be considered just and liberating. It is only if it is a praxis that contributes to the struggle for liberation of the poor and the oppressed that *lo cotidiano* is good, correct, salvific. To make *lo cotidiano* in itself a criterion, an ethical principle and norm, would be to idealize it. Yes, there is much that is good in daily life but there is also much that "obstructs understanding and tenderness, allowing an abundance of postures of self-defense to appear that are full of falsehoods, of lies, that turn *lo cotidiano* into a behavior that is not open to life."[22]

Having liberation as criterion means that we do not endorse a relaxed, vague, or loose morality as part of *lo cotidiano*. That type of morality is possible only for the powerful, for those who are so closed off in their social and political reality that they can live "unpreoccupied" only with those who think as they do. Such individuals can live with a vague sense of morality for they have the luxury of not needing to be open to others who know reality in a different way. A moral attitude that has as criterion satisfying the desires of the powerful is possible only in the world of those who live ignoring the world that surrounds them. Because the powerful view the rest of humanity as alien, they are incapable of conceiving new ideas, of creating different ways of organizing society; they are incapable even of understanding that if without radical structural changes they will not be able to maintain the status quo that benefits them so much. They are incapable of seeing that the present capitalist system that undergirds their status and privileges carries within it the seeds of its own destruction.[23]

Lo cotidiano in *mujerista* theology is not a "category" or "theory" in the essentialist, universal and/or idealist sense of this word. *Lo cotidiano* is not something that exists *a priori* under which we can classify what happens daily. We do not understand *lo cotidiano* as a universal experience, for to do so would mean that we do not take seriously the differences that exist among human beings and the way we experience and understand reality. Instead of thinking of common experiences we focus on "shared experiences" in an attempt to respect the subjectivity and agency of each person. At the same time, we use "shared" instead of "individual" to point to the interrelatedness that is intrinsic to *lo cotidiano*. The concept of shared experiences emphasizes that there are similarities in the way different persons and peoples experience and deal with *lo cotidiano*. Furthermore, to recognize similarities among the experiences of grassroot Hispanas/Latinas contributes to an understanding of differences that is relational instead of oppositional and exclusionary. The focus on shared experiences also helps us to be conscious that Hispanas/Latinas are not unique, that there is much we share with other communities of struggle and they with us.

Lo cotidiano does not support an absolute relativism that ignores the shared experiences that are part of our lives. On the contrary, the centrality of *lo cotidiano* in liberating historical processes and the need to be in the midst of reality as a central element of the process of knowing highlight the need not to dismiss a certain sense of relativity in an off-handed way. Instead we need to recognize that the limitations and historicity of all reality oblige us to deal with relativity in a positive way. "Responsible relativism," as we call the understanding of relativism that is operative in *mujerista* theology, is opposed to the objective universals that have undergirded many of the structures of oppression that exist in our world today.[24] Responsible relativism, recognizing the presence of subjectivity in all human thinking and knowing, makes clear that whatever is considered objective is merely the subjectivity of those who have the power to impose it as normative. Responsible relativism helps us to see knowledge and "truths" as different explanations of reality, explanations not necessarily exclusive of each other but often in agreement, at least partially. Such explanations do not necessarily do away with traditional ones or those elaborated by other communities. In responsible relativism it is very clear that those who endorse a certain version of reality have to be accountable in a specific and concrete way for those versions and the consequences they bring. Lastly, responsible relativism, based on the fact that it does not deny the viability of other possibilities, encourages the development of strategies that could be placed in common, that could be grounded in this or that explanation, that could contribute as much to the liberation of this community as to the liberation of that other one. But responsible relativism does not include or validate any understanding that would contribute to the liberation of a person or community at the expense of another one.

Lo Cotidiano, a Needed Category

Much has been said of *lo cotidiano* not included here, and much needs yet to be said about how it functions and how important it is in bringing about structural changes. This attempt to elaborate a *mujerista* understanding of *lo cotidiano* responds to two specific needs. First, there is a need for women's voices to be heard and to be recognized as important. The work women do, which is concentrated mainly in what is considered *cotidiano*, must be valued. I do not know any society in which women are valued sufficiently, in which we are considered as capable as men, in which the fact that we do more than half of the work needed for the survival of the human race is acknowledged. The insistence on *lo cotidiano* is a cry for the liberation of women.

In the second place, what moves us to heed *lo cotidiano* is the absolute need for radical changes in our world, in all parts of our world. Attempts to implement radical changes during the last forty years have failed because of a lack of attention and importance given to *lo cotidiano*. This conclusion is not a vague statement with no concrete reality to substantiate it. On the contrary, the experiences of grassroot Hispanas/Latinas confirm the need to pay attention and give importance to *lo cotidiano*.

Lo cotidiano embraces our struggles and our fiestas, our birthing, living and dying; *lo cotidiano* extends to our loving and, tragically, to our hating. *Lo cotidiano* is nurtured by our religious beliefs, the political, our utopias, and those eschatological glimpses we perceive when we are able to take a few steps towards justice. We create *lo cotidiano* when we walk, when we dance, when we work, when we make love. So, let us not forget *lo cotidiano* when we struggle for liberation. Let us not forget *lo cotidiano* as an intrinsic element of women-centered liberation theologies.

Notes

¹ Audre Lorde, "The Master's Tools Will Never Dismantle the Master's House," in *Sister Outsider* (Trumansburg, N.Y.: The Crossing Press, 1984), 110–113.

² Sheila Greeve Davaney, "Introduction," in *Horizons in Feminist Theology—Identity, Tradition, and Norm*, ed. Rebecca S. Chopp and Sheila Greeve Davaney (Minneapolis: Fortress Press, 1997), 3.

³ Structural changes proposed by different movements start with universal principles that try to mold societies accordingly. Whether these structural changes follow socialist or capitalist principles, for example, the insistence on principles as the foundation for structural changes leads to an aprioristic claim of validity that ignores the actual *cotidiano* of grassroot people and often excludes whole sectors of society. By insisting on *lo cotidiano* we are proposing that all principles need to be submitted to a criterion of effectiveness for people's struggles for liberation. See Franz Hinkelammert, "Por una sociedad donde quepan todos," in *Por una sociedad donde quepan todos*, Cuarta Jornada Teológica de CETELA, ed. José Duque (San José: DEI, 1996), 364–365.

⁴ I explore another aspect of this idea in Chapter 9 of this book, "*Burlando al Opresor:* Mocking/Tricking the Oppressor: Hispanas/Latinas' Dreams and Hopes."

⁵ Ivone Gebara, *Teologia a ritmo de mujer* (México City: Ediciones Dabar, 1995), 121. This is my own translation from the Spanish edition of this work, which is itself a translation from the Portuguese.

⁶ Ibid.

⁷ In other words, we are not suggesting that a conscienticized *cotidiano* is one that supports this or that ideology but one that describes, relates to, and identifies the reality of grassroot people.

⁸ Daniel Levine, *Popular Voices in Latin American Catholicism* (Princeton: Princeton University Press, 1992), 317.

⁹ Clifford Geertz, "Common Sense as a Cultural System," in *Local Knowledge* (New York: Basic Books, 1983), 84ff. This description of *lo cotidiano* uses some elements of Geertz's analysis of "common sense."

¹⁰ Ibid., 85–86.

¹¹ Ibid., 87.

¹² Ibid., 90.

¹³ Ibid., 91.

¹⁴ Ignacio Ellacuría, "Hacia una fundamentación del método teológico latinoamericano," *Estudios centroamericanos* 30:322–323 (agosto-septiembre, 1975): 419. I use this schema several times throughout this book, applying it in different circumstances. See Chapter 7, "In a Time Such as This: 9/11/01."

[15] A more complete explanation of the role that narrative plays for Hispanas/Latinas is discussed in Chapter 4 in this book, "Creating a Liberating Culture: Hispanas/Latinas' Subversive Narratives."

[16] See Paul Ricoeur, "Life: A Story in Search of a Narrator," in *A Ricoeur Reader: Reflection and Imagination*, ed. Mario J. Valdés (Hertfordshire: Harvester, Wheatshef, 1991), 425–437.

[17] We are assigning a function to hermeneutics that goes beyond the usual one because we do not think one can deal with meaning if one does not face what is happening with it. We are amplifying the meaning of hermeneutics by assigning to it some of the functions of rhetoric. See J. D. H Amador, "Feminist Biblical Hermeneutics: A Failure of Theoretical Nerve," *Journal of the American Academy of Religion* 66:1 (Spring, 1998): 39–57.

[18] Otto Maduro, *Mapas para la fiesta* (Buenos Aires: Centro Nuevo para la Promoción Social y Pastoral, 1992), 137.

[19] And in *mujerista* theology we are very clear about our partisan perspective. We make a clear option for the perspective of Latinas based on the fact that we believe the Christian message of justice and peace is based on an option for the oppressed.

[20] I have here adapted Maduro's synthesis about knowledge. See *Mapas para la fiesta*, 136–138.

[21] This scheme is proposed by Ellacuría, 419.

[22] Ivone Gebara, *Conohece-te a ti misma* (Sao Paulo: Ediciones Paulinas, 1991), 24. This is my own translation from the Portuguese.

[23] I recognize that this evaluation is enormously complex. Here I simply wish to point out that the need for ever-expanding markets, essential to capitalism, will undoubtedly in the long run destroy it. For markets to expand there needs to be people who consume in big quantities. Given the finite resources of our world, this need for some to consume so much, goes hand in hand with reducing the number of people who can do so.

[24] What I call "responsible relativism" is an adaptation of the ideas of feminist philosopher Lorraine Code. She does not use this phrase and the following development of this term is not based on her ideas. See Lorraine Code, *Rhetorical Spaces—Essays on Gendered Locations* (New York: Routledge, 1995), 185–207. In Chapter 12 of this book, "*Identíficate con Nosotras: A Mujerista* Christological Understanding," I apply this understanding to the values that are intrinsic to being part of the kin-dom of God.

7

In a Time Such as This

9/11/01

The Twin Towers[1] once stood about forty miles from Drew University, where I teach ethics. A few days after the September 11 tragedy, when the Manhattan bridges opened and I was able to get to the university, I took time in my classes to analyze what had happened. Virtually every person I had talked to or heard in the news used four words to describe what they felt, to describe their reaction to the tragedy: anguish, pain, fright, and loss. The students also expressed these overwhelming feelings and emotions.[2] Since that day I keep asking myself and others again and again, "How did we get from anguish, pain, fright and loss to the bombing of Afghanistan? Answer me this," I insist, "how come it is considered patriotic to exact vengeance instead of extending forgiveness? How come it is considered patriotic to curse those responsible for the tragedy of September 11 instead of feeling compassion for them?"

Answers like "we must not show weakness" or "we need to make sure that something like this never happens again" simply do not ring true. Such responses avoid looking at all that happened before September 11. They refuse to take into consideration what led to that day of disaster. These answers avoid analyzing USA policies that are so devastating that people are willing to follow orders at the expense of their own lives. When the nightly news, for example, have shown non-Afghan men crossing into Afghanistan to join the Taliban forces, I have asked myself, Why are they willing to risk their lives? I can understand that a few men, and even more than a few, are fanatics bent on destroying others to forward their cause. But when there are significant numbers of people who are willing to follow those extremists, something is happening that the rest of us cannot dismiss or ignore.

Virtually every opinion I have read or heard that has dared to question the response of the USA government (a point where I find myself in this article right now) has made it clear that what happened on September 11 is not being condoned in any way whatsoever. I join them. I denounce all violence, I denounce all taking of human life and, therefore, unequivocally, I denounce and protest, I abhor and condemn what happened on September 11. But precisely for the same reasons that I cannot in any way whatsoever excuse what happened then, for those same reasons I denounce and protest, I abhor and condemn the bombing of Afghanistan and any and all actions that are death-dealing instead of life-giving. If we designate as fanatics and extremists those who planned, approved, and executed the dreadful acts of September 11, what do we call those who bomb a country where the majority of its citizens are women and children, a country with no means of defense against such bombing?

The people of New York City, soon after September 11, turned Union Square into one big altar full of candles, signs and symbols of their anguish, pain, fright, and loss. At the edge of the zone in lower Manhattan closed for weeks after the tragedy, Union Square became a sort of open-air church where we went to be with others, to console one another, to see if we could help one another understand what had happened, to attempt to help us all find ways of moving on with our lives. I happened to go there the evening city officials had decided it was time for us to move on, to go back to being consumers, a role they have reminded us of repeatedly since the early days after the tragedy. The night a colleague and I went there, the city had cleaned the place, filling dozens of garbage bags with the mementos and symbols the people had created to ritualize their fright and pain, their loss and anguish. But New Yorkers are a fierce brand of people. There they were, setting up the altar again, posting signs, lighting candles, discussing and preaching, crying and finding comfort in the arms of strangers. Nothing impressed me more that day than a flyer pasted in different areas of the park that said, "Not in my son's name." A mother refused to allow her son's death to be used by the authorities as the reason for bombing Afghanistan, as the reason for the USA to engage in acts strikingly similar to those of the terrorists on September 11.

Another day begins. The sun is about to rise above my horizon, a horizon crowded with the buildings of upper Manhattan. But for those of us who live in this city for the time being, and I suspect for a long time to come, there is no longer just "another day." Instead, the precariousness of life that became so palpable on September 11 has made us fill our days with such intentionality that every day now has its own features, characteristics, and goals. Each day has to be faced specifically so we can live through the anguish, pain, fright, and loss that subsume our lives. And each day, which we now live so carefully, gives us the opportunity to understand ourselves, individually and as a people, in a very different way from the lighthearted reflections of those lazy days of the summer of 2001.

In the days and weeks after September 11, as I drove across the George Washington Bridge, I would look at the scarred skyline of Manhattan and pray for those who died and their families. The fully armed men who patrolled the sidewalks of the bridge remind me of the other military personnel who carried out the orders to bomb Afghanistan, and those who invaded it and continue to engage in ground combat. Those who patrolled this Manhattan bridge with machine guns reminded me how the illusion of safety has disappeared from my life, how, from now on, I stand with the millions of women, children and men who day after day, all around this world of ours, live in danger of dying an untimely death.

Knowing in a Different Way

I have purposefully laid out the themes of this essay in a long introduction in a way different from the one traditionally used in academic discourse. I have done this in an attempt to gather first feelings and emotions, and only secondarily, understandings and reasons. I follow this structure to highlight the role of emotions and feelings in learning and in the work of ethics.[3] The anguish, pain, fright, and loss so prevalent in our lives nowadays make it more obvious than ever that emotions and feelings play a role in what we know, how we know it, how we process what we know, and how we allow it to impact our lives. I am here trying to go beyond the mere assertion that our worldview or ideology, the position from which we know, and the implications of our knowing affect or determine what we know. In a way my assertion is simple, not at all extraordinary or new, but inescapable all the same: Our emotions and feelings, and not just our ability to reason and to understand, are central elements of our knowing. Our emotions and our feelings, as a matter of fact, put us in touch with reality in a way our intellect does not. The wrenching emotions and feelings that the September 11 catastrophe aroused in us do not cloud our thinking and understanding but rather illumine it. Without them our knowledge is incomplete, our understanding is severely hampered, our reasoning is faulty. It is precisely our emotions and feelings that make it possible for us to be involved in such a way that we can claim to know, to have learned something from the situation we have experienced and about which we have some information.[4]

To know reality, I believe, one has to be, first of all, enmeshed in a situation, one has to be impacted and affected by it.[5] Many things we come to know are not part of our immediate experience. In this case solidarity becomes key, for solidarity is what allows us to become enmeshed in situations that are removed from us experientially but that impinge on our lives. The farther from our experience, the more difficult it is for us to be touched by the reality of things instead of merely being in touch with ideas about reality. To be touched by reality one has to be in touch with its materiality and since our personal experience is limited, since our touching others and situations in which we are not involved is limited by the finitude of our humanity, the only way we can come to "touch" this reality is through a deep sense of solidarity. Emotion, then, makes it possible to become enmeshed in the materiality of situations and other people's lives in ways that intellect does not.

I did not know personally, as far as I have been able to ascertain, anyone who died in the Twin Towers, the Pentagon or the airplane crash in Pennsylvania. Yet the physical immediacy of what happened, its enormous scope, the images seared into my mind by television replays, the surreal image of smoke rising from lower Manhattan, the absence of the Towers in the Manhattan skyline, the increased security at airports and train stations—all of this enmeshes me in what happened and makes it possible for me to know this devastating reality in a much better way than if I only read about it.[6]

The second necessary element of knowing involves taking responsibility for what has happened in the sense of shouldering what it requires, what it demands, what it exacts from us. This is the ethical component of knowing that one cannot effectively evade. And here is where we need to look carefully at what public officials, the government and the media have done with us, with you and me personally. For what has happened is that our anguish, pain, fright, and loss have been abducted and turned into violence. What has happened is that we have been told that the best—and only?—reaction possible is a violent one, one that demands retribution. Let us be very clear, retribution is but a thinly disguised version of vengeance, and vengeance is never an ethical action. It is wrong to seek vengeance in and of itself. Furthermore, it has been proven time and again that vengeance generates only more violence. Violence does not satisfy those seeking to exact some sort of payment for what they have suffered.

The day after the disaster, I went out in my neighborhood in upper Manhattan to buy fruit and vegetables. I went into the little neighborhood stores where I have been going for the last twelve years. The sense of anguish, pain, fright, and loss was so obvious. People looked at each other and simply sighed. We sensed that we each knew what the other was thinking, what the other was feeling, what concerned us all. The usual assertiveness and impatience of New Yorkers were gone. Incredulity seemed to have replaced our brashness, and all we could do as we looked at each other was shudder. Then I returned home to the lone functioning television station to face the barrage of violent language that had become standard by then, to watch how our emotions were being hijacked by the government in an attempt, I believe, to keep us from thinking about how part of the responsibility for what happened lies squarely on the shoulders of this nation.[7] Government officials could have chosen to react in some other way, but instead, all we heard from them was an immediate declaration of war, language that debased others, that offered no solution but vengeance and that equated patriotism—love of country—with military action. Indeed they continue to assure us this is the only possible solution. Would we not know better and understand more clearly what happened on September 11 if our anguish, pain, fright, and loss had been channeled a different way? Would we not know better if our emotions had been used to help us understand those who were attacking us instead of turning them into enemies that we, as a nation, vow to destroy, that we, as a nation, vow to obliterate from the face of the earth?

The anguish, pain, fright, and loss we felt can very well be placed at the service of making us go beyond our regular pattern of analyzing and dealing with situations in which we are involved, in which we place ourselves always at the center, making ourselves the main point of reference. The profound emotions that gripped us on that frightful September 11 have made us vulnerable, and when we are vulnerable we are able to allow into ourselves what in our regular state of mind we persistently keep out: people, events, and ideas that challenge our priorities and make us lay aside our rational/cost-analysis/how-does-this-benefit-me way of confronting reality. Here is an opportunity for us to go beyond ourselves and in so doing to grow in the best of ways possible. Here is a moment where the intensity of emotions and feelings has made it socially acceptable for us to lead with our hearts. It could have been possible or easier for us to break through our usual way of thinking and to shoulder part of the responsibility for what has happened. We might have understood it in a different way. However, this new and untried way of thinking was immediately made impossible by the leaders of our communities who have had one unswerving message for us: the best way, the only way to cope with the situation, to act in a responsible way, is by endorsing a military response. Because our anguish, pain, fright, and loss were transformed into feelings of revenge, our knowledge of what took place on September 11 has been distorted. It has been perverted. The one ethical response that has been envisioned and endorsed by our governmental representatives and, yes, even by most of our church leaders, leads us to ignorance of what really happened and makes our political actions questionable.[8] The total unwillingness of those who speak for us and to us to look for other alternatives than a violent response to the events of September 11 has left us bereft of moral decisions that enhance life and expand goodness and kindness, trust and love, solidarity and compassion in our world.

Acting in a Different Way

The third element of knowing reality has to do with the action-oriented pole of knowing, for we have long left behind the idea that we can know in the abstract or that we can claim to know and understand and not do anything about it. Here I affirm that *not acting* on what we claim to know is not neutral. It is a positive something in the sense that it results in our endorsing the way proposed. This action-oriented moment of knowing follows on the heels of the ethical component of knowledge that requires us to take responsibility for reality in order to really know it. Perhaps here is where we can begin to unmask and deconstruct the "knowledge" of September 11 that has been elaborated by the government and the media. As we reject the solution, as we attempt to influence the way the USA as a nation is acting, we begin to create a different narrative—a different discourse—of what happened September 11. We begin to honor the anguish, pain, fright, and loss that we experience day in and day out; we begin to allow ourselves to lead with our hearts and to come to know reality in a different way. But we cannot do this unless we act in a different way. The "official" interpretation of what happened is so potent and pervasive that we cannot just sit in front of our television sets and attempt to think differently from what we are being told. We have to allow ourselves to act into knowing, to feel into knowing, in a different way. This is the ethical and epistemological challenge facing us. Our responsibility is to act differently so we can know differently. How do we "act-know/know-act" in a way that makes us agents of life, of fullness of life, instead of dealers of death? Knowing that how we act towards others and what we know is constitutive of who we are, how do we love ourselves in the present situation so that we can love others?

Thich Nhat Hanh, the Vietnamese Buddhist monk, prophet of peace, spoke at Riverside Church shortly after the September 11 tragedy. In his address he took our anguish, pain, fright, and loss and led those present to a different place from where we have been made to go by the government and the media. Instead of using violent language and war images, the Buddhist monk helped his audience to lead with their hearts, to be in touch with and to understand the desperation behind the acts of September 11. To be in touch with and to try to understand the situation that gave rise to the attacks in no way means condoning what happened or attempting to excuse from responsibility those who planned them and carried them out. However, it does mean that we take responsibility for asking the hard questions instead of leaving them for others to ask and then condemning them for doing so. It means that we honor our anguish, pain, fright and loss, but that we do so knowing that we now simply join the vast numbers of people all over the world as well as marginalized groups in this country who feel and have felt this way for generations. Thich Nhat Hanh took our anguish, pain, fright, and loss and made us realize that the way we respond to what has happened definitely colors our understanding of those events, understanding that we then turn into a rationalization for what we do. The Vietnamese Buddhist monk proposed that we respond differently from the present course. He suggested that instead of bombing Afghanistan we should flood with aid that country and other countries in that part of the world poor beyond our comprehension. This aid, coming from people made vulnerable by fear and pain, would not be self-serving, an aid with strings attached, one that would help us to control others in a more efficient way, but rather a respectful aid that would enable those nations to stand on their own.

In a time such as this, Thich Nhat Hanh's presentation suggests, how different would be our world if instead of becoming cheerleaders for war the USA would lead the world in efforts to respect one another and our different ways of life! To be able to act in such a way we have to know "those people" as intrinsically connected to us, as indeed they are, and ourselves intrinsically linked to them, as indeed we are. To submerge ourselves in the process of "knowing differently-doing differently" we have to recognize, appreciate, and cherish the common interests that we have as human beings. To "know differently-do differently" we have to realize that the globalization process, which is so beneficial to us in this country, also creates an interdependence that carries with it the same responsibilities characteristic of all mutual relationships.

If our knowing does truly depend on our ability to be in touch with the reality we claim to know, and if it depends on our taking responsibility for it, it is no less true that our knowing depends also on our taking action on the reality in which we are enmeshed and for which we are responsible. All reality that touches our lives in some way changes us and is changed by us. Therefore, what we do following on what we comprehend throws light back on what we have understood. The way in which we are actively present in any given reality affects how we know that reality and, consequently, what that reality is for us, what it means for us, how it affects us. Concretely, if we had spent the millions of dollars the bombs dropped over Afghanistan have cost us in humanitarian aid for the people of Afghanistan, we would come to know what happened on September 11 in a different way, a difference that would then ground our future actions in this moment in history. Yes, if we had been convinced to act humanely—even if we were not very sure it was going to be effective, even if we were not convinced that it was going to stop future acts of terrorism in our world—if we had acted differently, we would know ourselves and the tragedy that we suffer differently. We would know those who inflicted such wounds on us and the tragedy that they have suffered in a very different way.

The anguish, pain, fright, and loss that have been turned into a patriotism that exacts nothing but vengeance and leads only to violence should instead have led us to compassion. Yes, compassion for those who have hurt us, compassion for those whose way of thinking and believing led them to overcome the human instinct for self-preservation, is a befitting way, a moral way to be present in the reality that we know as September 11. Compassion is an ethical attitude and praxis that in a time such as this is indeed redemptive not only for those to whom we show compassion but also for ourselves who have the opportunity to be compassionate.

In Times Such as This: Compassion

Compassion in a time such as this is indeed a brave and courageous act. Compassion in a time such as this is not an extraordinary act. Neither is it an inappropriate response for public—political—acts. Compassion is a necessary disposition and way of acting in the present circumstances, for it helps us to understand the needs and relationships that are part of this situation.[9] Furthermore, it is my contention that without compassion we cannot see the real consequences of the response of the USA government to the September 11 attack.

Compassion demands of us beneficent actions that have to arise from a concrete concern for the good of others. Compassion is what in ethics we refer to as a virtue, that is, a habitual disposition concerned with choosing both how to act and how to feel.[10] Compassion, as well as any other virtue, does not exist in the abstract. One who is compassionate is so only because she or he does compassionate acts, and such acts are born from a way of feeling, from a disposition that has to be rooted in the heart as well as in the mind. How do we acquire such a disposition? How do we become compassionate people? How do we act in a beneficent way towards those who have harmed us? How does being compassionate help us to know the dreadful reality of September 11?

The virtue of compassion does not arise solely from an act of the will. Neither does it come solely from a kind heart. The virtue of compassion—feeling and action combined—needs to be practiced time and again so it can become second nature. The practice of compassion starts with our ability to feel with and for others and, in order to do that, we have to value the other, we have to believe that those "others" have something to contribute to us and to the world, something intrinsic to our well-being. We act in a compassionate way; we have concern for the good of "others," for their own sake as well as for our own sake.[11] To have compassion towards others, therefore, we need to allow ourselves to be vulnerable or, rather, we need to recognize that we are vulnerable instead of pretending that we are impenetrable and self-sufficient. Vulnerability is openness to being affected, moved, and convinced by someone else. Openness here refers to an attitude and a belief that our truth is not necessarily the only truth and even that our truth might be wrong, which means that the truth of other persons might be right.

Again, I am not suggesting, by asking us to be compassionate towards those who attacked us, to condone what they did. I am asking us, however, to leave behind the imperialist position that rules every aspect of the USA as a nation and of our lives as a people. The USA is a great nation, but to others it may be only the most powerful, not necessarily the greatest. Most probably each person believes her own nation is the greatest! For us, this may be the best system in the world, but for others—with other cultural and historical backgrounds—this system may not necessarily be what they want for themselves. We have every right to defend our way of life but not at the expense of other people, of placing them all at the service of our way of life, of imposing upon them our way of life.[12] We need to see ourselves in relation to these "others," and we need to respect their way of life and their beliefs.[13] The anguish, pain, fright, and loss that the events of September 11 have caused give us a window of opportunity for being vulnerable to others and, therefore, for feeling the need to be compassionate. Anguish, pain, fright, and loss can indeed provide for us the opportunity for "emotional thinking," for turning to others in a different way, for de-centering ourselves and considering the situation as others see it and in view of others. September 11 provides us with a rich opportunity to practice courageously the virtue of compassion, a virtue that is needed if we are to attain the fullness of humanity for which we were created. We may not be in the habit of being compassionate but here is an opportunity to move in that direction, an opportunity we cannot waste, an opportunity for which we will be held accountable.

We must be compassionate and concerned for those who attacked us and hurt us in such a grievous way, if for no other reason, at least because of the interconnection that exists among us. In this day and age the interconnection among all peoples is more obvious than ever. Globality is a reality at many levels of our lives.[14] Consider communications: there is almost instantaneous accessibility to worldwide information and one can reach almost every corner of our planet in less than forty-eight hours. Think of the economy: before Wall Street opens here in Manhattan, we are told how it will be affected by markets in other parts of the world. Of course, the economy of the USA buoys up or drags down the economies of many other countries. What about ecology? Acid rain does not stay inside any given country's borders; global warming does not occur in only one area of the planet; and the deterioration of the ozone layer responds to practices in many different countries. Consider health: the AIDS epidemic certainly has no boundaries. These realities affect all of humanity regardless of the country in which we live. Therefore, compassion for those who attacked us, being concerned about them and acting towards them in a beneficent way has specific and immediate repercussions for everyone. We should indeed be feeding the people of Afghanistan, not as part of a propaganda blitz aimed at turning them against the Taliban, but out of a deep sense of compassion. The Afghanis have suffered and continue to suffer in unspeakable ways partially because of our own dealings with them—using them as chess pawns—for several decades. Our lives are very much intertwined with theirs; we have furthered our cause, our economic wellbeing and our political influence, by using the Afghanis.[15] It is now obvious that we have explicitly tied their destiny to ours. In a time such as this when thousands are in refugee camps, in which so many Afghani men have died that a disproportionate number of women and children make up the population, when they face harsh winters and widespread famine, in a time such as this, we are called to be compassionate. We do have another option than the one we have embraced. As a nation we must reverse ourselves and become compassionate toward Afghanistan.

Finally, compassion is a much more life-giving way of channeling the anguish, pain, fright, and loss that we all feel. Compassion respects and honors those feelings while revenge and vengeance betray them. Violence and revenge lead only to more violence and play into the hands of those who have done violence to us. Religious leaders, immediately after the September 11 tragedy, expressed this concern. We must "face deep and profound questions of what this attack on America will do to us as a nation," they said. They asked, "Are we to respond in kind and therefore continue the circle of violence in which those who committed the violent acts of September 11 were caught and promoted? Instead we are called to assert the vision of community, tolerance, compassion, justice, and the sacredness of human life, which lies at the heart of all our religious traditions. . . . Let us make the right choices in this crisis—to pray, act, and unite against the bitter fruits of division, hatred, and violence. Let us rededicate ourselves to global peace, human dignity, and the eradication of injustice that breeds rage and vengeance."[16]

In a time such as this, we must honor our anguish, pain, fright, and loss and work to increase goodness in the world instead of violence. In a time such as this we must concentrate on being as generous as possible, on being as compassionate as possible for the sake of all of humankind. We are always called to be the best we can be. We are always called to be life-giving and not death-dealing people. In a time such as this, let us grow in stature in the eyes of our children and of the rest of the world. Let us welcome and embrace the call and the grace to be compassionate.

Notes

[1] I dedicate this article to the youngest in my family, Julia, Mikey, Katie, Alec and Caroline. Others may not agree with what I say in this article, but these children are the ones that have the right to hold me accountable for what I think and do in a time such as this. To them I owe a world where the greatest possible number of people can live to their fullest potential instead of a world where less than one third of us live at the expense of all the rest. In a time such as this, Julia, Mikey, Katie, Alec and Caroline, you keep me honest. I thank you for this.

[2] Of course, another word often heard was "anger." I do not use anger as a point of reference in this article for several reasons. First of all, I did not feel angry, my students did not mention anger, and when I checked with close friends, they were not feeling angry. Second, all those I heard on television and radio who mentioned being angry also mentioned feeling anguish, pain, fright and loss but not all those who felt these emotions mentioned anger too.

3 For a fuller explanation of the role of emotions in ethics and ethical behavior see Chapter 10 of this book, "Justice and Love Shall Kiss."

4 I want to make it perfectly clear that I am talking here about epistemology and not only about hermeneutics, though the latter impinges on the former.

5 I am using here Ignacio Ellacuría's explanation of the process of knowing reality. See Ignacio Ellacuría, "Hacia una fundamentación del método teológico latinoamericano," *Estudios centroamericanos* 30:322–323 (agosto-septiembre, 1975): 419–421.

6 Of course we can and do become saturated or "sick and tired" of what we see repeatedly and then we ignore it, we do not allow it to touch us, we become callous. Here is where we rely on habits—virtues— of caring and compassion that are kept alive and operative only if we practice them. Often, the beginning of our caring and being compassionate starts with making ourselves be attentive to what we see, and, so much of what we see is what we watch on television in the comfort of our homes, that we have to make an effort not to watch as a mere spectator. We need to watch to know, and we need to remember that to know we have to become emotionally engaged, which in turn leads us to take responsibility for what we know and to become involved in what we learn.

7 I do not have cable TV and in Manhattan the television antennas of the main networks were on top of one of the Towers. All that I was able to see for several weeks was a local station that obviously had an antenna somewhere else and transmitted non-stop about what was happening in New York City.

8 The use of justice as a code word for retribution, for punishing the guilty, for retaliation, is unpardonable on the lips of anyone but particularly of religious people. The moral indignation of common, ordinary people over the misuse of the word "justice" around the events of September 11 came to the fore in a stunning way over the suggestion of some in the government to use for the war against Afghanistan the code name "Operation Infinite Justice," an idea that they had to abandon for its blatant hubris!

9 Jodi Dean, *Solidarity of Strangers—Feminism after Identity Politics* (Berkeley: University of California Press, 1996), 92–101.

10 Diana Fritz Cates, *Choosing to Feel—Virtue, Friendship, and Compassion for Friends* (Notre Dame: University of Notre Dame Press, 1997), 2. I thank the Drew University students in my course, "Contemporary Ethical Issues: Love and Reconciliation," for their insights during our class discussions the fall semester, 2001.

11 Ibid., 133–136.

¹² Consider this regarding our way of life, something that many might think quite insignificant but that has enormous repercussions all over the world. Consider how our way of life is marked by our use of paper. The fact is that all the trees of the world would disappear in two years if the whole world were to use the amount of paper that is used in the USA, where only 6 percent of the world population lives. Why then should we not learn from the way of life of those who use paper in a much more limited way instead of imposing our way on them? Pedro Casaldáliga, "El Pregón del Jubileo," *Presencia Ecuménica* 46 (enero-marzo 1998, Caracas): 23.

¹³ Respect for the way of life and beliefs of others does not in any way mean that we accept situations of oppression and violence in other cultures. As a woman I am very aware of the fact that in the name of cultural differences, women have been the victims of oppressive and violent practices such as genital mutilation, not being allowed to receive an education, and dress codes that are abusively confining. These I unequivocally denounce as unjust, as simply wrong.

¹⁴ For a fuller explanation of the idea of globality and how it is different from globalization see Chapter 8 of this book, "La Habana: The City That Inhabits Me."

¹⁵ This is not the place to review in full facts that many of us are now learning but that the USA government chooses to ignore. I only offer the following to substantiate what I say about the USA use of Afghanis and their situation.

Bin Laden is a Saudi Arabian millionaire who "became a militant Islamic leader in the war to drive the Russians out of Afghanistan. He was one of the many religious fundamentalist extremists recruited, armed, and financed by the CIA and their allies in Pakistani intelligence to cause maximal harm to the Russians . . . though whether he personally happened to have direct contact with the CIA is unclear and not particularly important. . . . Bin Laden . . . [and his followers, many of them are not Afghanis,] turned against the US in 1990 when . . . [this country] established permanent bases in Saudi Arabia — from his point of view, this was a parallel action to the Russian occupation of Afghanistan, but far more significant because of Saudi Arabia's special status as the guardian of the holiest Moslem shrines." Noam Chomsky, "Interview with Noam Chomsky by Radio B92 in Belgrade," September 18, 2001 (received via the internet from an undisclosed source).

¹⁶ "Deny Them Their Victory: A Religious Response to Terrorism," September 20, 2001. This statement was signed by nearly four thousand persons. The full text may be found at http://www.ncccusa.org/news/interfaithstatement.html.

8

La Habana:
The City That Inhabits Me

A Multi-Site Understanding of Location

"Who are the Cubans here?" asked in a most authoritarian voice the government official who headed the project we were visiting. I raised my hand, as did the couple that was hosting our group, and the driver of our bus. "Come with me." I got up but our host, smiling discreetly, said to me, "Not you. He means those of us who live here." I did not feel embarrassed but I had a sense of being "dis-placed," without a place to call my own. Born and raised in La Habana, Cuba's capital, I have lived feeling that I left my heart there, just as the song says, when I became an *exiliada* at age eighteen. I have lived for decades thinking of the day when I will be able to live again in Cuba. If all of this does not qualify me as a Cuban, what does? What will?

* * * * *

"That is Don Luis," I said to myself. Stopping the car I jumped out saying, "Don Luis, what are you doing here?" Six months earlier the parish had thrown him a goodbye party. He was retiring and was going to do what he always said he would do, move back to Puerto Rico. "*Pues*, things did not turn out the way I expected and, here you have me, back in Rochester, New York."

* * * * *

I had just finished giving a low-key critical analysis of the USA economy to a friendly group. I had been asked to give the information needed to those who were gathering signatures opposing congressional plans to end the "welfare laws." The third person to ask me a question said, "You speak about the USA that way because you are not an American." That night I thought to myself, how much more American can I be? I vote in general elections, in primaries and in local elections; I pay city, state, and federal taxes; I enjoy the privileges of living in New York City, I carry a USA passport, and my economic fate is tied to that of the USA. But she is right, I admitted to myself in the safety of my bed, in one sense I am not an American. This is not where my "first" loyalties lie.

* * * * *

Maggie has cut my hair for the last fifteen years. She is beginning to retire. She now works a month and spends the next one in Puerto Rico where she is building a house. "I hope to be able to move back home for good in two years." Maggie has lived in New York City for over 25 years. Yet, her "real" home has always been her country of origin, that little island in the Caribbean that they call "the island of enchantment." Maybe I will retire to the island where I was born!

* * * * *

In La Habana, after going through immigration, you notice a group of uniformed persons looking over each one of us going by. Feeling somewhat uncomfortable by what I considered government surveillance — they are from the Ministry of Health — I lower my eyes and try to pass unnoticed. "*¿Se siente bien? ¿Quiere que le tome la presión?*" No, I do not want my blood pressure taken; I am feeling fine. Hearing me answer in Spanish she says, "*¿De dónde eres?*" I am not prepared for the question. It sticks in my throat but I finally stutter, "*Soy Americana,*" thinking that will protect me from having to submit to any tests.

"*Pero, ¿dónde tú naciste?*" I tell her I was born in La Habana. Her whole attitude changes and, drawing me in with a very intimate tone, she says, "*No digas eso; tú eres cubana.*" I want to cry. She is right: I am not an American; I am a Cuban who lives in New York. I want to embrace her and kiss her and broadcast far and wide what she has said. I look at her and holding back my tears I say, "*Tienes razón, tienes razón!*" You are so right!

* * * * *

Lupe writes, "I am back from our yearly trip to Texas. Once we are back here in Michigan we always say that it is too far to keep driving there. But there is something that almost forces us to go. It is as if we need to touch the land where we were born to have the strength to keep living far away from it. I don't know; maybe we are getting old and sentimental but though right now we are saying we cannot do this again, I know we will. Maybe next time my niece can come and help us with the driving. That way we can show her all the places back there that we are always talking about. That would be so nice!"

* * * * *

I am with a group of students in the "Plaza de la Revolución" posing for a picture where Fidel stands to review military parades and speak for hours. All of a sudden I see a man I know from back in the USA walking towards me. We embrace. "What are you doing here?" "I brought a group of students for an immersion experience," I reply. "And you?" "I just had to come at least for a few days. I simply could not stand any longer being away from La Habana."

* * * * *

September 11, 2001. I feel deep sadness. I am not angry, I am just sad. I am so distraught about this human race to which I belong. I am sad.

September 14, 2001. The Manhattan bridges are open and I drive to work in New Jersey. Coming back I am anxious to get to the point in the highway where I can see the city: first the Empire State Building and then, looking south, the Twin Towers. I slow down and pull to the side to take a good look. There is the Empire State and further south: just smoke. October 25, 2001. Today was the first time the smoke over southern Manhattan was light enough for me to see the gaping hole in the horizon where the Twin Towers used to be. Great sadness comes over me. "How could they do this to this city?" No, wait. I did not say, "this city." I said "my city!"

* * * * *

Para Ana Velford
Lourdes Casal

Pero Nueva York no fue la ciudad de mi infancia
    But New York was not the city of my infancy
no fue aquí que adquirí las primeras certidumbres
    it was not here that I grasped truth for the first time
no está aquí el rincón de mi primera caída
    the corner where I first fell is not here
ni el silbido lacerante que marcaba las noches.
    or where I heard the piercing whistle that
        signaled night.
Por eso siempre permaneceré al margen,
    This is why I will always remain at the margins,
una extraña entre estas piedras,
    a stranger among these stones,
aun bajo el sol amable de este día de verano,
    even under the kind sun of this summer day,
como ya para siempre permaneceré extranjera
    just as I will always remain a foreigner
aun cuando regrese a la ciudad de mi infancia.
    even when I return to my childhood city.
Cargo esta marginalidad inmune a todos los retornos,
    I carry this marginality that is immune to
        all returns,
demasiado habanera para ser neoyorkina,
    too much from La Habana to be a New Yorker,

demasiado neoyorkina para ser,
        too New Yorker to be,
 —aun volver a ser—
        —even to be again—
cualquier otra cosa.
        any other thing.

Displaced/Multi-Sites Persons

As we move ahead into the twenty-first century, where do we turn to find elements with which to create a *proyecto histórico* that will move us from terrorism to Biblical neighborliness, from frustration to possibilities, from unfulfilled wants to the resources we need to satisfy them? The future that we need to create to make these moves possible is indeed utopian—not utopian in the popular sense of a chimerical dream, but in the sense of being a reality that "is not but yet will be." The *mujerista proyecto histórico* of this article refers to is precisely that: a utopian project that seeks to embody the preferred future of many Hispanas/Latinas living in the USA. This *mujerista proyecto histórico* works as a motivator and organizing framework for our hopes for fullness of human life-liberation, which is the criterion and hermeneutical lens of all *mujerista* praxis. Our *proyecto* refers to a reality we are working to create: a concrete reality in a given place, with specific contours and content having as its guiding principle the firm commitment that no one will be excluded.[1] The goal of our *proyecto* is to change radically, little by little, the oppressive society in which we live into a society from which no one is excluded.

When I refer to a Hispanas/Latinas *proyecto histórico* I am talking not only about a vision of a preferred future but also about a whole spectrum of "utopian work," which in many small ways has already started: formulating utopian plans, delineating utopian processes, enabling utopian projects, creating utopian spaces and institutions. I am referring here to projects that include as part of their goals contributing in specific and effective ways to the material wellbeing of the poor, which will not happen apart from a radical change in the economic structures of most of our world. I am referring to programs and institutions that are run and administered in ways that contribute to the enablement of Hispanas/Latinas, including us not only in their implementation but also in conceptualizing them. This means that the way society operates will include the way Hispanas/Latinas "do things," which does not obviate our cultural values and ways of understanding reality. Hispanas/Latinas' utopian projects are those that are conceptualized as ways of enabling our fullness of human life-liberation in a way that does not exclude others or is not at the expense of others.

There are many elements at play in a utopian project, in a *proyecto histórico*. Here I want to concentrate only on one, a key one: the social human person who needs to relate to others and needs to be keenly aware of the fact that we live and move and have our being within and in relation to the rest of creation, in relation to the cosmos.[2] I want to concentrate on the human person that understands herself in relation to her community and to those beyond her community that need and are creating a different world. Basing my reflection on the reality of lived-experiences and understandings embedded in the stories above (and they are but a handful of a possible flood of stories), I want to talk here about the Hispanic/Latino people—particularly about Hispanas/Latinas—as "displaced" people.[3] For economic or political reasons, either as migrants or refugees, Hispanas/Latinas have had to leave our places of origin—abroad or in the USA—to look for another place to call "home."[4] Little by little we learn that once we leave home we never settle down completely. Hispanas/Latinas are always "on the move," creating a constant "from there to here" that results in living in many places but never fully being at "home." This "from there to here" is also part of our multiple, shifting identities, a fluid social ontology[5] that is one of the constitutive elements of *mestizaje-mulatez*, the racial-ethnic-cultural-historical-religious reality that is the *locus* of the Hispanic/Latino community in the USA.[6]

Several clarifications are needed about using the word "displaced" in relation to Hispanas/Latinas. What shall we say about the largest group of Hispanas/Latinas, the Mexican-American women who are not physically displaced, who live in the USA, the country where they were born and where their families have lived for generations? What about other Hispanas/Latinas that are second- and third- and fourth-generation USA-born? All these, in my view, are "displaced" persons, for I am using "displaced" not as a category but as a heuristic device to describe how Hispanas/Latinas are "displaced" from our cultures/countries of origin as well as from what is normative in the USA.

As a heuristic device, "displaced" points to our permanent condition of living/being in the interstices of society. It reflects a condition of dissonance that we struggle to turn into a positive element in our thinking and way of acting. Otherwise we would have to submit to understanding and practices that exclude us. "Displaced" refers to our sense of not belonging that is part of our conscious selves. "Displaced" refers to what we have brought with us and hold on to, letting this richness evolve and be transformed as needed, even as we displace ourselves from our communities/countries of origin and are not given a "full" place in the mainstream of USA society.

Since our *proyecto* **is** *histórico*—material—I have chosen to use the word displaced as a heuristic device to point to its physical reality, to indicate that our *proyecto* is a *topos* and not a non-place. Hispanas/Latinas' *proyecto histórico* has a geographic base: we were displaced from somewhere concrete and our "original" selves—our **first** selves as well as our **creative** selves—continue to be displaced not only from where we came but also from where we have arrived or have always been. The preferred future we are creating is likewise to be viewed as a "space." It is a turning our "displace-ness" into a multi-sites space/place that includes from where we come from and where we are—both of which are in themselves many places that harbor spaces. We are working to create our multi-sites *proyecto histórico* here where we live, in the USA. We are also helping to create a multi-sites *proyecto histórico* in our communities/countries of origin.

What does our "displace-ness" contribute to the creation of our Hispanas/Latinas *proyecto histórico*? I want to suggest that we bring four gifts to this utopian project—each of them subdividing into whole baskets of gifts. The first gift is the lived-experience mentioned above. The community, city, country in which each of us lives is never single/one: it is always a multi-sites place. This is one of the main characteristics of the twenty-first century that enriches humanity. I call it globality. Globality is not globalization, that ideological stance, production, and mode of consumption that oppresses and marginalizes most of our world. Globality refers to the interconnectedness of all areas of our world, of all spheres of our world—ecological, animal, human, and of all the people in our world. Hispanas/Latinas "displace-ness" reminds others as much as ourselves that economic and political isolation are impossible in today's world. To talk about ourselves as displaced persons indicates that we have to take responsibility for the consequences of our actions for they spread out like ripples that reach every single corner of a pond.[7]

The second gift we displaced people have to offer is the understandings and ways of thinking about life and fullness of human life-liberation that emerge from our cultures/ countries of origin. These conceptions enrich the places where we have arrived, the spaces where we hope we will be safe and to which we will fully belong. This implies, of course, that there is a multiplicity of truths that can co-exist in the same physical-historical-political-social space. This is indeed possible as long as none of these truths sets itself up as arbiter of the other truths. The multiple conceptions of life and fullness of human life-liberation that exist indicate this is not a static concept but a principle that can become flesh in many different ways. Our second gift, then, has to do with making this claim in the face of hegemonic understandings of "the" good prevalent in the USA. If taken seriously our gift can help to counter the violence created by the claim that the USA is the best country in the world and that only if others do as is done here will they be able to flourish.

The third gift we bring to our *proyecto histórico* is that of "dangerous memory": one must never forget where one came from.[8] Why? I could allude here to all sorts of psychological and sociological reasons but I will refer only to a religious one since it is the most important for me. I believe that we are not born in a given country or to a given mother and father in a haphazard way. I claim that there is a purpose for my having been born in Cuba, to my Díaz mom and my Isasi dad. And this purpose, for me, is linked to my understanding of the divine and to what is, for me, life and fullness of human life-liberation.[9] What was/is the purpose? As I analyze how my life has evolved, it appears to me that at least a part of it has to do with making known to and reminding the USA that this country has done harm to Cuba,[10] for example, by imposing on the original Cuban constitution an offensive and demeaning amendment that gave the USA government the right to invade Cuba whenever order—as the USA interests saw it—was endangered.[11] Remembering and making known the oppressive and exploitative ways in which the USA has dealt (and deals) with our cultures/countries of origin will remind Hispanas/Latinas that our *proyecto histórico* is not a matter of our participation in oppressive structures but rather of replacing those structures with all-inclusive structures. Dangerous memories help us to keep this perspective clear. Dangerous memories do not have an accusatory tone nor do they indicate a relishing of the past for the past's sake. Dangerous memories make the past present so that we will not repeat the crimes of the past, so that we will continue to seek ways of organizing ourselves socially, economically, and politically that allow fullness of life to flourish for all.

The fourth gift that displaced Hispanas/Latinas bring is recognizing the danger of closure inherent in all utopian projects. Once a preferred future begins to unfold and to take hold *in* our reality and *of* our reality, how do we refrain from closing ourselves to other possibilities? And if we do not remain open, how can we claim that we are not excluding anyone? How do we move from the "either/or" that a preferred future is thought to need—for if it remains always open to change it never becomes a concrete reality—to a "both/and" that affirms our choice but continues to contemplate the possibility of evolving and even radically changing as "others" seek to be included?[12] I believe that we, displaced persons that live in the geographic-cultural interstices formed by our back-and-forth movement between the USA and our cultures/countries of origin, we who carry constantly with us the preoccupations and dreams of those "others" (and those "others" include us as well as the people back "home") who are excluded from life and fullness of human life-liberation, we are a reminder of the danger of closure. We are a reminder that closure can never be definitive and final, for we represent the excluded.

To be able to present these gifts as part of a preferred future, we Hispanas/Latinas have to ground ourselves in our original space-reality. Why? First of all, to ground ourselves thus helps us not to idealize our communities/countries of origin. Part of this process of idealization is, I believe, a mechanism of defense against the lack of value the USA—as a country and as a people—assign to all other nations and cultures.[13] So we counter how little they value our native communities/countries by telling ourselves and others "tall-tales" and romanticizing the places from where we came. At the same time we always need to renew our knowledge so as not to freeze in the past our communities/countries of origin. Just as we have changed in the time we have been away, our people and the culture back there have also evolved. Space and time—distance—make us long for what we have known, tricking us into thinking that the past was better than the present, and insisting that we hold on to what was.[14] As a countermeasure we need to stay in touch with what is in our communities/countries of origin and not just with what was by reinserting ourselves there as often as possible. Third, we need to realize how enticing are the privileges and benefits of the USA society. The myth that anyone who really wants to can prosper in this country is extremely powerful—though no less of a myth because of that. Therefore, staying close to our communities/countries of origin can be an antidote to the desire to "make it" here, a needed antidote since success in the First World is always—to a smaller or larger measure but always—at the expense of Hispanas/Latinas or other Third World people. To "make it" we have to participate in present oppressive structures. Only if we stay close to our origins, only if we continue to experience ourselves as "displaced," will we stand against oppressive structures and work to radically change them.

This idea of keeping in physical proximity to our communities/countries of origin is almost instinctive in the Hispanic community. We seem to know instinctively that we need to keep in physical touch with the space-reality of our communities/countries of origin—with their space-reality—for, as the stories I related at the beginning indicate, our people do everything to return "home" as often as possible, whether home is Cuba, Texas or Puerto Rico. And if we fail to return alive, the community will make sure that at least we are buried back home.[15]

What are the cultural realities that hold us and, at the same time, send us forth—that inhabit us?[16] What concrete realities have been harmed and are being harmed by the marginalizing and exploitative attitudes prevalent in the USA towards our communities/countries of origin? How do these same attitudes affect us here in the USA? To know the reality of our sites of origin necessitates our seeing with our own eyes and experiencing in our own flesh.[17] For me, for example, this means returning to La Habana, analyzing La Habana. What about La Habana do I need to make present in the USA? What can I learn from La Habana that will be beneficial in the construction of our *proyecto histórico*? How will the immediacy of being in La Habana help me evade total closure? How will it help me invent ways of remaining open to future possibilities while making a firm commitment to a specific future for Hispanas/Latinas in the USA?[18]

The description of places and ways of life in La Habana that follows is an attempt to give specifics regarding the meaning of being grounded in the physical reality—the geography—of one's communities/countries of origin. These descriptions offer "outsiders" important insights into the above questions, which are essential to me as a displaced person, and provide, if not answers, at least clues. My hope as a displaced person is that readers will also appropriate at least some of what I describe, changing in the process whatever needs to be changed because of differences between La Habana and whichever place the reader calls home, but allowing my description of La Habana to challenge and expand their horizons.

La Habana, "The City That Witnessed My Birth"

The sea that I was imagining more than seeing was an undefined gray mass way down there. Only slightly more than half an hour had gone by since taking off from Miami when I saw dim lights. I knew that in no time I would be landing for the first time in twenty-seven years in my homeland, in the land of my birth, infancy, and youth. I was not scared nor was I apprehensive.

Indeed what I felt was an immense desire to be back in Cuba. I had enormous expectations of reconnecting physically with my birthplace.

A huge sign with the name of the airport, the same one I had seen out of the window of my departing airplane in 1960, now seemed to spell "welcome." There was no jet way connecting the airplane to the terminal. I came down the stairs of the airplane with great intentionality, quietly but decisively claiming the right to be "home" regardless of the fact that the government of Cuba, even today, places obstacles to this right. So many thoughts were crowding my mind; so many emotions were caught between my chest and my throat! I felt so much a stranger in that airport, surrounded by what seemed an inordinate number of uniformed people given the small number of travelers arriving that morning. But then, I also had a profound sense that I belonged there. I wanted so much to feel at home.

Volunteering to be the first in our group to face the immigration officer, I stepped up to the window. My USA passport says I was born in La Habana but he still had to ask. "Go to the end of the line so I can process the rest of the people and then I will take care of your papers," he said. Some document I needed—who knows what!—was missing. My traveling companions, fellow seminarians, agreed to be processed and to meet me on the other side of the door. While I waited alone leaning against the wall, I could not help becoming a bit scared but it was mostly sadness that I felt at being required to present so much documentation and to get permission before being able to walk the streets of my native city, La Habana, to get my passport stamped. Finally the officer called me back. I had to go to some government agency in La Habana. "You will not be allowed to leave the country if you do not have that stamp," he warned me. (When I left Cuba two weeks later, the immigration officer never looked in my passport for the stamp I had dutifully gotten that first day in La Habana.)

The moment the minibus in which we were traveling left the parking lot of the airport and turned left, I knew where we were: I could have driven us to La Habana! That gave me an enormous sense of relief for I had wondered how accurate my memories were. No, I was not a stranger. I was home and even if that sense of belonging was to be tested and even marred during my two weeks in Cuba, my time there confirmed my conviction that, though I hold American citizenship and live in New York City, I am a Cuban and the city of La Habana inhabits me.

After that first trip back to Cuba I did not return for ten years. Then, starting in 1997, I have been able to go and actually work there every year. La Habana has changed much during these seven years and I certainly see it through much different eyes than I did that first time I went back. What has not changed, however, is my feeling of being at home in La Habana. Regardless of the fact that I do not live there, despite the fact that I do not earn a living there and that my family does not live there, despite having to petition for an entry permit every time I go and being allowed to stay for only a month (to stay longer I have to petition and pay for an extension of my visa), despite the fact that the US dollars in my pocket make my life while there different from that of the majority of Cuban people who have no access or very limited access to hard currency—despite all of this, I walk endlessly around La Habana knowing this is my city, reveling in the fact that I am more Cuban than anything else.

"Aeropuerto Internacional José Martí" is fifteen miles from La Habana. Often when I arrive in La Habana instead of going north into the city I go further south. The mother of the friend who always picks me up at the airport lives in Santiago de Las Vegas, a small town a few miles from the airport, and I go visit her. The people there who have to go into La Habana face one of the most difficult parts of everyday living: transportation. Before 1990, subsidies and favorable trading terms with the Soviet Union and Eastern Europe made it possible to have a good public transportation system that linked all areas of La Habana. However, when the economic help came to an end with the unraveling of the USSR and the radical changes in governments and economic systems in Eastern Europe, gasoline, which had been rationed even before, became almost non-existent. This, together with the lack of spare parts for buses that had been imported from the Soviet camp, brought the system of public transportation to a virtual halt. Though the system is back on its feet, Cubans have to face long waits in the tropical heat and, when the bus finally comes, they pile in like the proverbial sardines in a can.[19]

Taxis provide another means of transportation, some of them for tourists (you have to pay in US dollars) and others for Cubans. The latter ones, most of them "vintage cars" left from pre-1959, crowd in as many as possible, picking up and dropping people along a set route. In Cuba's roads and streets one sees every imaginable motor-driven or humanly-propelled contraption with wheels: bicycles—most of the time with two, even with three persons riding them—"rickshaws" for one or two persons, motorcycles with sidecart. Though not as much in La Habana as in other cities and roads away from the capital, one sees every sort of animal-pulled cart imaginable, some of them fitted with benches and a roof to protect against the sun. Then there is hitchhiking—*coger botella*. Everyone, young and old, women and men, tries to get a ride with anyone going by. In the main streets of La Habana, at all times but particularly when it is time to go to work and return home, people stand on both side of the streets and even in the middle, between the rows of cars. One of my friends still gives rides to people in her Russian-made Lada. Another one stopped doing so after the number of people who crowded in ruined the back doors and seat of her car.

Why is it that Cubans cannot buy new cars? Of course, much has to do with the fact that what they earn, not only now but during these last forty-five years, has never been enough to be able to save to buy a car. But there is also another reason: the government did not want some to have what others could not, the idea being to try to make everyone equal. I am not sure if one would need special permission to buy a new car. But just to make sure this is not possible, the sales tax on a new car is 100 percent. Instead of buying new cars, therefore, Cubans keep recycling cars and constructing them from pieces salvaged from others or made by themselves. I have traveled in a car that had an American pre-1959 body with parts of the motor belonging to a Russian-made Lada, and other parts salvaged from a Russian-made Moscovich. Drivers have to have available on demand their sales receipt and the government permits for the various parts out of which they have created their cars. Policemen stop them randomly just to check them.

After visiting my friend's mother I go a few miles further south, to an area where there are several military camps, to El Cacahual. I have made this a "required" stop for myself and those

I take to Cuba. There, in an elevated spot from which one can see the whole city of La Habana, is a huge rotunda the size of a football field. It contains the tomb of one of the heroes of Cuba's War of Independence fought against Spain starting in 1895, Antonio Maceo.[20] Next to him is buried his aide-de-camp, Francisco Gómez Toro. I go there for the view of La Habana and to reminisce, for this was a site where we used to go in school outings. I go there to remember the mother of Maceo, Mariana Grajales—the Cuban "mother of the Maccabees"—for history and myth tell us how she encouraged each of her sons to be willing to die for Cuba's independence.[21] However, the main reason I go there is to keep in mind that Cuban history does not start in 1959 with the triumph of the revolution of which Fidel (as we Cubans call Castro) was one of the leaders.

The other place I go before heading into La Habana is El Rincón. There I visit the "Santuario de San Lázaro," one of the most important pilgrimage sites in Cuba. San Lázaro is the patron saint of the sick, and his feast is on December 17, when no less than fifty thousand devotees come to give thanks to the saint and ask for new favors. This was one of the places visited by Pope John Paul II when he came to Cuba in January 1998. The story of San Lázaro says a great deal about the relationship between the official theology and liturgy of the Catholic Church and Cubans' popular religion. The latter is not church-based, definitely not church-sanctioned, and very much mixed with *Santería*, a Cuban version of the Lucumí religion the Yoruba slaves brought from Africa to Cuba when it was still a colony of Spain. Catholicism provides the iconography used by *Santería* while the Lucumí religion provides the deities. The Catholic saints are seen as "incarnations/representations" of the Yoruba *orishas* and provide a cover for religious practices officially banned. So, San Lázaro is the *orisha* Babalú-Ayé. But this is not the only sleight-of-hand going on here, at this Catholic church. As you approach the "Santuario" you notice that the statues of San Lázaro being sold in the street are of a man on crutches and covered with sores. However, the image of San Lázaro inside the church is that of a bishop. The San Lázaro to which Cubans are devoted is the lame beggar with sores in the parable told by Jesus of the rich man who refused to help Lázaro, the beggar at his door.[22]

Because saints in the Catholic Church are persons who have lived virtuous lives and are proposed to the faithful as exemplars, the church in the 1960s, when liturgical reforms were implemented, removed the statues of the man in crutches from its altars. But when the people simply would not stop praying to San Lázaro, the church began to promote in Cuba another St. Lazarus, a bishop, who was in its roster and whom lepers and victims of the plague in Europe had invoked centuries ago.[23]

Once we light candles to San Lázaro in thanksgiving for the good things that have come into our lives and ask for help with the difficult things, my friend and I are ready for the drive into La Habana. Shortly after leaving El Rincón we see "Los Cocos," Cuba's first sanatorium to house people infected with HIV/ AIDS. In the early 1980s Cuba started massive testing of its population and quarantined everyone who was HIV positive. HIV/ AIDS was seen as "a health problem/public health problem with human rights dimensions rather than a social problem/human rights problem with health repercussions."[24] By 1994, when mandatory testing was stopped, nearly all of the adult population had been tested. Mandatory confinement, from the perspective of the Cuban government an attempt to stem the spread of AIDS and to provide the best care to those who were sick, was seen by many as a violation of human rights. Since 1993 patients can choose to live in the sanatoria—there are several others in the island besides "Los Cocos"—or at home. The sanatoria serve now as residences for HIV/AIDS patients as well as outpatient facilities. "Community based education, case finding, and treatment is now being stressed." At present, "infection rates are slowly rising. . . . HIV infection among the homosexual population constitutes the fastest increase, as well as spread through prostitution. The expanding tourist industry has created new channels of spread of the virus."[25]

The road into La Habana houses numerous light industries and it is one of the few places where there are commercial billboards. Almost all billboards feature slogans and quotes from Fidel encouraging people to remain faithful to the revolution. One of the students I took to Cuba decided to write down all the slogans we saw on billboards convinced that he could piece together from them a pretty accurate picture of the ideology of the government. He was right! Billboards often have pictures of dead heroes of the revolution, particularly Che Guevara, the Argentinean doctor who fought against the dictator Batista; Camilo Cienfuegos, a popular leader who fought with Fidel and Che and who was killed in a mysterious airplane crash shortly after Fidel came to power in 1959; and Julio Antonio Mella, a student leader, one of the founders of the Cuban Communist Party, murdered in Mexico while in exile in the 1920s.

The old two-lane highway that brings us into La Habana ends in a huge fountain, now without water, that serves as a traffic circle. There to your right is the old "Palacio de Los Deportes" and behind it a huge sports complex with other stadiums and sport fields. Ahead of us is the "Plaza de la Revolución" with an imposing statue of José Martí, the father of our country, as centerpiece.[26] The tower behind the statue is the highest point in La Habana and at present it houses a splendid museum of Martí; the top of the tower has windows from which you can see fifty miles in all directions. At the feet of the statue and tower there is a massive review stand and podium from which Fidel addresses the masses. I went to the Plaza in 2000, on one of Cuba's main holidays, Labor Day celebrated on May 1st, at the height of the Elián affair.[27] Though in the past the celebration consisted of military parades and Fidel's endless speeches, recently the festivities have changed. The year I was there, there was a party-like atmosphere with music and poetry reading, dances with flags, and, as always, a long speech by Fidel. That day I moved around the crowd watching intensely the faces of the people. Certainly there were some who were enthusiastically participating but there were many who waved their Cuban paper flags and repeated slogans on cue without much *ánimo*—fervor. These mass gatherings are obligatory. Workers report to their jobs, children and youth to their schools and, after attendance is taken, they are bused to the Plaza. In his speeches Fidel instructs the people, announces policy changes and government programs, interprets national and international events, and "consults" the people, something he has done since he first entered La Habana triumphantly on January 8, 1959, days after Batista had fled. That day, during a long speech, Fidel "announced he had a question for the 'people,' thereby inaugurating a new approach to the art of governance: a dialogue with the masses, through which they would affirm his policies by chanting responses to his 'questions.' Soon he would call it 'direct democracy . . . of the marketplace,' cleaner and more honest than the old-fashioned corrupt electoral procedures of the past."[28] Undoubtedly Fidel's government by rhetoric is without precedence and it has proven to be effective, being one of the main reasons for the staying power of his government.

As you travel around La Habana you often see long lines of people in front of stores waiting their turn to buy the limited goods available. The long lines have existed since the early 1960s but they have grown longer since the beginning of the "Período Especial," the "Special Period in a Time of Peace," an unprecedented austerity plan announced by Fidel in January 1990. The government had to take strong measures in 1993–1994 to stop Cuba's economy from shrinking any further (between 1989 and 1993 the "economy shrunk 35 to 50 percent"[29]). One such measure was the legalization of the US dollar, allowing "free markets for agricultural products and light consumer durables."[30] Despite these and other changes, feeding a family in Cuba today is a heroic deed requiring immense patience, dogged perseverance, limitless time, and a huge dose of Cuban ingenuity. I have eaten lobster at a friend's house because the day I came to visit someone, knowing she has access to dollars, came to her door selling lobster tails, though it is illegal both to fish and sell lobsters. I often have *café con leche* for breakfast because my friends get milk from *campesinos* that sell it illegally, or buy powdered milk in the black market, for milk is permissible in Cuba only for children under seven, the elderly, and people on diets because of health problems. The best bananas I have ever eaten are grown by one of my friends in her backyard where she also keeps chickens. When driving outside La Habana I have learned to keep my eyes open for fresh cheese and garlic sold by *campesinos* who do not approach your car until they are sure you are not a government official stopping to confiscate their goods and impose a stiff fine for selling without a government permit.

I have stood in line outside a store where one has to pay with dollars to buy food to contribute to the family that was hosting me. Those in line with me—the line was needed because of the crowds—were quiet and somber, a total reversal of the loudness and lightheartedness of Cubans. I spent a long time pretending to examine merchandise on a shelf near the checkout counter so I could observe what people had bought and how they paid for it. Most of them bought small quantities of food, often imported canned goods and toiletries, and they paid generally with one dollar bills. My friends later explained that most of the one dollar bills I saw were tips from tourists staying at the nearby hotel or simply money the people had hustled who knows how. I have also gone with friends to the "*agros*" — the agricultural markets where you find cheap produce, pork and chicken in government-subsidized stalls, and more expensive — and better — goods at stalls where you pay a higher price. Quantity and variety is not much of a problem in these markets but, obviously, many Cubans cannot afford to buy there. Then, how do Cubans manage to eat? Since 1962 when food rationing was begun, *la libreta* — the rationing book — allows each person to buy for pennies a certain amount of staples like rice, beans, coffee, lard, cooking oil, household detergent, soap, matches. Most of the time, some of these staples are simply not available or are not available in the quantity allowed, and Cubans complain constantly about the bad quality of what they get. Some items like cooking oil, household detergents and soap have been missing for a long time. People get whatever is available and then the process of exchanging what one has for what one needs begins.[31] Something still available every day is a very glutinous small bread roll, one per person. I always smile when I eat them remembering the daughter of a friend of mine baptized them "*pan del Comandante*" — bread given by "*el Comandante*," as Fidel is called.[32]

That first time I went back to La Habana in 1987, after an early breakfast at the old "Habana Hilton," now the "Habana Libre," when the driver turned right onto Calle 23, I knew that in seconds we would be in "El Malecón" — a winding avenue by the sea, six lanes wide and five miles long, starting in "La Habana Vieja" — old La Habana — and ending at the Río Almendares, the river where the other municipality of metropolitan La Habana begins. El Malecón, which refers to the avenue as well as to the seawall, was designed as a jetty wall by a Cuban architect in 1857, while Cuba was still a Spanish colony, but its construction was not started until 1902 while Cuba was a USA military protectorate. It took fifty years to complete it. The wall is about three feet high and two feet wide providing one long continuous "*sofá*" for the delight of all. All along the wall one can see the remains of square baths hewn from the rocks, "about 12 feet square and six to eight feet deep, with rock steps for access and a couple portholes through which the waves of this tideless shore wash in and out."[33]

On the other side of the avenue, El Malecón has many faces, many personalities. The first section of the avenue borders on one side "La Habana Vieja" with its colonial buildings, and on the other the very narrow entrance of La Habana's bay.[34] The second zone of El Malecón starts at El Prado—a kilometer-long boulevard with a park lined with trees running down the middle—and finishes at the "Parque Maceo." This section of El Malecón, about a mile long, is called the "traditional Malecón" and it is lined with stunningly beautiful residential buildings in great disrepair.[35] This "long urban façade wall, with a continuous pedestrian arcade,"[36] is in the process of being reconstructed. The centerpiece of the park where this section ends is a huge statue of Antonio Maceo on horseback. The third part of El Malecón ends at Calle 23, in El Vedado—one of La Habana's main sectors. In this area there is a noticeable variety in the sizes and styles of the residential buildings and there are some businesses, including a European car dealership. The fourth zone starts on a rocky promontory on top of which sits the Hotel Nacional, a beautiful building with Moorish-influenced architecture built in the 1930s. Other more modern hotels might be more attractive to tourists but for Cubans El Hotel Nacional continues to be the "grand dame." At the foot of the small cliff is the "Monumento al Maine," in honor of those who died when the American warship exploded and sank in La Habana's harbor in 1898, providing the excuse for the USA to declare war on Spain.[37] The next structure on El Malecón is a park recently constructed specifically for demonstrations against the USA, next to a modern glass structure that used to be the USA Embassy, now the USA Interest Section. Following this tall building there are some beautiful private homes set further back from the ocean. The fifth and last zone of El Malecón starts at the Monument to Calixto García, another hero of the Cuban War of Independence.

Two hotels and what used to be a private social club dominate this zone. The houses and residential buildings in this area are also set further back from the sea. The Malecón ends with a military fortress (today it houses a restaurant) built to protect La Habana from the west in the eighteenth century. The road at this end disappears into a tunnel under the Río Almendares, coming out on the other side as a beautiful boulevard named Fifth Avenue.

The physical description anchors what El Malecón represents and the role it plays for La Habana and its residents. El Malecón has been described as the "gateway" of La Habana, and it certainly is a symbol and, in many ways, a synthesis of the city. El Malecón serves as "the porch" for many of La Habana's residents. Children play and ride their bikes on its wide sidewalk and leave their clothes with their parents while they bathe in the sea. This is a favorite place for lovers—young and old—and for thinkers. Fishermen try their luck here, and it is a place where one can safely discuss politics, for the sea drowns voices. The houses bordering El Malecón might have belonged to people of economic means but *el muro del Malecón*, the wall of El Malecón, is a democratic place from which no one is excluded.[38] When I talk about La Habana as the city that inhabits me the first image that comes to my mind is that of El Malecón and the description that I first think of is my mother's. She went on a cruise to Panama for her honeymoon in the 1920s. The ship returned at night and I remember my mother telling us that the lights along El Malecón were like a string of pearls around La Habana.

Being a Displaced/Multi-Sites Person

La Habana is the city that inhabits me most fully. It is not the only city that inhabits me because as a displaced person I am a multi-sites person. However, La Habana is, undoubtedly, the city that provides most of the resources for my "imaginary," for my gaze into the present and the future, and a main point of reference in how I position myself in relation to the past.[39] Going to La Habana is a way of refurbishing—renovating, renewing, revamping—my resources for day-to-day living (*lo cotidiano*).

Though as a multi-sites person I do not belong fully in La Habana, the ways I do feel at home in La Habana renew my desire to make the USA, where I spend most of my time, a place I can also call home. Being in La Habana gives me new impetus for the struggle (*la lucha*) to create a *mujerista proyecto histórico* where La Habana as well as the USA will be home. Having walked the streets of the city where I was born and grew up, I return to New York more sure of who I am, less foreign to myself. Many parts of me that in the USA mark me as foreign, make me in Cuba simply "part of the bunch." The centering or grounding that being in La Habana gives me in many ways makes me a better citizen of the USA, for I return here with a renewed vigor for life, for my work, and for the multiple commitments that mark my life.

Every time I go to La Habana I go with preoccupations and questions that emerge, as they always do, from what is happening in my life, from my interpretation of world events, from my commitments to issues of justice, from my dedication to those I love. Returning from La Habana I have new questions and new insights into my questions. I have new preoccupations that I do not leave behind but instead add to my *cotidiano* in the other multi-sites where I live as a displaced person. One of the last times I was in La Habana I began to see the importance of paying attention to globality and globalization, to learn what they mean, how they operate and how they impact our present communities.

What made me turn my attention to these phenomena is the fact that in La Habana, contrary to most places in the world, globality does not work very well. To start with, telephone communications even within Cuba are limited since many people still do not have telephones. Communicating with the rest of the world is very restricted. Calls to any place outside Cuba are expensive and, with rare exceptions, you cannot dial an international call from telephones in private homes. Those who can have a second telephone with a special line allowed by the government.[40] Mail simply does not work. The most common experience is for letters not to arrive—either coming or going—and if they arrive the news will certainly not be fresh. Use of the Internet is severely limited. The number of people with computers is extremely small and access to the Internet has to be authorized by the government. News about Cuba and abroad are limited to what is provided on official TV channels, radio stations and newspapers. The physical insularity of Cuba is replicated at all levels of contact and communication with the rest of the world. Cuba, in many ways, does stop at the wall of El Malecón.

Cuba's lack of communication with the rest of the world is a result of its political and economic isolation, partially self-imposed, partially imposed by the policies of the USA. Its insularity is broken by people who visit Cuba,[41] those who leave legally or illegally,[42] and those who live outside the island and keep in touch with relatives and friends, sending them medicine and money to the tune of one billion US dollars a year.[43] Through these kinds of contacts Cuba becomes part of globalization, a "global economic matrix" that encompasses not only the production and distribution of goods but also "a worldwide system of governance and power."[44] In us and through us who live outside but are indeed part of Cuba, our island interacts with the world in ways that it does not do officially. Unfortunately much of the interaction is not positive, for, though some Cubans and Cuban-Americans benefit from globalization, a great number of us Cubans who live outside the island—the majority—belong to the middle and working classes and are the ones used and abused by globalization.

Being used and abused is the reality not only for the majority of Cubans but also, of course, for all Hispanic/Latinos in the USA. Therefore, it is important—as we, Hispanas/Latinas, create our preferred future, as we work on our *proyecto histórico*— to pay attention to the role globalization plays in our oppression. The fact is that globalization creates a "demand for lower-paid workers," a category that includes most Hispanas/Latinas. The "global cities" that are the key links in the network of globalization are "most often supported . . . by large populations of immigrant workers who perform the blue-collar, industrial, low-wage, dirty work of the global economy as the valets, the coffee-stand servers, the janitors."[45] In the "global cities," like New York, London, Frankfurt, Bangkok, Santiago (Chile) and a few others, global capital is not the only element present. There is also a workforce made up of "women, immigrants, people of color . . ."[46] without which these cities could not perform the highly specialized transactions that are intrinsic to globalization. This makes these cities attractive to those who are searching for jobs. In other words, "some of the infrastructure that enables globalization enables and indeed may induce migration."[47]

Though much has been said about globalization in relation to capital, little or no attention has been paid to the "transnationalization of labor" it needs. The "global cities" need the support of labor coming from communities such as ours: the Hispanas/Latinas communities. These communities, instead of the cities and the countries in which they live, provide the principal source of identification to these workers, most of them being displaced/multi-sites people. Given that these "global cities" are sites not only for global capital but also for a "global workforce," they also contribute to "the formation of transnational identities."[48] The global cities are characterized not only by "their telecommunication infrastructure and international firms, but also . . . [by] the many different cultural environments they contain. . . . An immense array of cultures from around the world, each rooted in a particular country, town, or village, now are re-territorialized in a few single places, places such as New York, Los Angeles, Paris, London, and most recently Tokyo."[49]

These global cities, therefore, have the effect of "unbundling" the territoriality of nations, for they relate among themselves and depend on each other much more than they relate to other cities in their same nation or to the nation in which they are located.[50] This unbundling of territoriality also leads to the "unbundling of sovereignty." "We are seeing the relocation of various components of sovereignty onto supranational, nongovernmental, or private institutions."[51] Also, because the working class that supports globalization in New York, for example, has much more in common with those who support globalization in, let's say São Paulo, Brazil, than with the elite population of New York, "new notions of community, of membership, and of entitlement" are emerging linking workers across national boundaries.

Another element generated by "globalization," a non-intended element but an element nonetheless that plays a significant role in the way transnational labor continues to relate to the people "back home," is that of family remittances. Cubans are not the only ones to send monies back to our country of origin. Hispanas/Latinas as a whole practice this "philanthropy of the poor"[52] that often is the main sustenance of our families and friends back home. The need for family remittances is to a large extent a consequence of globalization. "As the global north has put increasing pressures on governments in the global south to open their economies to foreign firms, these countries have become poorer even as certain sectors within them have gotten very rich. Government and large sectors of the population in many of these countries have come to depend more and more on the remittances of immigrants in the global north, which overall are estimated at an annual 70 billion US dollars over each of the last few years."[53] This sort of sharing/deployment of resources also takes place in Hispanic/Latino families born in the USA. Though I have never seen statistics I am sure that the monies sent back to their families by those of us who move to cities to improve our earnings are economically important to the local communities, particularly if we come from small towns. The fact is, then, that the poor of the world are maintaining the poor of the world. The poor of the world in the USA are maintaining families and friends back home as well as contributing in a significant way to the economies and governments of our communities/countries of origin.

These mechanisms of globalization, at work in many of the cities where there are great concentrations of Hispanas/Latinas, have created new ways, meanings, and understandings of the back-and-forth characteristic of displaced/multi-sites people. Globalization is not only about transnational economic spaces but it is also about transnational people, and that is what many of us Hispanas/Latinas are. Definitely, globalization is exploitative, benefiting only 20 percent of the world population. However, if we look carefully at the mechanisms of globalization, I propose that we can use some of the unintentional side effects of globalization in constructing our *mujerista proyecto histórico*.

First, as these global cities of the globalization network concentrate larger and larger numbers of Hispanas/Latinas (and of course, also Hispanic/Latino men), we begin to be a critical mass that can organize to pressure the government for our rights and the benefits we have earned by being productive members of this society. This will be useful for the *mujerista proyecto histórico* only if we are clear that our goal is to create a society from which no one is excluded and not to participate in oppressive structures. Second, with the growing dependence of Third World governments and USA town, city and state governments on remittances from those of us who work outside their parameters, can we not turn our generosity into influence? Can we not find effective ways of using the economic leverage that remittances give us to reverse the structural adjustment programs imposed on governments by the World Bank and the International Monetary Fund that have cut health, education, and other social programs? Third, the transnational labor force of globalization of which Hispanas/Latinas are a part contributes a basis for identity that makes clear we have to see ourselves in relation to our communities/countries of origin. We have much more in common with women in our communities/countries of origin than we have with the privileged women of the global cities. Being conscious of this and finding effective means of maintaining close contact with each other across the physical distance that separates us can provide a most effective way of finding ways to struggle to create a *proyecto histórico* from which no one is excluded.

La Habana, the city that inhabits me, is the city that challenges me, the city that makes me ask new questions, the city where I dream dreams and see visions. La Habana is the city that is home—but not completely, for La Habana also displaces me, sending me forth to be a multi-sites woman. La Habana is one of the key organizing principles in my life: who I am/want to be, what I want to do with my life—a life which will always have to honor the discontinuities and ruptures created in me and for me. La Habana is the place that precludes me from returning and fragments me, but this fragmentation is not problematic to me. Rather it facilitates the interstices through which I can reach our *mujerista* utopian project, or where I can stand free of the objectifying gaze of those who insist on constructing me as "other."⁵⁴ La Habana has its all-encompassing effect on me as I walk its streets, manage its heat or its surprising coldness (having fallen prey to the propaganda that in-January-it-is-hot-in-the-tropics), maneuver its still somewhat unfamiliar systems in order to get food, find transportation, make a phone call, buy an airline ticket. La Habana, with its sad buildings holding on to a splendor that shines through crumbling walls, imposes itself in irrevocable beauty on my heart and mind and soul: this is the city/place/locality/human geography that was and continues to be my starting point as a displaced/multi-sites person committed to a *mujerista proyecto histórico* that will exclude no one. La Habana: *"si no existieras yo te inventaría, mi ciudad de La Habana."*[55]

Notes

[1] *Una sociedad donde quepan todos*—"a society in which everyone fits," is a leitmotiv of the Zapatistas in Chiapas, southern Mexico, and pointedly expresses the goal of their struggle.

[2] I thank Carlos Sintado for pointing out the need to articulate this understanding.

[3] I certainly do not consider my reflections as applicable only to the Hispanic/Latino community living in the USA. However, this is the community I have as my point of reference and as my context and to whom I am accountable, particularly Hispanas/Latinas.

[4] There is a difference, of course, between the categories of migrants and refugees but in this paper I include all of us under the rubric "displaced persons."

[5] Catherine Keller, "Seeking and Sucking—On Relation and Essence in Feminist Theology," in *Horizons in Feminist Theology—Identity, Tradition, and Norms*, ed. Rebecca S. Chopp and Sheila Greeve Davaney (Minneapolis: Fortress Press, 1997), 55.

[6] See, Ada María Isasi-Díaz, "A New *Mestizaje-Mulatez:* Re-conceptualizing Difference," in *A Dream Unfinished: Theological Reflections on America from the Margins*, ed. Eleazar S. Fernandez and Fernando F. Segovia (Maryknoll: Orbis Books, 2001), 203–219. A different but no less important analysis is that of Manuel Mejido, "The Fundamental Problematic of US Hispanic Theology," in *Nuevas Voces/New Voices: Horizons in U.S. Hispanic Latino(a) Theology*, ed. Benjamín Valentín (Pasadena, Texas: Pilgrim Press, forthcoming).

[7] I heard Franz Hinkelammert make a distinction between globality and globalization years back at a meeting in Germany. Hinkelammert was born in Germany. He is an economist who for the last forty years has lived first in Chile and then in Costa Rica. He is a part of DEI—The Department of Investigation in San Jose, Costa Rica. Though the distinction I make here between globality and globaliza-

tion is based on what Hinkelammert said, the elaboration I present is my own.

⁸ Johann Baptist Metz, *Faith in History and Society* (New York: Seabury Press, 1980), 184. This phrase is used extensively. I refer to Metz because this is where I first saw it used years ago.

⁹ There is a sentence in a prayer to Jesus that I have said for the last forty-three years that captures what I am saying here in a succinct way. Referring to Cuba it says, *"Tú nos la diste y por eso es para nosotras un legado sagrado"*—you gave it to us and that is why it is for us a sacred legacy.

¹⁰ I am not ignoring the fact that Cubans have also done enormous harm to our country. My point here is that we have to contribute to building a preferred future that is "situated" in the USA and, therefore, I am pointing out what needs to change in the USA. I realize fully that there is much also that needs to change in the communities/countries of origin of Hispanas/Latinas.

¹¹ The USA government asked the members of the Cuban constitutional assembly to write this into our constitution. When they refused to do so, even if Cuba was at the time under USA military rule, it was imposed by the USA government as an amendment to our constitution. Franklin Delano Roosevelt abrogated this amendment in 1934. Marifeli Pérez-Stable, *The Cuban Revolution: Origins, Course, and Legacy* (New York: Oxford University Press, 1999), 4, 7. There was a military occupation of Cuba lasting from 1906 to 1909. Marines landed in 1910 to protect USA interest and citizens, and in 1917 to persuade Cuba to enter World War I. To protect USA properties, the marines remained in Cuba until 1923. Tad Szulc, *Fidel: A Critical Portrait* (New York: Harper and Collins, Avon Books, 1986), 96.

¹² See David Harvey, *Spaces of Hope* (Berkeley: University of California Press, 2000), 182–196.

¹³ The view prevalent in this society is that the USA is the best country in the world and that everyone else should follow its example.

¹⁴ Nowhere is this idea expressed better or more beautifully than in the first *copla*—couplet—of the elegy Jorge Manrique, the fifteenth-century Spanish poet, wrote on the death of his father. See Jorge Manrique, *Obras Completas*, 2nd edición, edición y prólogo de Augusto Cortina (Buenos Aires: Espasa Calpe, 1942), 135.

¹⁵ A few years ago there was a wave of murders in New York City, the victims being Dominican taxi drivers. In each and every case the community raised funds to send their bodies back to the Dominican Republic for burial. Cubans living in the USA have asked to be cremated when they die so their ashes can be taken back to Cuba as soon as possible. The ashes of many have already been returned to the island. Most

of them have been taken by relatives in their handbags; a few have been returned through the expensive official process that has been set up. Undoubtedly, many Latinas and Latinos do not wish to return to their communities/countries of origin and are happy to die and be buried in the land to which they have moved. However, I think statistics uphold the claim that we have a very high rate of visiting our communities/ countries of origin and taking our dead back to be buried there. Will this be different in the future? It remains to be seen, of course, but the fact that there is a continuous flow of people from our countries of origin coming into our communities in the USA, I believe will keep fresh our links to where we came from.

16 I borrow this phrase, and the title of this article from the title of the book by Magali García Ramis, *La ciudad que me habita*, 2nd edición (Río Piedras, PR: Ediciones Huracán, 1997).

17 I realize that returning/visiting one's country of origin might not be possible for some Hispanas/Latinas or Latinos or that some might simply choose not to return. Those who are not able because of whatever reason I believe fit into the schema I present in this essay. Those who choose to return might very well exclude themselves from this schema.

18 Though many Cubans living in the USA would disagree with me, maybe even the majority, I continue to believe that we all have something to learn from today's La Habana, from how it deals with space, from its radically different way of organizing its socio-political-economic structures—radically different from the way they are organized in the USA—and from the struggles of the Cuban people there.

19 Cuban inventiveness is legendary and how effective we are in dealing with crisis is seen everywhere in La Habana when a *camello*—camel— comes into sight. This is a bus made by adding bodies to two articulated flatbed Mack trucks. The place where the bus "articulates" dips lower than the bodies. This camel-like feature accounts for its name. *Camellos* weigh twenty tons, adding terrible wear and tear to the streets of La Habana. They cost about $30,000 and carry 220 persons, though usually no less than 300 cram in. Those who travel by *camellos* know that they are not very safe. It is not uncommon to have wallets and anything else you might be carrying lifted and the women always complain of being molested physically and verbally. Much of this kind of information I have gathered during the years I have been going to Cuba. See Christopher P. Baker, *Havana Handbook*, Moon Travel Handbooks (Emeryville, Calif.: Avalon Travel Publishing, 2000). Of all the travel guidebooks I find the "hermeneutical lens" of this one to be the most balanced and I still have to catch a single mistake in the information it provides!

20 Maceo since the time of his death has been called *"El Titán de Bronce"* — The Bronze Titan — a reference to the fact that he was black and to his military acumen. As a young man he led troops in the first Cuban war for independence called the Ten Years War. He refused to accept the armistice that brought that armed conflict to an end because the Spaniards would not abolish slavery nor give Cuba its independence. His renewal of the armed struggle at that time is known as *La Protesta de Baraguá* — The Protest of Baragua — the place where Maceo met with the Spanish general to discuss his demands. In three months, however, Maceo had to abandon his efforts. Refusing to surrender, he left Cuba (was allowed to leave Cuba by the Spanish general) while his followers accepted the armistice Maceo had refused to embrace. (Since 1990 Fidel has used *La Protesta de Baraguá* in his speeches — it can be seen in La Habana's billboards — to indicate his refusal to give in and bring about political and economic reforms in Cuba.) In the 1895 Cuban War of Independence Maceo was the insurgents' army second-in-command. Bypassing La Habana, he was able to bring the fight for independence to the western part of the island. He was killed in battle, together with his assistant, on December 7, 1896.

21 Her parents had come from the Dominican Republic and settled in Santiago de Cuba, in the eastern part of the island, where she was born June 26, 1808. With her first husband she had four sons. After he died — though contemporary research indicates maybe they divorced — she married Marcos Maceo, who was a Venezuelan. With him she had five sons — nine sons in all. It is said that when her husband died fighting in the first Cuban war for independence she cried out to the youngest of her sons, then a little boy, "Stand up tall; it is already time that you should fight for your country." She herself took to the battlefield, to help whichever way she could. In November 23, 1893, less than two years before the start of the Cuban War of Independence, Mariana Grajales Cuello died in Jamaica. Thirty years later her remains were taken to Cuba and buried in the Cemetery of Sta. Ifigenia, in her birth city of Santiago. See, Raúl Ramos, "Mariana Grajales" available at http://www.ain.cubaweb.cu/mujer/mariana.htm; accessed August 25, 2002; María Elena Balán, "Mariana Grajales, madre mayor de Cuba" available at http://www.nnc.cubaweb.cu/historia/historia27.htm; accessed August 25, 2002; J.A. Sierra, "The Timetable. History of Cuba. The Antonio Maceo Timeline" available at http://www, historyofcuba.com/history/mactime1.htm accessed on August 25, 2002.

22 See Luke 16:19–31.

23 This may very well be the Lazarus of the Gospels, brother of Martha and Mary, whom Jesus raised from the dead. A derivation of his

name, *lazaretto*, is given to places where lepers are cared for. This move by the church not only removed a non-historical character from the roster of the saints but also attempted to distance San Lázaro from Babalú-Ayé, who is represented in Africa as an old man with a wooden leg. Jorge Castellanos and Isabel Castellanos,*Cultura Afrocubana 3: Las Religiones y Las Lenguas* (Miami: Ediciones Universales, 1992), 57–59.

24 Tim Holtz, M.D., M.P.H., "Summary of Issue of HIV-AIDS in Cuba—APHA Cuba Tour, August 1997" available from http://www.cubasolidarity.net/cubahol12.html accessed September 1, 2002.

25 Ibid.

26 Born in 1853 in La Habana, José Martí was the soul of the Cuban War of Independence, advocating equality for all Cubans and the establishment of democratic processes. He worked in the USA to bring together all the factions of Cuban exiles and raised funds to finance the war. He landed in Cuba with a few others and, gathering supporters along the way, he was finally able to link with Antonio Maceo and his army, but died in battle shortly thereafter, May 19, 1895. Martí's copious writings have been the inspiration of every single struggle for freedom in Cuba. He was also a poet and is one of the key figures of Latin American literature.

27 On November 22, 1999, Elizabeth Brotón illegally left Cuba for the USA in a 16-foot motorboat with her son, Elián González. The boat capsized the next day and Elizabeth and Elián survived hanging to inner tubes. On November 25 two of the other survivors came ashore and Elián was rescued at sea near Ft. Lauderdale. His mother had died. The next day Elián was entrusted to his great-uncle who lives in Miami. On November 27, Elián's father in Cuba demanded his return. The Immigration and Naturalization Service in the USA decided that the father in Cuba had the right to custody; the Attorney General upheld this decision. Elián's Miami family did everything possible to keep the six-year-old child here: they applied for political asylum for him, applied for temporary custody, filed suit in federal court to challenge the INS ruling. Elián became a battleground between the Cuban government and the large and politically powerful anti-Cuban-government Cuban community in Miami. The federal government in the USA never wavered in its decision regarding the right of the father to custody. His father was granted a visa and came to Washington, D.C. After months of public demonstrations in Cuba and Miami, of legal procedures, and of meetings with Elián's family in Miami by well-known community and national leaders trying to find a solution to the situation, on April 22, 2000, federal agents stormed the Miami house of Elián's family and took him to his father in Washington. On June 28, after the US

Supreme Court refused to block his departure, Elián returned to Cuba. The political machinations at work in this case are many. What is often lost is that the González family is an example of the terrible divisions that exist in Cuban families. The grandfather of Elián and his family are sympathizers of the Castro regime. His brothers who exiled themselves in Miami are not. Elián became embroiled in the painful divisions that had split the family years before. The day I was at the *Plaza de La Revolución*, Fidel from the podium placed a phone call to Elián's father, who already had the child with him in Washington, D.C. After the ceremonies at the Plaza, Fidel led the people in a march of several kilometers to the staging area that had been recently built outside the USA Interest Section in La Habana. Here demonstrations took place almost daily during the time of the early months of 2000 with children being brought from school and workers from their workplaces to participate. For the chronology of the events see, "Elián González Chronology;" available from http://www.washingtonpost.com/wp-srv/nation/sidebars/elian_timeline.htm accessed September 2, 2002.

[28] Szulc, *Fidel*, 469.

[29] Pérez-Stable, *The Cuban Revolution*, 174.

[30] Ibid., 176–177.

[31] Food subsidies are one of the reasons why Cubans had been able to live with such small salaries. Since staples are now not always available, Cubans' monthly salaries are said to allow people to live for two weeks. The rest of the time, those who have dollars manage, the rest have to rely on their creative resourcefulness and simply have to be hungry. Workers and students do receive free meals but, again, the quality is so terrible that many simply do not eat them.

[32] Fidel holds the rank of major in Cuba's armed forced. The rank of general was created for his brother Raúl who heads the Ministry of the Interior, controlling the army and the security apparatus of the government.

[33] Baker, *Havana Handbook*, 108.

[34] This part of El Malecón is called Avenida del Puerto, and it is not considered to be officially part of El Malecón. However the seawall continues in this area and many of us consider it to be part of El Malecón. In my description I am following the division of El Malecón used by a course taught at Harvard Design School in Cambridge, Massachusetts. See Lelan Cott, "1511: Havana, Cuba III: El Malecon," Harvard Design School — Spring 2002 Courses;" available from http://courses. gsd.harvard.edu/2002/spring/1511.html; accessed on September 2, 2002.

[35] Though a few of the buildings have been torn down for safety reasons, many of them still stand with the help of scaffolds, which

Cubans refer to as "crutches." When I look at those old buildings I always have the sense that they are standing against all odds to show us the honor and grace inherent in the act of surviving.

[36] Cott, "1511: Havana, Cuba III: El Malecon," 2.

[37] The eagle that was on top of two forty-foot-tall columns was toppled in 1961 by an angry mob on the occasion of the USA-sponsored invasion by Cubans aiming to overthrow Fidel's government, known as the Bay of Pigs.

[38] Jorge Mañach, "El Muro del Malecón," in *Estampas de San Cristóbal* (I) (Cuenca, Spain: Editorial Trópico, 1995).

[39] Stuart Hall, "Cultural Identity and Diaspora," in *Colonial Discourse and Post-Colonial Theory: A Reader*, ed. Patrick Williams and Laura Chrisman (New York: Columbia University Press, 1994), 392–403.

I am using here "the imaginary" as a noun. This usage as a noun is quite extensive in contemporary Spanish writings — *el imaginario* — and it refers to the "inventory" of ideas, images, symbols that exist or are possible to imagine or conceive by a group of people or a person.

[40] In La Habana I stay with a friend who has a telephone and just outside her house, on the sidewalk, there are two public telephones from where I can make long distance calls using cards bought at kiosks of ETECSA, the Cuban telephone company (that is a partnership with an Italian company). Last year I went to the sidewalk outside my friend's house to call the USA and found that the phones were broken (the children from across the street play with them). So I started to walk trying to find another phone. I finally found three phones about ten blocks away. One was broken and the other two were being used. I waited. After ten minutes the woman using the phone allowed me to make my call before she made her next call. Gratefully I dialed but it took me no less that five minutes of constant dialing to be able to get a line and have my call go through. I ran back to the house, for my host was waiting for me. As I tried desperately to make my legs go faster, I started to laugh remembering that, when I went to China for a women's meeting a few years ago, I found a telephone on top of the Great Wall. The friend that was with me thought it would be wonderful to call her daughter in Geneva from the Great Wall. So she picked up the phone and using her Swiss credit card got a hold of her daughter, having had to dial only once! My friend lives in Cuba.

[41] The Cuban government indicated that in 2001 120,000 Cubans and Cuban-Americans traveled to Cuba. The money spent by those who travel to Cuba, plus the remittances sent to the island from abroad, provide 14 percent of the hard currency available to the Castro govern-

ment. Pablo Alfonso, "Castro necesita más dólares del exilio"; available in http://futurodecuba.org/Castro%20Necesita%20Mas%20Dolares%20del%20Exilio_.htm; accessed August 25, 2002.

[42] The lowest estimate as to those who have left Cuba illegally in boats and rafts since 1959 is 78,000. (Personal e-mail from Holly Ackerman, 8/28/2002.) See Holly Ackerman and Juan M. Clark, *The Cuban Balseros: Voyage of Uncertainty* (Miami: Policy Center of the Cuban American Council, c. 1995). No less than one fourth of them have perished. This number does not include those who left by boat with permission of the Cuban government in 1965 through Camarioca (5,083) and in 1980 through Mariel (120,800). See Cuban-American Military Council, "Support for a Democratic Transition in Cuba (excerpts)"; available from camcocuba.org/news/lyndon.html; accessed September 1, 2002; and US Coast Guard Office of Law Enforcement, "Mariel Boatlift," available from www.uscg.mil/hq/g-o/g-opl/mle/mariel.htm; Internet; accessed September 1, 2002. Besides the estimate of 78,000 leaving by boat, there is no estimate as to the Cubans who have deserted, who having been allowed to leave Cuba to visit families or to go to different events—whether representing Cuba officially or on their own—and have not returned.

[43] Exact figures are impossible to obtain. The best estimate is that Cubans send to the island between 830 million and one billion US dollars. Oscar Espinosa Chepe, "El estado real de la economía cubana," *Cuba en Transición* 10 (2000), 15. Seemingly three years later a much higher amount is being sent to Cuba by those of us living outside the island. "A government economist . . . says that remittances from Cuban-Americans topped $1 billion last year. . . ." In "The Dollarised Revolution," *The Economist* (August 2, 2003), 37.

The remittances have to be sent through third countries and now there is a way of sending money through the Internet for those with a credit card. See "International Money Transfer;" available at http://www.international-money-transfer-consumer-guide.info; accessed June 8, 2004.

The government in Cuba indicates that approximately 62 percent of Cubans have access to dollars. These are not only the ones who receive money from abroad but also a small number of Cubans who work in key industries like construction and oil and receive stimulus in US dollars. It also includes those who work in tourism. See Pablo Alfonso, "Castro necesita más dólares del exilio."

[44] This understanding of globalization is that of Saskia Sassen. See her book *Globalization and Its Discontents: Essays on the New Mobility of People and Money* (New York: New York Press, 1998). Here I am quot-

ing from Charlotte Snow, "Saskia Sassen calls for a democratic approach to globalization's impact," in *University of Chicago Magazine*; available at http://magazine.uchicago.edu/9812/html/invest2.htm; accessed June 8, 2004.

45 Ibid.

46 Saskia Sassen, "The Global City: Strategic Site/New Frontier;" available at http://india-seminar.com/2001/503/503%20sassen.htm; accessed June 8, 2004.

47 Ibid.

48 Saskia Sassen, *Globalization and Its Discontents* (New York: The New York Press, 1998), xxx. Though Sassen does not apply her theory to workers from less economically advantaged areas within the USA, I do. I believe that Mexican-American and USA-born Hispanas/Latinas are indeed part of this transnational labor pool to which Sassen refers.

49 Ibid., xxx–xxxi.

50 Ibid., 24–25 and many other places throughout the book.

51 Ibid., 92.

52 This use of "philanthropy" was shared with me by Yolanda Tarango, to whom I am grateful for conversations on several points of this article. She heard it from Barbara Ehrenreich in an interview about her book, *Nickeled and Dimed—On (Not) Getting By in America* (New York: Henry Holt and Company, 2001).

53 Sassen "The Global City."

54 Gayatri Chakravorty Spivak, "'Questions of Multiculturalism,' interview by Sneja Gunew (August 30, 1986)," in *The Post-Colonial Critic: Interviews, Strategies, Dialogues*, ed. Sarah Harasym (New York: Routledge, 1990), 66.

55 "If you did not exist I would invent you, my city of La Habana." Closing verse of a poem by Fayad Jamis.

9

Burlando al Opresor:
Mocking/Tricking the Oppressor

Hispanas/Latinas' Dreams and Hopes

¡Te digo yo a ti![1]
The prevalence of hyphens, slashes, dashes, and parenthetical expressions in contemporary academic discourse points to the shifts that have been taking place in the world for decades, but only recently (twenty years seem recent to me) have we in the academic world paid attention to these shifts, most probably because they have begun to interrupt our *cotidiano*—the daily reality that impinges on our routines making us notice what is going on "out there."[2] Hyphens, slashes, dashes, and parentheses indicate that we are in-between times—we find ourselves in a situation where the explanations of what is and the reasons for it (theories) that we created and have depended on to make sense of our world, are less and less apt to help us deal with reality, if not ours, at least the reality of the great majority of the world, which we find less and less capable of ignoring.

¡Ay Dios mío!
The hyphens seem to have a predilection for connecting "post" with a variety of words used to explain how we have been thinking and functioning—"we" here being those of us who seem to believe that we are the avant-garde of the human race. At times, "post" does not do the trick appropriately and we then have recourse to the prefix "neo" hoping always, I would like to

suggest, not to ignore what has been. (Rightly so, no?) Why leave behind a way of interpreting reality and dealing with the material world that is beneficial to those with power and privileges? But perhaps I should give at least some of us with power and privilege the benefit of the doubt. The fact is I need to do so. So I would like to propose that some few of us are willing to consider a "post" here and a "neo" there because we have finally realized that our fate is tied up inexorably with that of the more than two-thirds of the human race that do not have time but to think about how to survive today.[3] And if this is so, then we need to consider ways of leaving behind what is so detrimental to many. Not such a bad thing this preoccupation with self, for (in the Gospel message of Jesus and also in my books) love of neighbor —the only thing that really saves us from destroying ourselves together with destroying them—is grounded in love of self: so we better love ourselves or there is no possible way out for anyone.[4]

¡Vaya usted a saber!

The hyphens, slashes, dashes, and parentheses created by the constant flow between continuity and discontinuity constitute the space where we place ourselves (well, perhaps at times they are simply the spaces where we find ourselves to be). As a matter of fact, what is key always as one moves on (and not to move indicates the one final thing we humans can count on: death!) is to figure out the right proportions between what has been and what will be. Too much of the past means the cake will be hard, too much of the future means it will turn out runny. What about the present? The present is but the moments (and because it is made up of moments does not mean that it is immaterial or non-important, for the present is precisely the conscious now in which we live; the present has continuity becoming the present-past and the present-future) that we grab to construct our lives, to make up our *cotidiano* and the narratives about it that we create to explain ourselves to ourselves.

¡Tenlo por sentado!

The hyphens, slashes, dashes, and parentheses likewise are indicative of our fluid social ontology,[5] which is based on the hybridity and diversity that are key realities/understandings we need to deal with in this twenty-first century (and I am being optimistic in not calling them "problems"). *Mestizaje-mulatez* is the Hispanic/Latino incarnation of hybridity and diversity and it has been considered, in *mujerista* theology, from its initial immature enunciations, our *locus theologicus*.[6] The interstices in which we stand (not any less "real" in and of themselves in spite of their constant movement/evolvement into the next one; their flux and temporality not making them any less capable of yielding reality and truth as we deal with them/become involved in the process of changing them), need to be recognized and embraced (ah! yes! embraced, as in *un abrazo fuerte*, with not even a little bit of air between the embracer and the "embracee") as a way of exposing and subverting the liberal hegemonic paradigm that continues to control society and the academy, as a way of revealing the power differences that keep many at the mercy of a few, and as an antidote to a self-aggrandizement that will make us explode (well, maybe implode). The problem is that though the blasts are often not enough to kill us, they leave us diminished more than anything else, I would like to suggest, because they affect those around us as well as those not so close by (like the Mexican-American woman who harvested the tomatoes I had in my omelet this morning)—those "those" with whom I am intrinsically bound whether I realize/accept it or not.

¡Avanza!

Coming from one of the communities that lives on the hyphen,[7] I want to capitalize on the interstices—and that is what I have been doing all along. By this I mean that I want to make it count: I want to stand on the "in-betweens" fully conscious that it is not only a matter of acknowledging that is where I am, but also knowing that I have to decide "how" I stand there and "which way" to turn. I stand in these spaces as a protagonist—a non-sovereign *sujeto histórico*—needing to contribute to the "meanings" operative in society and wanting to resist any attempt to leave me out of this enterprise. (Yes, to post-modern and post-colonial I indeed add post-structural![8]) I stand there always turning whichever way best makes it possible for me to engage in *la lucha*—*la lucha* for life, for fullness of human life (life, fullness of human life is another way of talking about liberation; liberation is the hermeneutical lens/ideological stance/worldview of *mujerista* thought/theology). From the interstices I look back and I look to the "backward" in the now: to the neo-colonial forces at work in the present. I do this only in so far as it helps *la lucha cotidiana hoy*, for the present situation of my main community of accountability—the Hispanic/Latino community living in the USA, particularly Hispanas/Latinas—is too precarious (Come on! It is outright dangerous!) to dally in what has been. The present is often death-dealing and from the space the present provides I look back and "backward" in order to decolonize[9] myself and my community. I look back to critique, and this means that I stop to denounce and deconstruct only insofar as I need to for the sake of the future.[10] To denounce and deconstruct is a raiding action: it is a taking hold of what I find useful in my colonized condition for building the future (this recognizes the fact that we Hispanas/Latinas can speak and have spoken; that our interstices have not been and are not silencing spaces but rather fertile in-betweens from which to gather rich understandings/praxis).[11] I denounce and deconstruct to find and salvage the "dangerous memories"[12] of the personal and communal experiences where life has been begotten and birthed despite the death-dealing situations in which we have lived. I denounce and deconstruct only to rescue what is mine, recognizing that to do so I have to embrace the life-long process of freeing myself of the internalized oppressors. To denounce and deconstruct is a way of actively remembering what I do *not* want the future to be like. However, to tarry in the colonial past and the neocolonial present, even if it is to critique it, is one of the key impediments to liberation for it feeds the oppressors within. This is why looking back and "backward" is necessarily a "memory forward,"[13] not a "back and 'backward'" for their own sake, but a re-membering myself and my people only to make it possible to move ahead.[14]

¡*Nena, por favor!*

Engaging in *la lucha* for fullness of human life-liberation, however, is much more a matter of "creating a-new," of looking forward in order to participate in creating a future that is life-dealing, from which no one—starting with myself and my community of accountability, of course—no one group of persons (turned into "a group" by capitalizing on whichever characteristic/feature they or the rest of us consider desirable) is excluded. Looking forward from the interstices we have created as refuge or where we had been exiled but have turned into our own is an exercise of the imagination. It is a strategic way of engaging in *la lucha*—of struggling by expanding the imaginary, of looking ahead. I look forward and by doing so I recognize how Hispanas/Latinas have created spaces interstitially as the beginning moments of "a hopeful utopian project,"[15] our *proyecto histórico*.[16]

¡Imagínate! ¡Más!

To claim that our *proyecto histórico* is a utopian project indicates that I intentionally move away from post-modern understandings to a way of understanding reality—you cannot understand/know reality unless you take responsibility for it and change it—that is liberationist. Regardless of the many ifs and buts that post-modern thinking has introduced about meta-narratives, I hold on to the need for a *proyecto histórico* as a necessary element of any true liberation thought—and *mujerista* theology is, among other things, a liberation theology. Since we are talking about a *proyecto*, what we are dealing with is, first and foremost, a process that turns the confinement of the smallest of in-betweens into a stepping-stone for the future. Then, precisely because this *proyecto* is *histórico*, our utopian project struggles with what is as it tries to become a concrete way of life in a given geographic space for the largest number of people possible. Hispanas/Latinas' *proyecto histórico* is indeed, as the prophet Joel said, a dreaming dreams and seeing visions by the powerless: the old and the young, the maidservants, the menservants.[17] Our *mujerista proyecto histórico* is enmeshed in materiality, beginning to become a reality whenever the hungry are fed, the thirsty are given to drink, the homeless are sheltered, and those who are sick and in prison are visited.[18]

¡No lo puedo creer!

Often I have the sense that the rejection of utopian projects by those with power and privileges is a way of imprisoning so-called minorities in the in-betweens. Often I know that we, Hispanas/Latinas, let them think they are dominating us while we in the interstices create a meaningful *cotidiano* that makes our lives worth living—and I am not ignoring or lessening the reality of the pain and sorrow of oppression of my community of accountability. In other words, *nos burlamos del opresor* for, though they exploit us, we in turn not only survive despite them, but also change their material world and are learning to influence their discourse about the world at large and even about themselves. *Mujeristas* are archeologists (yes! in the Foucault-fashion) and *nos burlamos del opresor burlando al opresor:* we mock the oppressor by tricking/evading the oppressor. This does not mean that we do not take to heart the advice that "the master's tools will never dismantle the master's house."[19] Rather than using the master's tools what we are doing is turning the confinement/spaces to which we are assigned into creative/liberating spaces. In other words, we are trying not to let the will of the masters (and mistresses) define the tiniest of space which initially was not ours but which little by little we turn into our own, partially because masters and mistresses are scared to come into them once we inhabit them.

¡*Acaba, chica!*

Nos burlamos del opresor burlando al opresor: mockery as a "power of the weak"[20] is an intrinsic element of our *proyecto histórico* and though I wish it did not have to be so (for I am often boringly straight-faced), the fact is that the mischievousness of mockery is a most healthy antidote for any sense of "victimhood" that we might be tempted to embrace. The even more important thing is, however, that *nos burlamos del opresor* in order to *burlar al opresor*.[21] Hispanas/Latinas mock the oppressor—and often "they" do not even notice!—as a way of confronting the oppressor. *Burla*, meaning mockery, is another way of asserting ourselves as *sujetos históricos* engaged in *la lucha* and refusing to value suffering in itself. *Burla*, meaning tricking/evading, makes it very clear for us Hispanas/Latinas that our *mujerista proyecto histórico* cannot be a repetition of what is—for much of what is, is worthy of mockery, right?—that we cannot become like the oppressors or imitate the way they create, understand and interpret reality (well, at least most of the way they do it!). This is our ultimate *burla:* to turn the elements of confinement in the tiniest of interstices into those needed to create *una sociedad en la que quepan todos*,[22] a society in which all fit, from which no one is excluded.[23]

Our *Mujerista Proyecto Histórico:*
A Hispanas/Latinas' Utopian Project

Hispanas/Latinas in the USA are oppressed and excluded. Given that reality, it is not surprising that we hope for a different future, that we look ahead and work for what is not part of our reality: liberation. Our *mujerista proyecto histórico* clearly indicates that we understand our ethical-theological enterprise as praxis: Hispanas/Latinas' critical reflective action process centered on our lived-experience that uses and embodies a liberation hermeneutics. Our *mujerista proyecto histórico* is a utopian project and this immediately distinguishes us from post-modernism, which insists that utopias are invalid totalizing narratives. Also distancing our *mujerista* enterprise from post-modernism is our (hopefully) clear and effective commitment to moral agency.[24] Post-modernism offers no position from which to speak[25] and our *mujerista proyecto histórico* is precisely that: a place/position/ commitment from which to speak as well as a place/worldview/societal organizational framework that we are committed to create and inhabit. I am not totally ungrateful to post-modernism, for I know that it certainly has contributed to breaking the hegemony of modernity in which Hispanas/Latinas could not get a foothold. However, it is my humble opinion that by the time post-modernism began to be elaborated as an understanding/ theory in the academy, the struggles of poor and marginalized people all over the world during the 1960s and early 1970s against dictatorial governments and colonial oppression as well as three socio-political movements in the USA—for civil rights of African Americans, against the war in Vietnam, and for nuclear disarmament—had gone a long way in questioning and beginning to deconstruct modernity as a social, political and philosophical period/condition. *Mujeristas* are grateful to these people's struggles and movements for breaking the hold that modernity had on our understandings and ways of conceptualizing our world and ourselves. So, though it might be academic post-modernism what gets me invited to write this article, it is the struggle of peoples against modernity that gave me a start in the struggle for liberation.

In regard to post-colonialism I will simply say that *mujerista* ethical-theological enterprise certainly includes what is central to this discourse: the "dismantling [of] the Center/Margin binarism of imperial discourse."[26] Likewise, our *mujerista* enterprise has a strong political motivation that necessarily has to start being oppositional (the looking back and "backward" is precisely part of the oppositional movement in our work). This is also true of post-colonialism.[27] There seems to be, therefore, affinity between post-colonialism and the *mujerista* enterprise. Though it is very rare to find reference to utopias in post-colonial text, it is a theory—maybe theories—that in and of itself does not seem to contradict the possibility or even the need for a utopian project. One of the most interesting and helpful elements of postcolonial thought for our *mujerista* enterprise has to do with the difference being made between "place" and "space." In many ways the utopia that is created by our *mujerista* struggle is not a different place but a different space, a space often assigned to us by the dominant group in society, but also space we have been able to clear for ourselves and inhabit in the midst of a very oppressive place—today's USA society. This space is not an abstraction but rather a spatio-temporal reality that we create in order to have the freedom to envision our preferred future. As this preferred future takes root in us as a community of struggle and as it begins to become tangible in concrete projects, our *mujerista* space begins to influence society, contributing to a radical re-definition of "place" in general by re-drawing the concrete characteristics of this place—today's USA society—where we struggle to find and/or create our Hispana/Latina's space.[28] Perhaps in the future critical post-colonial theory will work to bring the concept of utopias into its discourse. Be that as it may, I unabashedly now turn, equipped with a liberation lens and a hermeneutics of suspicion, to an elaboration of some of the key elements of a Hispanas/Latinas utopian project: our *mujerista proyecto histórico*.

Utopias, Desire, Hope

Utopias have served humankind as a way of focusing and organizing hopes for changing the world, for making it a better world. The present day rejection of utopias seems to me to confuse utopia as an inspiring and organizing concept/image, with given forms of utopia that have resulted in the exclusion and oppression of vast number of people. Utopias in reality will never disappear. They will never go away, for they are "hidden signifiers"[29] of our needs and our desires, and without needs and desires humans fall into mortal apathy. Utopias have to do with the hopes and expectations of the poor and all the marginalized as they face the everyday reality of oppression. As a matter of fact, utopias provide for us the ability to really see and understand *lo cotidiano* and our daily struggles to survive, for "only in a concern to transform the present situation shall we ever be able to acquire an authentically realistic view of the situation."[30] Part of the driving force of utopias is their subversive character, which is precisely why they threaten those who support the *status quo* at any cost.

Utopias relate not to an imprecise future but to the present reality in which we are immersed.

> But this relationship to historical reality is neither simple nor static. It appears under two aspects which mutually require each other. . . .
>
> Utopia necessarily means a condemnation of the existing order. Its deficiencies are to a large extent the reason for the emergence of a utopia. It is a matter of a complete rejection which attempts to get to the root of the evil. This is why utopia is revolutionary. . . .
>
> But utopia is also a proclamation, an annunciation of what is not yet, but will be; it is the forecast of a different order of things, a new society. It is the field of creative imagination which proposes the alternative values to those rejected. The condemnation is to a large extent made in function of the proclamation. But the proclamation in its turn presupposes this rejection, which clearly delimits it retrospectively.[31]

Utopia weaves desire, hope, feasibility, and pleasure in a way that sustains the struggle to reach our preferred future: life and fullness of life-liberation for Hispanas/Latinas. In our *cotidiano* it is impossible to separate hope, feasibility, desire and pleasure. Therefore we separate them only as a heuristic device in order to be able to analyze what they mean and explain how they are present in our lives. Desire is the starting point. Desire is a way of reaching out for what we believe is good for us. This means that desire has an ethical component, for desire involves "selective intentionality and responsiveness" and, therefore, "seems to be a part of our humanity worthy of respect and voice."[32]

Desire operates in the interstitial spaces to which we are often confined as the "yeast" that activates us, that moves us to begin to imagine—thus beginning to change—those in-between spaces from confinement to platforms for struggle.[33] To understand and value desire is to pay attention to the beginning of the processes that make it possible for us Hispanas/Latinas to create our own meaning of reality by exploding, confronting and subverting precisely these same processes that have been created and are sustained by those who oppress and marginalize us. Desire helps us to come to terms with ourselves, making it possible to confront the categories of meaning of the dominant group in society which exclude Hispanas/Latinas. In this sense, desire is a tool used in the archeological work we do that enables us to move from oppression to liberation.[34] Desire unmasks the discourse of destructive abnegation/self-sacrifice and pain/sorrow and shows them for what they are: anti-values. Hispanas/Latinas create meaning for ourselves by paying attention to our desires, thus beginning to be self-defining moral agents by being self-reflective. This is why if we understand "desire as revolution, desire as love and hope for a different kind of future," desire becomes "a medium for social change."[35] We need to trust our desires instead of suppressing them, as we have been taught, for desires are what make it possible not only to unmask anti-values but also to move in a different direction, to enunciate our utopian vision.

Hispanas/Latinas' desires make it possible for us to recognize how social practices to which we have not been allowed to contribute and which we are forbidden to question have been forced upon us: upon our bodies, our personal lives and the lives of our communities. In this sense desire is not only a tool for discovering and unmasking the discourse of sacrifice and pain but it also helps us to analyze how this discourse has been "written" on Hispanas/Latinas' bodies. Desire, then, has not only an archeological function but also a genealogical one, following Foucault's usage, grounding our utopian vision in the history we have lived and live everyday as marginalized women living in the USA.[36] The genealogical function of desire, however, not only enables us to uncover the social practices that marginalize Hispanas/Latinas but also allows our utopian vision to surface, enabling the desires we have experienced—lived here and there, this time and that one, in private and publicly, personally and as a community—despite the oppression we suffer. Desires move us from the interpretations we have been taught to give our experiences—the interpretations we give our desires, who we are, and what we do as well as the interpretations that are imposed on us—to the experiences themselves. In this sense desires are "energies, excitations, impulses, actions, movements, practices, moments, pulses of feeling"[37] inscribed on Hispanas/Latinas' bodies, in our *cotidiano*, enmeshed in the materiality of who we are and what we do and in what we dare to imagine. In the interstitial spaces we occupy, desires make it possible for us to break loose from oppression in order to resist, oppose and transform. If we do not begin to resist and transform we cannot imagine differently. This imagining differently is part of the process of conscientization that anchors our struggle to be self-defining, to become subjects of our own history, to struggle to make our utopian vision a reality.[38]

Desire not only plays a role in starting this process of self-definition for Hispanas/Latinas but it also is central to sustain our struggles to bring about our *mujerista proyecto histórico*. Once we cease to desire, our motivation for staying in the struggle grows faint and our ability to keep our eyes set on liberation diminishes. Desire also helps us to evaluate our utopian vision, for "if the vast majority" of Hispanas/Latinas "characteristically and pervasively and over a long period of time did not desire" the *mujerista* utopian vision, we might still think that such utopian vision is good but we would have lost a key element needed to turn it into a realizable project, a political project. Our *mujerista* insistence on self-definition necessitates a process of reflection and deliberation, intrinsic steps in choosing for oneself. Choice also has to do with what people want, with what we desire. Desire is as much a human component of choice as are reflection and deliberation. Desire, therefore, has an important role at the level of implementation of our utopian vision as well as being key in helping us to imagine a preferred future different from present oppressive structures and motivating us to struggle for our personal liberation and the liberation of Hispanas/Latinas communities.[39]

A second moment in imagining and creating Hispanas/Latinas' future is that of hope. Once desires help us to recognize something different, making it possible to give credence to what we imagine, hope emerges leading us to work to make our desires a reality. Hope begins to make our desires concrete. Hope is a virtue because it is a disposition that creates a passion that results in actions. Hope is a passion for something that is not but yet will be. Hope is also a praxis that makes reality what one passionately desires. Hope is a virtue that is absolutely necessary for humans to remain alive. It is necessary for life (certainly for fullness of human life-liberation) because hope is what makes us believe that we can and will live beyond this very minute. In this sense hope is what makes possible transcending the present and moving into the future. Hope lies "midway between knowledge and willing . . . where absolute knowledge fails, wishing and willing intervene in a creative act, to take the chance or the risk. . . ."[40] This wishing and willing that somehow move us ahead into the future are "elements" of hope. Hope is "the fundamental knowledge and feeling that there is a way out of difficulty, that we as human persons can somehow handle and manage internal and external reality, that there are 'solutions' in the most ordinary biological and physiological sense of that word."[41] Hope operates at the personal-interpersonal level as well as at the social-political level. It operates in our dealings with each other from the most intimate to the most formal, and hope operates in the social and political institutions that organize and govern the lives of communities.

Utopias are precisely projects that result when the desires of the people fuel hope for bringing together ways of organizing and governing our lives with the means necessary to begin to do so. Hope fills us with optimism, providing us the energy to pursue their implementation—the realization of our utopian vision. However, utopias become indeed "no place" if the hopes that create them have no materiality, if they have no way of being incarnated in political, social and economic systems, processes and organizations. Hope itself is impossible to maintain—dissolving into confusion, futility, anguish and frustration: despair—if it does not have at least the tiniest of footholds in the world of the tangible. Hope—the wishing and willing that move us on—in many ways is ourselves acting within our own beings in order to make us move outwardly. If hope remains something within with no way of being exteriorized, hope simply dies, leaving the utopia it had birthed as something impossible even to imagine. The need for hope to have a foothold in the material world in order to have a reason for continuing to be alive is paralleled and made known by the need utopias have for historical—material—mediations. These material mediations are the conditions and means necessary for a given utopian project to be feasible and to become a reality. If the project is not feasible it runs the risk of becoming "a pseudo-prophecy with unlimited ethical exigencies sustained by an anthropological presupposition of human beings who are generously committed to social ends, which they are waiting for someone to propose."[42]

Feasibility and Effectiveness

The third element in the work to create our preferred future is feasibility. Feasibility becomes key in shaping dreams, sustaining hope, and moving to make our *mujerista* utopian project a reality. Feasibility points to the rationality of utopias, to the socio-political-historical grounding of utopias that does not preclude imagination and hope. Feasibility has to do with the technological, political, social and economic means to carry out *mujerista's proyecto histórico*. Often what we have chosen, decided, judged to be life-giving and just and adequate is simply not feasible for us to work for or to attain. At times we do not have the technological know-how/expertise to implement projects that make it possible for us to create or inhabit spaces where we can be self-determining. Other times we do not have the expertise to organize ourselves to carry out needed projects in our communities while those who exploit our communities have the political savvy and means to mobilize the community even if they are promoting anti-life goals. Frequently we do not have access to newspapers, radio, and television to make known and publicize our messages. In no way do I want to suggest that Hispanas/Latinas are incompetent or lack leadership qualities. However, the lack of economic means to carry out projects often simply makes materializing our goals unfeasible. We find ourselves repeatedly in situations where we have no way of moving from what we know we should do to doing it.[43] This means that often we have no way of making our hopes tangible. It means that repeatedly we find there is no way for us to attain the material means needed to make our utopian project a reality.

Our *proyecto histórico* has many facets to which to tend. It is a process that is not linear and the facets intersect and influence each other in many ways and at different moments. But there is—there has to be—a concrete process or we would not be able to talk of taking seriously the need for historical—material—mediations.[44] The first step in the process is to establish clearly the meaning of our goal: life and fullness of human life-liberation.[45] This has to be conceptualized in a possible/feasible way: if we do not see how we can accomplish it, then we cannot do it.[46] Then we have to begin to elaborate means to make that end come about: projects that will begin to create spaces, processes and institutions where our goal can become operational. Our starting point for all of this has to be the reality in which we are immersed. In other words, our experience is our starting point and our point of reference to check out the "rightness" of how we are proceeding.

The next step has to do with procuring the material means to be able to implement our *proyecto*. Here is where we have to face the fact that if we do not have what we need to carry out our tasks then our *proyecto* is not feasible. However, we also need to take into consideration that simply because something is doable it does not mean that it should be done. In other words, at all of these levels our *mujerista* ethical principle is at work. We have to ask ourselves constantly if what we are doing or hoping to do contributes to life and fullness of human life-liberation for the largest possible number of people.

The elaboration of projects to bring about our goal based on our experiences and made possible by having the social-economic-technical means to carry it out, with a constant ethical evaluation of the way the means fit our end and the end informs the means, also needs to pay attention to effectiveness. In other words, how effective are we in doing what we do, and how effective is this that we are doing in making our goal a reality? The best of good will and the best of intentions will not carry the day. Feasibility and effectiveness are intrinsic to the process. As we hopefully begin to see our efforts bear fruit, we must not forget the last two steps on the process. Once we make some gains we need to consolidate them, we need to institutionalize them. Somehow, to change oppressive structures and systems we have to counter with liberating structures and systems. Many times what we have worked very hard to accomplish, after a few years, disappears precisely because we have not been able to institutionalize it, because we have not been able to turn what we have accomplished into obligations, norms, and rights respected by all. If we are not able to do this, we cannot obtain civil legitimacy for our goals. No doubt we might be able to get some laws passed that protect what we have worked so hard to accomplish. But we also need for people at large to embrace the fact that whatever step we have been able to take towards liberation benefits all, that it has to be a norm for all. Unless the rest of society embraces what we accomplish as promoting life and fullness of human life-liberation for all, legal legitimacy will be an empty move.

The need to watch for effectiveness of the work we do does not disappear when projects are institutionalized. We need to stay ever vigilant so that institutionalization does not turn what we have accomplished into an inappropriate means given the goal we have in mind. Institutionalization, which means in many ways bureaucratization, can pervert the stated goal of any project. Insisting on carrying out our projects in a way acceptable to society and doing them whichever way those helping us with the funding insist they must be done, can make us lose sight of the reason for the project, of the values that we are trying to uphold given the goal we have in mind. I am not suggesting a "holier than thou" attitude which makes it impossible for anyone to help us or cooperate with us. Nor am I suggesting that we get paralyzed and insist on not moving unless we are perfectly sure of every step we need to take along the way. On the contrary, I believe that given the limits we humans have, the only way to proceed is to accept all kinds of help, move on partial solutions, and to take risks even when we are not sure of the results. But all of this has to be done within parameters of responsible action, of responsibility to our *proyecto*, knowing that our goal will become clearer as we move to accomplish it, that our *proyecto* will be modified many times by new understandings, new obstacles, and the ever present realization that nothing in our world is permanent. Being responsible to our stated goal does not mean immutability; on the contrary, responsibility to our *proyecto* means that we see what we do always as a process that evolves and becomes more precise as we go along. However, this in no way means that we adopt an anything-goes attitude. We insist on the need to be clear about what is the ethical principle that guides us, the principle that we have to constantly work to define and refine as we move with tiny but persistent steps towards life and fullness of life-liberation

Pleasure and Happiness

Feasibility as a characteristic of the praxis that mediates utopias has to do with what makes life possible and what facilitates life: "to live one has to be able to live, and in order to do that the criterion for choosing ends has to be the satisfaction of needs."[47] However, more and more we have come to realize that it is almost impossible to separate needs from wants though we must, I believe, continue to be able to differentiate one from the other, for in times of extreme deprivation, we must hold on to our right to have our needs satisfied. The satisfaction of wants as well as of needs is grounded in the importance we give to desires. Replacing abnegation/self-sacrifice—a negative/death-dealing attitude and understanding we have been tricked into believing is a "virtue"—with desire will help us to understand even more fully the goal of our *mujerista* utopian project: not only life but *fullness* of human life-liberation.[48]

Desire, hope, feasibility—they all make us realize that the struggle for fullness of life necessitates that we denounce also as

a negative/death-dealing attitude and understanding the idealization of pain/suffering, which is quite popular in religious circles, replacing it with the human desire for pleasure. Yes,
Hispanas/Latinas have the right to *"una existencia cotidiana
agradable y . . . [el] derecho al gusto de vivir"*—a pleasant daily
existence and the right to a pleasurable life.[49] We claim the right
to pleasure and happiness, knowing that one cannot be without
the other, always considering them as elements of our *proyecto
histórico.* By pleasure we refer to gratification and, in this context, we are using it to refer particularly—though not exclusively—to bodily gratification: sensual and sexual. By happiness
we refer to fullness of satisfaction and, in this context, satisfaction refers to the gratifying sense that comes from understandings, attitudes, and commitments. Of course such satisfaction is
not apart from material reality. Material gratification—bodily
gratification—is necessary for experiencing satisfaction, pleasure,
and happiness. The degree and kind of material gratification
needed depends on the persons involved but, I insist, material
gratification is essential to satisfaction. Yes, gratification and satisfaction, pleasure and happiness, exist in a circular fashion, spiraling towards human fulfillment and fullness of life.

Insisting on pleasure and happiness does not mean that we
are embracing a hedonistic attitude that concentrates on or
restricts happiness to pleasure but, again, we are insisting on
pleasure as an intrinsic element of happiness and fullness of life.
Nor are we espousing eudemonism, claiming that the highest
ethical goal is happiness and personal well-being. However, we
are indeed saying that happiness and personal well-being are
intrinsic elements of fulfillment and fullness of life. We will look
at key elements of what we call fullness of life below but here we
must at least explain that we base embracing and promoting
pleasure and happiness on the theological understanding that
love of self is **not** necessarily a selfish act. Love of self is a positive act that serves as the measuring rod for the love of neighbor required by Christian Scripture. The Gospel of Matthew 22:
34–40, places on Jesus' lips the then already ancient commandment to love God and to love one's neighbors. But the way it is
phrased connects both of these requirements with love of self—

a motivational force, for we conceive love of self as promoting one's happiness (not achievable without pleasure): "You shall love the Lord your God with all your heart, and with all your soul, and with all your mind. This is the greatest and first commandment. And *the second is like it:* you shall love your neighbor as yourself" (emphasis added).

Happiness has been given, most of the time, a positive interpretation usually relating it to the goal of life, to what God wants for us. It is true that many times true happiness has been deferred —postponed, mostly for the poor and oppressed, to the next "world" as the reward for a life of sacrifice in this world. Happiness often seems to be what the rich and powerful have and the rest of us cannot obtain until we die. Yet, even this perverted sense of distribution of happiness has not imposed a negative attitude towards happiness. However, when it comes to pleasure, the contrary is true. Pleasure fell a long time ago into the hands of the negative side of dualism. Pleasure has been paired with the still prevailing negative understanding of sensuality and sexuality, with all sorts of excesses, of vices, with selfishness, with death. Pleasure has been made to refer mainly (only?) to "bodily sensations that have become divorced from or a stand-in for the pleasure of being a soul in a body living in connection with others."[50] This negative understanding of pleasure has resulted in splitting us from our desires (perhaps from our best selves?) and, I would suggest, by distancing us from our own humanity it has also brought about divisions among us.

The prevalent demeaning understanding of pleasure distances us from ourselves resulting in "a pervasive trauma . . . that leads to separate ourselves from parts of ourselves, to create a split within ourselves so that we can know and also not know what we know, feel and yet not feel our feelings."[51] Only a re-valuing of pleasure as "a sensation . . . written into our bodies . . . [an] experience of delight, of joy . . . a compass pointing to emotional true north" will cure the trauma most women, not only Hispanas/Latinas, suffer.[52] Only our insistence on regaining our pleasure-loving selves will allow us to become fully incarnated, to value our bodiliness, to embrace our sexuality, and to pay attention, appreciate and liberate our desires for our own life and fullness of life-liberation.

Life and Fullness of Human Life-Liberation as Universal Ethical Principle

The principle of our *mujerista proyecto histórico* is life and fullness of human life-liberation.[53] Since one (Please! I am saying this is only *one* of them) of the essential characteristics of human beings (Please! I am not claiming that this might not also be a characteristic of some other "forms" of life) is self-awareness/self-consciousness/self-reflection, and this ability of the human mind depends on the physical development of the brain (I use "brain" to mean, as it does in everyday language, all of the parts of the brain: the brain stem, the mid-brain, the cerebellum, and the cerebro-hemispheres), there is no way that we can dispense with the physicality of life. So when I talk about the principle of life I refer to the biological-physical aspect of life. Life is also sensations, feelings, emotions—which depend on physical life, as do also the evaluative functions of the mind (the basis for ethical thought), and the linguistic functions. Life also is/takes place at the historical, cultural, ethical-aesthetic, spiritual-mystical level—all of it indicating the necessarily social aspect of human life. Life as a principle for our *mujerista* utopian project "is not a concept, an idea, an ontological abstract or concrete horizon. Neither is it a 'mode of being.' Human life is a 'mode of reality;' it is the concrete life of each human being from which she or he faces reality, constituting [reality] . . . [and] actualizing it as practical truth."[54]

The mode of reality that we Hispanas/Latinas experience and create is *la lucha*—the struggle for survival. This struggle for survival is the material criterion for our *proyecto* (it is a material criterion because our *proyecto* is *histórico*). This *lucha* has to do with the *production* of life and fullness of human life-liberation in its physical-material aspect—including the functions of the mind; with the *reproduction* of human life; and with the *development* of human life in historical cultural institutions and values—cultural here referring to all that we humans produce to deal with reality.[55] All of this happens at the personal level—in each of us ("in" here does not mean "individually"—exclusively within—but rather "pertaining to each one"), at the communal level—in the inter-subjectivity that is another constitutive characteristic of the human person, and at the societal level—in the social, political, economic institutions that we create.[56] Production, reproduction and development of life and fullness of life-liberation depend on our struggles to liberate ourselves from social situations of oppression—exploitation, marginalization, cultural prejudices, powerlessness and institutionalized violence—that force us to live in sub-human conditions. We also need to work at our own personal transformation—from a psychological perspective—so we can face any and all kinds of internalized oppression and live "with profound inner freedom." For Christians this personal transformation also includes liberation from sin, from both personal sin and social sin—sinful structures—that perpetuate conditions that enslave us in so many different ways.[57]

Our *mujerista proyecto histórico* is based on this universal principle of life and fullness of human life-liberation that we have been explaining. In and of itself, however, the *proyecto* neither dictates nor prescribes other universally valid ethical principles nor specific forms of government, economic systems or societal arrangements. In embracing as the guiding understanding/criterion of our particular *proyecto* the concept of excluding no one and being open to including everyone,[58] which is the only way to make the principle of life and fullness of human life-liberation operative at all times and in all places, we are not "pretending to know which shape of society is the only right one."[59] We are not claiming to know exclusively—or even to be the ones who best know—"how can one make human beings happy."[60] This means that as long as the social, political, and economic institutions we develop/embrace/uphold do not exclude anyone, then those institutions are valid because they are not contrary to the principle of life and fullness of human life-liberation. All of our criteria/norms are submitted to this same kind of judgment: our decisions of what is right or wrong, obligatory or permitted not only have to respect but they have to promote life and fullness of life-liberation.

As we move ahead in the twenty-first century we have identified issues that need to be taken into consideration if the principle of life and fullness of human life-liberation is going to be respected. In other words, we turn into a criterion for our struggles the elimination of whatever effectively excludes us from contributing to societal norms. This is why we claim that our daily experience of exclusion and oppression and our cries and *lucha* against the death-dealing reality we face today is the starting place for giving shape to our *proyecto histórico*.

At this point, of course, we have moved from considering a utopian project into delineating a feasible *proyecto*, a concrete and practical program/praxis. Our praxis, our liberative praxis— the fully conscious work we do to change the oppressive and exclusionary reality of Hispanas/Latinas—has several important components. First of all, our liberative praxis happens in and defines spaces, situations, and moments. Our liberative praxis is entrenched in the world of possibilities, which is why effectiveness has to be one of its main criteria. This world of possibilities is a utopian vision and, I insist, it is also a "situated universal" because our *proyecto* arises from and is constantly renewed by *our* reality and *our* way of experiencing, understanding, and dealing with what is real. This reality is a "situated universal," not an abstract universal or a concrete universal that simply sees the concrete as a particular of the given universal.[61] It is *our proyecto* and we claim the right to have *our* experience be what defines it and grounds it. The insistence on the "*our*" does not mean that I believe Hispanas/Latinas are unique. However I do claim specificity: we experience reality in a certain way and that way is a very particular one. Particularity does not set us apart but, on the contrary, it is particularity that indeed constitutes universality and it is where we encounter universality.

Second, our liberative praxis *is*, and it has many different shapes. "Organic intellectuals"[62] like myself do not invent liberative praxis but rather contribute to the formulation of frameworks for understanding our praxis. As an activist-theologian I believe that my work in elaborating a theological discourse— *mujerista* theology—is praxis. Our discourse is an attempt to point to and bring together changes in ways of thinking and acting that inform our liberative praxis and arise from it. Our discourse also, hopefully, points to the fact that change happens gradually, for "political changes arise out of simultaneous and loosely coordinated shifts in both thinking and action across several scales" (either simultaneously or sequentially).[63] In our work as organic theologians we attempt to provide an impetus for setting adequate criteria to use in judging our liberative praxis. We see our theological work as one that "does not incidentally bring about freedom because it reflects on certain symbols or doctrines in certain ways; theology does not necessarily result in freedom because it offers theoretical arguments as to the nature of freedom. As a form of social and religious therapy, theology anticipates freedom, calling into question the way things are, seeking out distortions, provoking a new way of being and doing in history. As part of its practical nature, theology is inherently involved with emancipation and enlightenment, and its form must be critical: uncovering, revealing, hearing and enlightening."[64]

The particularities of Hispanas/Latinas' liberative praxis are not something anyone of us invents but rather they emerge from the reality in which we are immersed as Hispanas/Latinas who live in the USA. The multi-layer oppression we struggle against in our daily lives is what shapes our liberative praxis, including our theological enterprise.

Finally, all liberative praxis for us Hispanas/Latinas has to necessarily contribute to the process of conscientization that enables Hispanas/Latinas to become moral agents or to strengthen our moral agency. Conscientization respects and promotes the participation of Hispanas/Latinas in our own process of liberation. This is why in *mujerista* theology we have used a method that includes the voices of grassroots Hispanas/Latinas. *Mujerista* theology is a liberative praxis precisely because it does not objectify Hispanas/Latinas and our struggles but rather includes our religious understandings and practices and our ability to articulate their meaning in our lives. In gathering grassroots Hispanas/Latinas to reflect on their lived-experience and to share with one another their understandings and struggles, *mujerista* theology provides opportunities for conscientization—for self-definition, an intrinsic element of moral agency. Conscientization is a praxis in which, through reflective action, Hispanas/Latinas come to understand the world in which they live and the preferred future they envision in such a concrete world that they begin to deal with it effectively—undermining the present oppressive world while building the liberative future they desire. Conscientization is a liberative praxis because it makes it possible for us to move from seeing the spaces in which we are—

whether we create them or are placed there—as interstices in which we can embrace and nourish desire moving to a different kind of consciousness that makes it possible for us to break loose from the confinements of oppression in order to create our *proyecto histórico.*

Notes

[1] The use of Spanish throughout this article is an attempt to resist the hegemonic English language. Using Spanish for us Hispanas/Latinas helps us to "bring unprecedented modes of consciousness, agency, and collective action into being that (coactive with all other political formations) will provide us access to the *liberatory* global space as country people of the same psychic terrain." Chela Sandoval, *Methodology of the Oppressed* (Minneapolis: University of Minnesota Press, 2000), 6. The use of Spanish continues to be an identifying characteristic for Hispanas/Latinas, even if some of us know but a few words of it. Then there is the fact that there are understandings I simply cannot relate to fully unless I use the Spanish terms. For example: *cotidiano, proyecto histórico, la lucha.* See Chapter 2 of my book *En La Lucha—In the Struggle: Elaborating a Mujerista Theology,* 2nd ed. (1993; Minneapolis: Fortress Press, 2003).

[2] I have been saying this for more than two decades. Recently I found resonance in the work of another Latina. "[T]he primary impulses and strains of critical theory and interdisciplinary thought that emerged in the twentieth century are the result of transformative effects of oppressed speech upon dominant forms of perception—that the new modes of critical theory and philosophy, the new modes of reading and analysis that have emerged during the U.S. post-World War II period, are fundamentally linked to the voices of subordinate peoples." Sandoval, *Methodology of the Oppressed,* 8.

For an elaboration of *lo cotidiano* see, "*Lo Cotidiano:* Everyday Stuggles in Hispanas/ Latinas' Lives," Chapter 6 in this book.

[3] See <www.thehungersite.com> where an area of the world lights up in a map every two seconds indicating someone there has just died of hunger. The site indicates that one billion people live in "relentless poverty and chronic hunger," and that 75 percent of the 24,000 who die daily are children.

[4] See also Hugo Assmann, "Por una sociedad donde quepan todos," in *Por una sociedad donde quepan todos,* ed. José Duque (Costa Rica: DEI, 1996), 383.

⁵ Catherine Keller, "Seeking and Sucking—On Relation and Essence in Feminist Theology," in *Horizons in Feminist Theology—Identity, Tradition, and Norms,* ed. Rebecca S. Chopp and Sheila Greeve Davaney (Minneapolis: Fortress Press, 1997), 55.

⁶ Ada María Isasi-Díaz and Yolanda Tarango, *Hispanic Women: Prophetic Voice in the Church* (Minneapolis: Fortress Press, 1992), 5–6. For a much more complete elaboration of *mestizaje-mulatez* see "Reconceptualizing Difference—A New *Mestizaje-Mulatez*," Chapter 5 in this book

⁷ I borrow this from the title of a book by a fellow Cuban, Gustavo Pérez-Firmat, *Life on the Hyphen: The Cuban-American Way* (Austin: University of Texas Press, 1994).

⁸ I am informed by the clear and precise elaborations of Chris Weedon, *Feminist Practice and Poststucturalist Theory* (Oxford: Blackwell Publishers, 1987; reprint 1994). May the Goddess bless her!

⁹ See Emma Pérez, *The Decolonial Imaginary: Writing Chicanas into History* (Bloomington: Indiana University Press, 1999).

¹⁰ I am not interested in critique in the sense of "reflecting on the conditions of possibility of transcendental categories, of thought, morality, or judgment, universal values, cultural forms, linguistic structures, and religious a prioris [sic]." Nor am I interested in critique "as a pragmatist project" intended to reach understanding through certain procedures. Manuel Mejido, "Propaedeutic to the Critique of the Study of US Hispanic Religion: A Polemic Against Intellectual Assimilation" (unpublished article), c. 2001.

¹¹ I am addressing the famous comment of Spivak regarding the inability of the subaltern to speak. However, I think it is unjust to freeze such a gifted woman thinker in what she said, in a moment of despair, almost twenty years ago. For an explanation of how her thinking has evolved, see Gayatari Chakravorty Spivak, *A Critique of Postcolonial Reason: Toward a History of the Vanishing Present* (Cambridge, Mass.: Harvard University Press, 1999), 308–311.

Though he is speaking about a somewhat different sort of hyphen, Pérez-Firmat sees living in the hyphen as a place/situation that offers "opportunities for distinctive achievement." See Pérez-Firmat, *Life on the Hyphen,* 5.

¹² Johann Baptist Metz, *Faith in History and Society* (New York: Seabury Press, 1980), 184. This phrase is much used. I quote Metz because this is the place where I first saw it used years ago.

¹³ Ibid, 188.

¹⁴ The urgency to move ahead because of the precariousness of the poor and oppressed is something that I learned initially from the poor of Lima, Perú, with whom I had the privilege of working in the decade

of the 1960s. For some philosophical grounding for my claims in this regard, see Enrique Dussel, *Ética de la liberacion — en la edad de la globalización y de la exclusión* (Madrid: Editorial Trotta, 1998).

15 Emma Pérez, *The Decolonial Imaginary*, 33.

16 In Chapter 2 of *En La Lucha*, I introduced our *proyecto histórico* as one of the constitutive elements of Hispanas/Latinas' identity. I have kept working on the specifics of our utopian project. See, for example, "Solidarity: Love of Neighbor in the Twenty-First Century," and "*Un Poquito de Justicia* — A Little Bit of Justice," in my book *Mujerista Theology — A Theology for the Twenty-First Century* (Maryknoll, N.Y.: Orbis Books, 1996).

17 Joel 2:28–29 and Acts 2:17–18 RSV.

18 Matthew 25: 31–46 RSV.

19 Audre Lorde, *Sister Outsider* (Trumansburg, N.Y.: The Crossing Press, 1984), 110–113.

20 I borrow the phrase from the title of the book that first made me think about tricks/deceptions as a useful tool for those without power: Elizabeth Janeway, *Powers of the Weak* (New York: Knopf, 1980).

21 One of the most powerful uses of *burla* is that of Sor Juana Inés de La Cruz, "Respuesta de la poetisa a la muy ilustre Sor Filotea de La Cruz," in *Sor Juana Inés de La Cruz — Dolor fiero*, selección y prólogo de Fina García Marruz (La Habana: Fondo Editorial Casa de Las Américas, 1999). See the brilliant essay by Josefina Ludmer about what Sor Juana accomplishes in this letter, "Las Tretas del Débil," in *La sartén por el mango*, ed. Patricia Elena González and Eliana Ortega (Puerto Rico: Ediciones Huracán, 1985), 47–54.

22 This is a leitmotiv of the Zapatistas in Chiapas, southern Mexico, which pointedly expresses the goal of their struggle. Throughout this chapter translations from the Spanish are my own.

23 Allow me to stop here to clarify that most of what I say in this chapter has exceptions and needs modifiers in both directions: more and less. For example, when I talk of excluding no one, I am aware of the fact that I cannot even know all those who must be included, much less can I figure out how to include them all. Most of the issues that come to mind for not being able to include some have to do with material feasibility ("how" to include them); but then there is the finitude of all human enterprise including this one of knowing who are all the ones being excluded. The fact is that even if we were able to include all, the inclusion would be only for the time being, for we have no way of knowing how history will evolve and, therefore, whom it will exclude. This is the kind of "modulation" that I intended to introduce a few lines above when I wrote, "Then, precisely because it is *histórico*, our utopian project also struggles with the givens as it tries to become a concrete

way of life *for the largest number of people possible.*" Of course I introduced that modulation knowing that some would criticize me for not
including everyone!
For a philosophical explanation of this issue see Dussel, *Ética de la
liberación*, 412–422. I am also interested in grounding this understanding of inclusion-exclusion in the biblical concept of the *anawim*,
the poor of Yahweh, for I believe it is an element much needed in the
explanation of the preferential option for the poor. See Albert Gelin,
The Poor of Yahweh (Collegeville, Minn.: Liturgical Press, 1964); John
O'Brien, *Theology and the Option for the Poor* (Collegeville, Minn.: Liturgical Press, 1992).

[24] Linda Hutcheon, *The Politics of Postmodernism* (London: Routledge, 1989), 3.

[25] Ibid, 153. In all fairness, Hutcheon believes that postmodernism
has both a critical/resistance component as well as maintaining a com-
plicity with practices of representation that are exploitative. See also pp.
17–18.

[26] "Part IV: Postmodernism and Post-colonialism—Introduction,"
in *The Post-colonial Studies Reader*, ed. Bill Ashcroft, Gareth Griffiths
and Helen Tiffins (London: Routledge, 1997), 117.

[27] Linda Hutcheon, "Circling the Downspout of Empire," in *The
Post-colonial Studies Reader*, 130.

[28] See D. Landry and G. Maclean, eds., *The Spivak Reader* (London: Routledge, 1996), 21. See also Colin Wright, "Centrifugal Log-
ics: Eagleton and Spivak on the Place of 'Place' in Postcolonial Theory,"
Culture, Theory & Critique 43 (no. 1): 67–82.

[29] David Harvey, *Spaces of Hope* (Berkeley: University of California
Press, 2000), 195.

[30] Gustavo Gutiérrez, *The Power of the Poor in History* (Maryknoll,
N.Y.: Orbis Books, 1983), 81. For a most helpful thematic guide of the
work of Gutiérrez, see James B. Nickoloff, ed., *Gustavo Gutiérrez—
Essential Writings* (Maryknoll, N.Y.: Orbis Books, 1996).

[31] Nickoloff, *Gustavo Gutiérrez*, 201–202. I am quoting from Nickoloff because of his excellent editing of the original material. For the
original see Gustavo Gutiérrez, *A Theology of Liberation*, 2nd ed. (Maryknoll. N.Y.: Orbis Books, 1988), 135–136. I use in this section the
three elements Gutiérrez sees as characteristic of utopias: "relationship
to historical reality, its verification in praxis, and its rational nature"
(Nickoloff, *Gustavo Gutiérrez*, 201).

[32] Martha C. Nussbaum, *Women and Human Development: The Capa-
bilities Approach* (Cambridge: Cambridge University Press, 2000), 147.

[33] I am influenced here by Emma Pérez's understanding and use of
the concept of desire. Her work also led me to study and use Foucault's

understanding of "archeology" and "genealogy." See Pérez, *The Decolonial Imaginary*, xiii–xix; 106–125.

34 Michel Foucault, *The Archeology of Knowledge* (New York: Harper & Row, 1972). The following passages from this book are particularly helpful in understanding the meaning Foucault gives to "archeology," 128–129, 131, 135–140, 167, 195, 206–208.

35 Pérez, *The Decolonial Imaginary*, xix.

36 The following resources are helpful in understanding the meaning Foucault gives to "genealogy." Hubert L. Dreyfus and Paul Rabinow, *Michel Foucault: Beyond Structuralism and Hermeneutics*, 2nd ed. (Chicago: University of Chicago Press, 1983), 104–125; Michel Foucault, "Nietzsche, Genealogy, History," in *Aesthetics, Method, and Epistemology*, ed. James D. Faubion (New York: The New York Press, 1998), 369–391. I might very well ascribe much more materiality and historicity than Foucault does to "genealogy."

37 Elizabeth Grosz, "Refiguring Lesbian Desire," in *The Lesbian Postmodern*, ed. Laura Doan (New York: Columbia University Press, 1994), 78. My conclusion about the materiality and historicity of desire is not supported by Grosz.

38 Emma Pérez's concept of the "decolonial imaginary" and Chela Sandoval's understanding of "oppositional consciousness" are very similar to many of the elements I include in terms such as "conscientization," "liberation," "fullness of life."

39 Nussabaum, *Women and Human Development*, 150–156.

40 William F. Lynch, *Images of Hope: Imagination as Healer of the Hopeless* (Notre Dame: University of Notre Dame Press, 1965), 34–35.

41 Ibid., 32.

42 Assmann, "Por una sociedad donde quepan todos," 387.

43 Dussel, *Ética de la liberación*, 263. Here Dussel is explaining the understanding of feasibility elaborated by Hinkelammert.

44 I am informed and guided in this process by Dussel's discussion of Hinkelammert as well as Dussel's own elaborations. Dussel, *Ética de la liberación*, 258–280.

45 More on this in the section below.

46 I am in no way excluding dreaming dreams and seeing visions. I think imagination has an enormous role to play in creating/building utopias. However, the imaginable has to be harnessed into the possible in order for it to be effective in the struggle for life-fullness of life.

47 Franz Hinkelammert, *Crítica a la razón utópica* (San Jose, Costa Rica: DEI, 1984), 240; quoted in Dussel, *Ética de la liberación*, 262.

48 I am reminded here of the strike slogan in 1912 of the women textile workers made into a song in the 1970: "Give us bread, but give us roses. . . . Hearts starve as well as bodies, bread and roses, bread and roses."

[49] Assmann, "Por una sociedad donde quepan todos," 387.

[50] Carol Gilligan, *The Birth of Pleasure* (New York: Alfred A. Knopf, 2002), 10.

[51] Ibid., 8.

[52] Ibid., 159.

[53] Earlier on in my work I talked about our goal being survival. "Survival has to do with more than barely living. Survival has to do with the struggle *to be* fully. . . . This translates into two sets of questions: questions about physical survival and questions about cultural-historical survival." Ada María Isasi-Díaz and Yolanda Tarango, *Hispanic Women: Prophetic Voice in the Church*, 2nd ed. (Minneapolis: Fortress Press, 1992), 4. I have not departed from this insight that I articulated since the beginning, insight coming from my own experience and the experience of grassroot Hispanas/Latinas. The context in which this is said makes it very clear that "*to be*" is not at all meant in an essentialist way yet I continue to be questioned about this. In this article I have moved from *to be* to *life and fullness of human life-liberation* hoping to leave no doubt that I am not making essentialist claims and that what continues to be central is *la lucha*, which always is from a given perspective and is concrete.

[54] To complete here the quote in the text, "Human life has rationality as an intrinsic constitutive element (because it is human) and the intersubjective and verifying exercise of rationality is an exigency of life itself: it is an 'astuteness' of life. Human life is never 'other' than reason; it is the absolute-material-intrinsic condition of rationality. This is why there is the demand of not placing reason over life. . . . We defend, then, that human life is source of all rationality, and that material rationality has as criterion and last 'reference' of truth and as absolute condition of its possibility, human life." Dussel, *Ética de la liberación*, 618.

[55] See Dussel, *Ética de la liberación*, 622.

[56] See Ivone Gebara, *Longing for Running Water: Ecofeminism and Liberation* (Minneapolis: Fortress Press, 1999), 71–99; see also her latest book, *Out of the Depths: Women's Experience of Evil and Salvation* (Minneapolis: Fortress Press, 2002), 133–144.

[57] Gutiérrez, *A Theology of Liberation*, xxxviii.

[58] This is a clearer and more precise way of saying what we have said up to now, that liberation cannot be accomplished at the expense of anyone else and that we want and work toward radical change instead of merely wanting to participate in present structures.

[59] Franz Hinkelammert, "Una sociedad en la que todos quepan: de la impotencia de la omnipotencia," in Dussel, *Ética de la liberación*, 364.

[60] Ibid.

61 Mario C. Casalla, "El Cuarteto de Jerusalén," in *Márgenes de la Justicia* (Buenos Aires: Grupo Editor Altamira, 2000), 238 and 262 (footnote 11).

62 No matter how I think of myself, no matter what I call myself, I get rebuked by someone whose opinion I respect. If I refer to myself as an "academic" or the specific academic title given my specialty in the academy, "theologian" or "Christian ethicist," I am chided for using titles given by those who have power and privileges and by preferring to associate with book knowledge and not with knowledge arising from lived-experiences. If I call myself an activist because I believe the goals and methods I use in *mujerista* theology and ethics contribute to the liberation of Hispanas/Latinas, I am reproached for ascribing to my work possibilities that are beyond its scope. I am also taken to task for talking in a way that will allow academicians to ignore my work, which means I cannot influence—no matter that it might be a very tiny influence—ideas that become central in the public imaginary and in societal norms. I use "organic intellectual" for I can point to Gramsci and to Gustavo Gutiérrez's appropriation of Gramsci's idea for theologians—and that seems to make it more acceptable. (See Antonio Gramsci, "La formazione degli intellecttuali," *Scritti politici* [Rome: Editori Riunti, 1967], 830–40; and Gutiérrez, *A Theology of Liberation*, 10–11.) However, "organic intellectual" or "organic theologian" also seems to encounter resistance among some for they think I am being elitist, claiming intellectual or even moral superiority. I insist on using "organic intellectual" because it allows me to point to a hermeneutics of self-implicature that insists on a subjectivity that is not individualistic but rather points to social practices of grassroot Hispanas/Latinas as well as the way those in power see us and act towards us. (See Mark Kline Taylor, *Remembering Esperanza* [Maryknoll, N.Y.: Orbis Books, 1990], 3.)

63 Harvey, *Spaces of Hope*, 234.

64 Rebecca Chopp, *The Praxis of Suffering: An Interpretation of Liberation and Political Theologies* (Maryknoll, N.Y.: Orbis Books, 1986), 143.

10

Justice and Love Shall Kiss

There I was, marching in one more demonstration. Another attempt to convince public opinion that justice has to prevail. Volunteers, many of them elderly, had greeted me cheerfully when I arrived at the march's staging area. Their enthusiasm gave me the strength I needed to get my feet going, to begin waving my homemade sign, and to start chanting those catchy phrases that in a few words capture the urgency of our cause. A sense of despondency, a sense that what we did made absolutely no difference, had been taking over my spirit. Some of my friends soon arrived and I was happy to participate with them in the demonstration, discussing as we went along many issues in which we were involved. After about five hours the event was over and the now tired but no less cheerful elderly volunteers thanked us for coming as we made our way to the subway station.

That evening as I watched the skimpy media coverage the demonstration received, I thought about the lack of passion I had felt in the morning. I was not any less committed to justice but I was lacking the passion—the intense emotional charge— that had sustained me during the many years I had been engaged in different struggles for justice. The excitement, the aliveness I used to experience about being involved in justice issues seemed to have diminished. Of course I continued to consider the struggle for justice essential to my sense of vocation in life, believing it to be an intrinsic element of who I know myself to be. For me to struggle for justice has always been a way of being self-determining and making sure that the poor and the oppressed could likewise determine for themselves how to live their lives. However, reflecting on how I had felt when I arrived at the march that morning, I grew concerned about how I was going to motivate myself to continue my involvement if it stopped being deeply satisfying, if it became less life-giving. I knew that, at least for me, intellectual understanding and willful belief in justice would not be enough.

It was not until a few months later that I was able to take time to be by myself and go back to the questions and concerns that my lack of enthusiasm about marching in a demonstration had signaled. I am not the kind of person who can simply "turn the page" and keep on going without paying attention to unresolved issues. Though I do not need to have all the answers, I do need to be clear about the questions, to reflect on them so they do not turn problematic and weaken my resolve. I knew that what was unsettling me was how to be faithful to my commitment to justice if I was not passionate about it. In an attempt to recapture the driving conviction I had about justice I started by meditating on some of the biblical texts that had originally sparked and for years had sustained my concern for justice. I re-read a couple of books and several articles that had been helpful in providing me with the reasons for my participation in struggles for justice. I took time to carefully recall my time in Peru thirty some years ago when the poor of Lima had taught me a lasting lesson: without justice religious beliefs and practices could indeed become "the opium of the people." Justice had been for a long time one of my "most fundamental convictions and . . . [one of my] most fundamental loves,"[1] and I wanted this to continue to be. My commitment to justice not only intersects with my moral convictions and is intrinsic to my loves, it is not only an expression of them,[2] it is a constitutive element of them. To continue to have justice as central in my life I had to bring back the intense drive—the passion—that has had moved me for so long. It was the only way to hold back "the gradual flattening of emotional bonds into sheer obligation or duty."[3] I had to resist at all costs the lack of passion that was gnawing at my determination and was eroding my world view—the programmatic vision that holds and enlivens who I am and what I do—for to live ruled by obligation would destroy me.

Following Margaret Farley's advice in her book *Personal Commitments*, I fanned the flames of memory and hope so I could grow once again into a love of justice—a passion for justice—that had been so life-giving. A review of my participation in justice struggles made me aware that I was not stuck in the same "old" vision of justice. As a matter of fact, I had come to see justice itself as a process. Without much effort, out of the ever-evolving meaning that justice has had in my life, new expectations about justice and for justice in society have emerged during the years. Yet these new expectations did not seem to bring back my passion, my emotional involvement in the struggles for justice. Besides the need for memory and hope Farley also talks about the need for "relaxation of the heart." I had every reason to believe I was not fanatic about justice but rather that a "steady zeal" has given me staying power. What else was "relaxation of the heart" calling me to do? I had to remain clear-sighted about what the struggle for justice means for me. I had to be patient with myself and, instead of worrying about "failing in fidelity," I had to remain "present in hope" by not evading but rather embracing the struggle to light up the fire of passion for justice once again.[4]

Since life does not stop while we are going through a crisis, no matter what kind of crisis, I continued teaching, giving public lectures, writing, working with grassroot Latinas. One morning, in Cuba, where I go every year to teach in a Protestant seminary and work in a Catholic parish, I woke up with a verse from the Bible running through my head: "Justice and love shall kiss." I repeated the verse to myself all day long believing that it was important for some reason I could not see right away. I was surprised when I looked up the verse to find out that I had it wrong. Psalm 85:10 talks about justice and peace, not about justice and love. But the strong and persistent thought that had come into my mind and into my heart had been about justice and love, not justice and peace. I decided that instead of correcting myself I would allow "justice and love shall kiss" to stay with me, to nestle in me. I wanted to see where this thought would lead me. In the days that followed I began to understand little by little that I had indeed not paid enough attention to love as an important element in my commitment to justice. I came to realize that recapturing my passion for justice had to go hand in hand with bringing about a much closer relationship in my life between love and justice. I understood more and more that the passion—the intense emotion that compels me to be committed to justice—if it is to have staying power, has to come from love and be sustained by love.

I went back to Farley's *Personal Commitments*, re-read it carefully, and spent time meditating on several of its passages. Farley clearly indicates that commitment to justice is indeed commitment to persons and that "we need a way to keep us connected with, present to, the *object* of our commitments—what we love and have promised to love."[5] She talks about Susan whose commitment to the poor and homeless was not a matter of willful determination but rather the "result of her seeing, again and again, the reality of the persons, lovable and homeless and poor."[6] Farley insists that "every commitment to persons involves some form of mutuality."[7] She explains that even when we are committed to others who do not know about our commitment or do not accept our commitment to them, even then, mutuality is present. "Something in the other binds me to her or him, calls to me, makes it easier or more difficult for me to be faithful, places in sharp relief the painfulness of the forms of mutuality that are missing."[8] In her assertion about the need for mutuality in every commitment, it seems to me that Farley makes love central to any commitment, and given the issue I was wrestling with, this meant that love had to play a central role in my commitment to justice. Had I stopped loving the poor? Had I stopped loving oppressed and marginalized women whose life-struggles have been a source of strength and creativity for me for so long? Did I not care any longer about this earth of ours, so mistreated and disfigured by our greediness and destructive self-centeredness?

Thinking about love of neighbor in my life I remembered the first time my concept about what it means to love had been challenged. I was seventeen years old when I came from Cuba to live in the USA. As I began to have friends and became part of different groups in college, church, and neighborhood, I began to learn about cultural differences and the role they play in the way we love and in the way we express our love. I come from a culture that is very public about its emotions. We Cubans wear our emotions on our sleeves, we say laughing loudly.[9] It is very clear for us that we need to show our love way beyond words. For us, demonstrating our love is part of the love itself: showing love helps to bring it about. This is the sacramental nature of the expressions of love, of what Farley calls "the deeds of love."[10] Such expressions are part of the love itself and without them love suffers, is diminished. With time, as I had adapted myself to live in the USA, I had become much more guarded about expressing my emotions. In this society public expressions of emotions embarrass people. Expressing emotions makes us vulnerable, for it reveals what is deep in our hearts, what moves us and, in the USA, vulnerability unfortunately is often seen as weakness. I remembered how in those first years living in the USA I was pained by what I considered the coldness of friends, by what I believed were barriers they put up to keep relationships at this or that level instead of allowing relationships to flourish to the fullest. And now that I was faced with the task of rekindling passion for justice I realized that maybe I had killed that passion by not expressing it or by expressing it only in the quiet and private ways accepted by this society.[11]

Decades after arriving in the USA I became a social ethicist. One of the main reasons for this choice was because it was for me a way of being involved in the struggle for liberation of Latinas, of grassroot women whom society marginalizes, rendering them invisible and ignoring what they have to contribute to society. I have helped to formulate a theo-ethical discourse, *mujerista* theology, as a way of taking seriously the lived-experience of grassroot Latinas, their struggles to be self-determining persons with an important contribution to make to society. In elaborating *mujerista* theology, therefore, I have always worked extensively with the ethical understandings of the moral subject. I understand the moral person as being both an agent who takes decisions and acts on them, and a subject who perfects herself through those decisions and actions—all of this in the middle of and through the multiplicity of one's relationships.[12] Decisions are a taking hold of understandings and desires and translating them into action. At the core of any action is a decision, and at the heart of any decision is desire, for we never choose what we do not desire. Desires, in turn, are informed and formed by God's grace, reason, emotion and one's intuitions. Decisions and choices are a taking hold of one's desire and understandings, identifying with them freely, and translating them into action.[13]

As I analyzed my commitment to justice and worked to elaborate a *mujerista* understanding of justice, I realized that I still have very good reasons for the decision I took to make justice a priority in my life—I have very good reasons for my commitment to justice. Without the struggle for justice my life would be empty or at least much less fulfilling than it has been. I knew that this struggle played an important role in the sense I have of God's presence, of God's grace, in my life. The only element that had informed my commitment and now seemed to be absent or to have decreased was the emotional component. As I meditated on this, I realized that my dwindling emotional attachment for justice indicated somehow a weakened sense of self, for "there is an emotional bedrock of self-consciousness that constitutes the self, the person who makes moral decisions."[14] There was no option. I had to re-immerse myself in my culture and allow my emotional self to come forth and express openly what I felt so deeply.

To do this was no small task for, even in this first decade of the twenty-first century, not many think of emotions as a positive element of morality. Until recently emotions have been thought to be at odds with reason. The psychological model of human functioning most prevalent even today insists "first, that reasoning *can* be thoroughly detached from emotion; second, that only detached reasoning will be reliably objective; and third, that emotions will only bias, cloud, and impede moral decision-making."[15] But I was not to be deterred. My own personal needs plus my commitment to make present in the USA society through *mujerista* theology the valuable elements of Latina culture—as I believe expressing one's emotions is—spurred me on. I set out to recapture expressing my emotions not only as an element of my commitment to justice, but of my whole life. I decided to examine the role of expressing emotions in morality and ethics. I knew, however, that it was not only a matter of stirring up any emotion. Indeed, although negative emotions like anger, resentment, shame, disgust may also move one to action, still none of these have been strong motivational factors in my life. I knew that what I had to stir in myself was love, an "emotional love," a felt and expressed love, a passionate love. I knew that it was not only a matter of being committed to justice with my intellect and will, but of loving justice intensely. Love is the only emotion that has had staying power in my life, that has really inspired me, encouraged me, stimulated me time and time again. To stay committed to justice I had to once again love justice passionately.

The Poetry of Julia de Burgos

I wanted to recapture love and, because emotions are a different state of consciousness from the rational one, I knew that I could not reason my way into emotions. Where was I to turn, given that I live in a culture where reason and intellect reign supreme, where insights, imagination and emotions are not considered important? One night I surprised myself by wanting to write poetry. It was a first for me. In the poem I wrote, my "justice-self" speaks to my "love-self." Recently I had been introduced to the poetry of Julia de Burgos, a Puerto Rican poet, and I was undoubtedly influenced by one of her poems in which two "sides" of herself talk to each other.[16] The poem I wrote has my love-self, my emotional self, telling my justice-self, my rational self, that she has remained in the background long enough, that for years she has carried my justice-self and that now she wonders whether the justice-self has sacrificed her or instead provided her with a future by giving meaning to her life. Julia de Burgos' poetry was a godsend for me. Reading her poetry in Spanish took me back to my cultural matrix where emotions are nurtured and celebrated. The force and beauty of her poetry immersed me in Julia's world of emotions, particularly in her world of love and loving. Soon I was not only reading her poetry but studying it and learning about this poet who, for Puerto Ricans and for the rest of us who know her work, is "more than a writer, more than a national poet; she is a legend. . . ."[17] Julia's poetry has given me fresh insights into emotions and their role in my self-understanding and in the way I conceptualize my mission in life. Julia's poetry has validated my need to express my emotions, corroborating my belief that the expression of emotions is an integral element of the emotion itself. Julia's poetry has allowed me once again to embrace my need to express my emotions as part and parcel of communicating my ideas, of making who I am and what I do intelligible to myself and others. Her goal as a poet was precisely that, "to communicate her emotions, not to relate private anecdotes. . . . In her poetry one finds a woman who goes through an intimate process of dramatic highs and lows in the way she thinks as well as in her way of feeling."[18]

What made me turn to the poetry of Julia de Burgos when I needed to rekindle passion for justice in my life and to weave love into its understanding was that "love was a constant passion and goal of Julia's conscience."[19] Though many want to reduce her life to her failed relationship with a man, which they claim led her to become an alcoholic and to an early death when she was 39, there is evidence of precisely the contrary. There is proof of the "courage with which the writer struggled with hostile social conditions for each minute of her life and artistic potential. Looked at from this perspective, the work of Julia de Burgos is not a symbol of her defeat but of her struggle to create."[20] Her willingness to struggle, to be faithful to her need to communicate her emotions, became an integral part of Julia's moral horizon, of the person she believed she was called to be. And that was precisely what I felt I needed to focus on in order to rekindle my passion for justice.

Before an analysis of Julia's poetry, a short biographical sketch is in order. Julia de Burgos was born in 1917, in Carolina, Puerto Rico. She was from a very poor family, the oldest of 13 children, of whom six died as infants of malnutrition. She was a good student and her parents asked for financial help so Julia could attend high school and go to the university. When she was only 19, Julia received from the University of Puerto Rico a grade-school teacher diploma. She married when she was 20 but the marriage lasted only three years. Julia joined the nationalist party, which struggles for Puerto Rico's independence from the USA. In 1937 she was fired from her job as a teacher, perhaps because of her political activities, and she began to earn a living from her writings, publishing articles and poems in newspapers and magazines. That year she privately printed her first book of poetry but later decided that her work was not good enough and took back the copies she had sold or given away. The poems in this first book have been lost.

In 1935 her mother had been diagnosed with cancer so in 1938 Julia paid to have her second book of poetry printed and she went from town to town by bus selling the book in order to pay for her mother's medical care. This book of her poetry "offers the voice of a woman who rebels against her circumstances, who feels the socio-economic, political and cultural injustices as humiliating constraints that impede her free self-realization and that of her people."[21] Her mother died shortly thereafter.

In 1939 Julia met and fell in love with Juan Isidro Jiménez Grullón, a leftist politician from a well-to-do Dominican Republic family. Also in that year one of San Juan's leading cultural centers sponsored a recital in honor of Julia. At the beginning of 1940 she traveled to New York, probably following Jiménez Grullón, and later that year she followed him to Cuba. Jiménez Grullón never married Julia, for he already was married and his family had threatened to disinherit him if he divorced. After the couple lived together in Cuba for a while, the relationship ended and Julia moved back to New York in June of 1942. While in Cuba she wrote her third book of poetry, published posthumously, and sketched the outline for a fourth one that she never finished.

When she moved to New York she married a second time and lived for a while in Washington, D.C. During this time she earned a living as publisher of a weekly Hispanic newspaper and doing office work. In 1946 she was back in New York where she survived working at all kinds of odd jobs: office work, translator, salesperson, sewing in a factory. By then she was drinking heavily, and by 1951 she had been hospitalized six times. She collapsed on West 105 Street in New York on July 6, 1953, dying at Harlem Hospital. She was carrying no identification so her body was buried in the paupers' common grave. Eventually some friends found out about her death, her family was notified, and two months later her remains were taken to Puerto Rico where she is buried in Carolina, near San Juan, where she had been born.[22]

Julia's poetry has been studied from many different points of view. Perhaps the biggest controversy among scholars has to do with how much her poetry is autobiographical, how much her poetry reflects not only her socio-historical setting but also her personal life. As a neophyte when it comes to the work of Julia de Burgos and because of my interest in the role of emotions in her work, I tend to follow the proposal of a well-known expert on her poetry, María M. Solá, who insists that one cannot tie the poems of Julia directly to events in her life. However, Solá also indicates that "even though emotions are the main message of the lyrical text, poetry always includes meanings related to the historical circumstances in which it is written."[23] There is a certain distance between Julia, the woman, and the voice one hears in her poems, referred to by some scholars as a "lyrical speaker." I believe, however, that there is also a certain continuity between the two. Whether it was so or not for Julia, the lyrical speaker in her poetry suffers great sorrow and pain at being rejected by the beloved and having to leave him. Yet "to have lost trust in the fact that love can bring harmony, save the person from her struggles—that is even worse. . . . What disappears is the belief that love can save. . . . For the lyrical speaker, her main defining quality, what defines her, is her own ability to move with her word. To be able to create is the path she has to follow. The road that starts in herself and heads towards the future, beyond her death—that is the poetry her voice creates."[24]

I have chosen three poems written during different periods of Julia's life because of their personal appeal. As an admirer of her poetry, I will stay as close as possible to the text, noting how emotions, readily and passionately expressed, are never absent. I hope to show that emotions more than reasons are the vehicle she uses to communicate.[25] For Julia, emotions are a way of knowing and of expressing her being.

Her first extant book of poetry opens with a poem she dedicates to herself, *"A Julia de Burgos."*

To Julia de Burgos

v. 1   Already the people murmur that I am your enemy
because they say that in verse I give your I to the world.

v. 2   They lie, Julia de Burgos. They lie, Julia de Burgos.
Who rises in my verses is not your voice. It is my voice

because you are the dressing and the essence is I;
and the most profound abyss is spread between us.

v. 3   You are the cold doll of social lies,
and I, the virile starburst of the human truth.

v. 4   You, honey of courtesan hypocrisies; not I;
in all my poems I strip my heart.

v. 5   You are like your world, selfish; not I
who gambles everything betting on what I am.

v. 6   You are only the ponderous lady very lady;
not I; I am life, strength, woman.

v. 7   You belong to your husband, your master; not I;
I belong to nobody, or all, because to all, to all
I give myself in my clean feeling and in my thought.

v. 8   You curl your hair and paint yourself; not I;
the wind curls my hair, the sun paints me.

v. 9   You are a housewife, resigned, submissive,
tied to the prejudices of men; not I;
unbridled, I am a runaway Rocinante
snorting the horizons of God's justice.

v. 10   You in yourself have no say; everyone governs you;
your husband, your parents, your family,
the priest, the dressmaker, the theatre, the dance hall
the auto, the fine furnishings, the feast, champagne,
heaven and hell, and the social, "what will they say."

v. 11   Not in me, in me only my heart governs,
only my thought; who governs me is I.
You, flower of aristocracy; and I, flower of the people.
You in you have everything and you owe it to everyone,
while I, my nothing I owe to nobody.

v. 12   You, nailed to the static ancestral dividend,
and I, a one in the numerical social divider,
we are the duel to death that fatally approaches.

v. 13   When the multitudes run rioting
leaving behind ashes of burned injustices,
and with the torch of the seven virtues,
the multitudes run after the seven sins,
against you and against everything unjust and inhuman,
I will be their midst with the torch in my hand.[26]

In the beginning of this poem, social protest is presented by the lyrical speaker as a struggle to fulfill herself fully as a human being. The lyrical speaker, not necessarily the historical person Julia de Burgos, for one cannot read each poem as relating to a particular event in her life, seeks to express how she breaks with the social mores that keep women in bondage. Emotions for Julia de Burgos were not something pertinent only in the personal or private sphere as we see in the last part of the poem where the lyrical speaker "inserts her personal awareness in the situation of the people, delineating the rebellion of the masses as a revolutionary response to prejudices and class injustices."[27] She will struggle to find God's justice (v. 9)—"*horizontes de justicia de Dios*"—burning down anything that is unjust, as the poem ends—"*con la tea en la mano.*"[28] For Julia behind the personal struggles of the lyrical speaker there is a social space, and "emotions have their origin in the social practice and in a system of evaluations."[29]

Very early in the poem there is an explosion of emotions when the lyrical speaker accuses of lying (v. 2) those who identify her with a woman ruled by social conventions. It is impossible to think of reading this one line of verse 2 in any other way but as an emotional outburst.

> *Mienten, Julia de Burgos. Mienten, Julia de Burgos.*

The verse consists of the two shortest sentences in the poem, the repetition portraying vehemence. "This emphasis underlines a drastic opinion . . . and perhaps points to the attempt to call herself to conscience."[30] These two short sentences are like sharp arrows aimed at the thick cloak of social traditions and customs that limit who women are and how they can live their lives. The same sense of strong demand and great urgency will be expressed by the longest sentence in the poem, the last one, where a barrage of words leaves the reader breathless, conveying the passion of the lyrical speaker as she makes certain she communicates clearly that nothing will stop her from destroying the barriers society imposes on women.

> *Cuando las multitudes corran alborotadas*
> *dejando atrás cenizas de injusticias quemadas,*
> *y cuando con la tea de las siete virtudes,*

> *tras los siete pecados, corran las multitudes,*
> *contra ti, y contra todo lo injusto y lo inhumano,*
> *yo iré en medio de ellas con la tea en la mano.*

The body of the poem consists of a series of statements in which the lyrical speaker and the woman who abides by the social mores of her time—both of them are in Julia, are part of Julia—are set against each other. In all of the points/counterpoints the lyrical speaker never allows the other to speak, accusing her throughout the poem with sarcasm and derision of being nothing but a pretense while she is the essence of woman (v. 2). The first of the points/counterpoints describes the feel of each of the two women in the poem. The one who abides by social rules is "cold"; the one who struggles to be faithful to the essence of what it is to be a woman is a "virile starburst" (v. 3).

> *Tú eres fría muñeca de mentira social,*
> *y yo, viril destello de la humana verdad.*

"A starburst is a vivid but ephemeral light. By modifying it with the adjective 'virile' the semantic charge is augmented, giving the spark greater ability to illumine. . . ."[31] This adjective indicates a strong affective emotion.[32] The use of the adjective "virile" can be interpreted "as a linguistic betrayal since virility represents strength and control, qualities attributed to males. . . . The woman cannot be virile because society does not allow it. To be virile is the prerogative of the males . . . but the lyrical speaker can be virile because she is breaking with the established schemas for women."[33]

The lyrical speaker talks about how through her poems one can see her naked heart. She uses her emotions to fight rather than using logical argument or pointing to reasons (v. 4).

> *Tú, miel de cortesanas hipocresías; yo no;*
> *que en todos mis poemas desnudo el corazón.*

The lyrical speaker places feeling[34]—*sentir*—before thinking—*pensar*—(v. 7).

Yo de nadie [soy], o de todos, porque a todos, a todos,
en mi limpio sentir y en mi pensar me doy.

She refers to her heart—*corazón*—before talking about her thoughts—*pensamiento*—(v. 11). In this verse, in identifying herself as the one who decides for herself who she is instead of letting society order her around, her heart—emotions—comes before her thoughts—her head.

En mí no, que en mí manda mi solo corazón
mi solo pensamiento; quien en mí manda soy yo.

In this poem, Julia de Burgos shows that to be able to understand she has to feel. She moves away from considering reason and emotion in a linear or in a dualistic fashion and instead sees them as intertwined. The poem shows how she constructed her subjectivity using a different paradigm from the one prescribed by society. In it she breaks the false unity of the "bourgeois Cartesian subject" indicating not a binary possibility for different "kinds" of women, but signaling a dialectic reality that does not stop with the private but is also part of the public sphere.[35] Her poetry inserted in the social imaginary a valid sense of resistance on the part of women that does not leave behind the struggle against sexism but understands it as part and parcel of the struggle for the liberation of her people. Part of struggling for liberation from a woman's perspective is made clear by her unabashed reference to emotions as a positive element. Towards the end of this poem Julia chooses to identify with her people instead of with the aristocracy (v. 11).[36]

Tú, flor de aristocracia; y yo la flor del pueblo.

Julia's poetry "deconstructs the paradigms that organize the ethical and social fantasies of a common life at the same time that it offers a cartography of a freer community."[37] This is why scholars can claim that for Julia writing poetry was a morally subversive revolutionary activity.[38]

The second poem I have chosen is called *"Canción de mi sombra minúscla."*

Song of My Minuscule Shadow

v. 1   *Sometimes my life wants to explode in songs*
       of unexpected anguish!

v. 2   *I would like to stay in the secret of my pains*
       pricking like stars,
       but my soul can't reach the silence
       of the poem without words,
       and leaps through my lips made dust by intimate
          vibrations.

v. 3   *There is only one door open in the path where my life passes*
       unknown to smiles.
       I start to find its trail,
       as if the cosmos had concentrated its energy
       and my entire emotion would go there,
       like pieces of destroyed butterflies.

v. 4   *My emotion wheels through one of those savage islands*
       of pain.
       I have let myself arrive where
       happy songs die,
       and pain makes a date with the transparent paint
          of the sky.

v. 5   *The premature rose that fell in my eyes wounded by*
       rosy petals hurts me;
       and the last look of a bride of the air
       who died of chasteness upon feeling she was flesh
       for the kiss of man.

v. 6   *The pain of the twilight that won't woo again*
       the pale daisy of the woods
       bleeds in the pain of the evening fallen on my back.

v. 7   *Taken by a sprout of spray*
       a teardrop that rose to space
       cries from mystery in my cloud flight.

v. 8   *The pain that wheels in the abandoned instant*
       comes to dance its rhythm in my flesh tormented
       by cosmic anxiety.

v. 9   *And the emotion explodes in useless songs,*
       inside this mirage of greatness
       from which my shadow,
       minuscule,
       departs. . . .[39]

Scholars seem not to pay too much attention to this poem but I have found it to be the only one in which she speaks directly about her emotions and, through the use of metaphors, identifies with them. In this poem the lyrical speaker and the object to which she is referring—her emotions—are one and the same thing. It is as if no words existed that could express what she wants to say, as if the lyrical speaker identifies with what she is talking about through her emotions instead of by using ideas. Her emotions are the object of her contemplation and she does not simply talk about them but participates in them by identifying with them. This poem, then, makes it possible for Julia the woman-poet to satisfy her ontological need to express her emotions. Expressing her emotions, which is the same as having or feeling emotions, is an experience for her as real as the experiences constituted by events.[40] Writing this poem, then, is a liberative praxis for her, allowing her to be what she seemingly was not able to be in her day-to-day life.[41]

The poem starts with a similar emotional explosion to the one in the previous poems we analyzed, "*estallar*," made to stand out by making it the verb of an exclamatory sentence. The lyrical speaker then expresses her desire to stay inside herself with her emotions, but they are throbbing in such a way that they jump out of her mouth. Sorrow is the focus of this poem. The lyrical speaker talks about her emotion being shattered into pieces, and the pieces are of something—love—as beautiful as butterflies, the beauty making the destruction all the more painful (v. 3). She again refers directly to her emotions and acknowledges that they have led her to her death (v. 4). She speaks about sorrow, an emotion that causes pain, using various metaphors in an attempt to communicate not only the depth of the sorrow but also the fact that nothing will be able to take the pain away (vv. 4, 5, 6, 7). In the last verse, faced with the finality of her painful emotions, the lyrical speaker cannot but feel "cosmic anxiety" and experience great futility. Having started with an explosion of emotions, she returns to that same theme. It is important to notice that even in the midst of the pain, anxiety and futility that she experiences, the lyrical speaker acknowledges that through her emotions she has touched greatness. But the failure expressed in "useless songs" only allows a minuscule part of her, her shadow, to escape.

In the book that Julia worked on mostly when she was in Cuba, published posthumously, there is a poem called *"Canción hacia dentro."*

Inward Song

v. 1   *Don't remember me! Feel me!*
       There is only a warble between your love and my soul.

v. 2   *Both my eyes navigate*
       the same endless blue where you dance.

v. 3   *Your rainbow of dreams always has in me*
       an open meadow among mountains.

v. 4   *Once my sobs were lost*
       and I found them sheltered in your tears.

v. 5   *Don't remember me! Feel me!*
       A nightingale has us in his throat.

v. 6   *The rivers I brought from my cliffs*
       empty only on your beaches.

v. 7   *There is confusion of flight in the air . . .*
       The wind carries us in its sandals!

v. 8   *Don't remember me! Feel me!*
       The less you think me, the more you love me.[42]

This poem addresses someone who is only important in so far as the person is the object of the lyrical speaker's love. The readers of Julia's poem presume the beloved to be Jiménez Grullón, but despite the fact that most of Julia's poetry consists of love poems, little is known from them about the beloved. Her poems are really not about the beloved but about love, about the emotion of love that she feels and with which she identifies. References to the beloved in Julia's poems are rare. He appears mostly as an object of reproaches, reproaches which at times are sarcastic.[43] In this poem she tries to make the beloved understand that the important thing is not to remember the loved one but to feel her, that the less the beloved thinks about her, allowing feelings and emotions to be dominant instead, the more love will flourish. The tone of the whole poem is one of instruction, of trying to convince the beloved to do what is best for love: to feel, to have deep emotions on which the poem tries to capitalize.[44]

At the beginning, in the middle, and at the end of the poem the lyrical speaker repeats the leitmotif of the poem,

¡No me recuerdes! ¡Siénteme!

These two sentences are not exclamations but commands with exclamation points used for emphasis. The first sentence, in the negative, does away with the regular manner in which one deals with the beloved. It is as if the lyrical speaker were telling the beloved to throw away all her pictures, all the mementos that might feed the memory. Instead the beloved is ordered to feel the loved one. It is as if the lyrical speaker were commanding the beloved to embrace himself, to hold his arms tight around himself so he can feel her, so he can embrace the deep emotion that he feels for her. Such an insistence on not thinking might well have to do with the fact that for the lyrical speaker, it is in her emotions that her love can take flight. It is what is born within her—the emotions—that fulfills her. Only as a second step does she seek to "shape in the external world the emotion that is consuming her inside."[45] In these short imperative sentences repeated throughout the poem the lyrical speaker clearly indicates that "the act of sensual love is superior to remembering. She prefers an alienating amnesia to the absence of compenetration between the flesh and the spirit generated by a shared embrace. Love for Julia is passion; for her the falling in love of courtly love is equivalent to lack of willpower and indifference."[46] In these repeated verses remembering is an abstraction from which the lyrical speaker wants to flee while seeking the immediacy of the emotion of her love, which for her is life-giving.

This insistence of Julia in writing about the emotions is an element one finds in mystical writings. Though for some the mystical experience consists of union with the divine born of an intuitive sense of God, I believe that the mystical experience is "the experiential knowledge of the presence of God that has as its goal a sense of contact with God."[47] As experiential knowledge, then, the mystical experience involves the whole person and that can only happen if the senses are involved. In the mystical experience one is in the midst of God, experiences God in a way that far surpasses thinking about God. The mystical experience is not about understanding God but about apprehending

God, and this is what the lyrical speaker is asking for in this poem: to be apprehended by the beloved, not just to be remembered. The lyrical speaker has the same difficulty as the mystics, that is, of not being able to put into words what she has experienced. It is impossible to find words to express the intensity of love she has and that is why she calls for sensing and feeling, for emotions.[48] Words might indicate or teach but they fail when it comes to expressing what is inside her.[49]

Another mystical element in this poem comes in the second verse.

> Mis dos ojos navegan
> el mismo azul sin fin donde tu danzas.

The color blue, linked in this verse to infinitude, is a reference to heaven. Heaven, not the sky, communicates a religious sentiment.[50] Perhaps here it points to the immensity of the love or to the divinization of the beloved, divinization brought about by the love of the lyrical speaker. This is reminiscent of a verse by Delmira Agustini, the Uruguayan poet, a contemporary Julia never met, who speaks of love "as if I had the head of God in my hands."[51]

The interconnection and compenetration between the lovers are made explicit in the poem. The second line of this repeated verse holds the lyrical speaker and the beloved together. The first time, only the smallest possible distance, the wispy song of a bird, separates their souls. When the verse is repeated in the middle of the poem, the lovers are in the tiniest of spaces, the throat of a bird. These images try to convey the closeness desired. The last time the verse appears to end the poem, the insistence is on love that is not found in merely thinking about the one loved.

The poem struggles to communicate the oneness of the lyrical speaker and the beloved. Mostly it is the lyrical speaker— Julia—who moves to be in/with the beloved.

> Mis dos ojos navegan
> el mismo azul sin fin donde tu danzas. (v. 2)

> Una vez se perdieron mis sollozos,
> y los hallé, abrigados, en tus lágrimas. (v. 4)

Los ríos que me traje de mis riscos,
desembocan tan solo por tus playas. (v. 6)

Only once is the beloved the one who moves to be in/with the lyrical speaker (v. 3).

Tu arco iris de sueños en mí tiene
siempre pradera abierta entre montañas.

This leads to a verse that speaks about confusion, as if the lack of movement on the part of the beloved created a storm. The winds will only grow calm when they hold together the lover and the beloved. But, in the end, ideas expressed in words are not enough to communicate the compenetration that the lyrical speaker seeks with the beloved. Metaphors also fail her. All that she has left is to turn to emotions, to beg the beloved, for the third time, to affirm the emotions he has, to give himself over to the passion that the love between them has birthed.

For Julia de Burgos writing poetry was a way of being which was not apart from the need she had to communicate. What she sought to communicate were her emotions, which in turn constituted her primary way of knowing and relating to reality. When I read Julia's poetry, I often picture her with her emotions in her arms, embracing them, caressing them, receiving from them affirmation and affection. I spend time contemplating this picture Julia paints trying to grasp my own emotions, allowing them to come into consciousness, affirming them and feeding them by expressing them. I repeat time and again to myself the injunction the poet addresses to the beloved in the last poem I have analyzed, *"Siénteme."* I do so convinced that to love I have to feel deeply, I have to allow my emotions to break through to the surface of who I am and to let them be part of my decisions, of my way of acting and being with myself and with others. I have to express my emotions, making public what motivates me, what is most alive in me. In embracing my emotions I come to know, to live and to be more fully—that is why I am willing to risk being vulnerable. This is the key lesson I have learned from Julia de Burgos and this learning was what allowed me to turn my attention to the role of love in my work on behalf of justice. This learning has given me back my love for justice, the passion for justice that was birthed in me by the poor of Peru four decades ago. This whole journey into validating my emotional self and expressing it has led me to understand the importance emotions in general and those connected to love in particular play in morality and ethics.

Emotions, Expressing Emotions, and Ethics

Margaret Farley argues that love has to be at the heart of commitment. For Farley love is an emotion and it is something we do.[52] Emotions are a state of consciousness, a way of knowing and of being. Yet emotions command little attention (respect!), particularly in weighty matters, for they are volatile and voluble. Their less-concrete-than-we-would-like feel, however, should not lead to giving them less importance and to thinking of them as less relevant when dealing with reality—both routine and extraordinary reality. Their fluidity has to do with the fact that emotions attribute great importance to objects and persons outside ourselves, objects and persons that that we do not control, which makes us vulnerable. This makes us think that we cannot trust emotions: our lack of control over what is valuable and significant for us. At play in the lack of valuation of emotions is also the confusion in common parlance between "feeling" and "emotion." In this case "feeling" refers to generalized, nonintentional consciousness or sensation with little cognitive content. However, feeling also refers to sensations, perceptions or thoughts "with a rich intentional content . . . [that] may enter into the identity conditions for some emotions. . . ."[53] When used in this sense, whether we use "feelings" or "emotions," they are weighty matters and we risk cutting ourselves off from a way of being and a way of knowing that can enrich us, that can provide us with resources for the struggle to enable fullness of life for ourselves and others.

Emotions are a type of cognition, of way of knowing, for they are linked to the receiving and processing of information. That "elaborate calculation, . . . computation, or even reflexive self-awareness" are not part of emotions does not mean that they should be "demoted" from the category of intellectual function ("demoted" in quotes because I do not agree with the diminished value given to what is not purely intellectual).[54] This understanding of emotions rejects the more common view that they are "'non-reasoning movements,' unthinking energies that simply push the person around, without being hooked up to the ways in which she perceives or thinks about the world."[55] The fact that emotions "take place in a living body does not give us reason to reduce their intentional/cognitive components to nonintentional bodily movements."[56]

As cognitive functions emotions are about something, they are not unspecific or diffused but have an object in sight. Furthermore, the object of one's emotions is intentional, that is to say, "it figures in the emotion as it is seen or interpreted by the person whose emotions it is. Emotions are not *about* their objects merely in the sense of being pointed at them. . . . Their aboutness is more internal, and embodies a way of seeing."[57] This aboutness is part of the emotion's identity, the way the object is seen, what differentiates fear from hope, for example. Emotions have to do with what one believes about an object. This means that beliefs are not a simple way of seeing something but a complex and serious way of seeing a situation, an object, a person. When one connects thought to emotion one does so not simply as "a heuristic device" that reveals feelings, feelings being considered apart from thinking. If one sees thought as a mere heuristic device instead of putting the thought into the definition of the emotions itself, how could one discriminate among different types of emotions?[58]

The understanding that emotions have to do with what one believes places us already in the realm of morality and ethics. But the relevance of emotions for our moral life also has to do with the role value plays in them. "The intentional perceptions and the beliefs characteristic of the emotions . . . are concerned with *value*, they see their objects as invested with value and importance."[59] Moreover, "the value perceived in the object appears to be of a particular sort. It appears to make reference to the person's own flourishing. The object of the emotion is seen as *important for* some role it plays in the person's own life."[60] The object of the emotion has importance in and of itself and it also has importance for the person's ends and goals, for "the person's flourishing."[61] This means that emotions, as relevant judgments of value that have to do with assenting to the way we see things and with acknowledging it as true, are sufficiently internal to emotions to be "at least a part of the identity conditions of the emotion."[62]

Emotions, then, include judgments not as external causes but as constituent parts and these judgments have to do with the goal of one's life, with fullness of life. Emotions are part of our way of knowing and, therefore, the information emotions provide must be taken into consideration in the process of evaluating and deciding. The value judgment component of emotions that is linked to one's interests, to one's fullness of life, indicates how things are with this important aspect of our moral considerations. Emotions, therefore, undoubtedly are elements that morality and ethics need to take into account.

In short, emotions are "intelligent responses to the perception of value. If emotions are suffused with intelligence and discernment, and if they contain in themselves an awareness of value or importance, they cannot . . . be sidelined in accounts of ethical judgment. Instead of viewing morality as a system of principles to be grasped by the detached intellect, and emotions as motivations that either support or subvert our choice to act according to principle, we will have to consider emotions as part and parcel of the system of ethical reasoning. We cannot plausibly omit them, once we acknowledge that emotions include in their content judgments that can be true or false, and good or bad guides to ethical choice."[63]

This is why it is important to school our emotions, to shape them in a moral way, in a way that will serve our process of decision-making. Indeed we are clear about the fact that we need to assess our emotions; that we need to evaluate them in reference to a situation or to a possible course of action. But we also need to ascertain whether our choices are consistent with our moral self, a self in which we are invested emotionally as well as rationally. The lack of attention to emotions—and not expressing them plays a big role in ignoring them—allows us to become callous, not to empathize with others, to rationalize choices that ignore the negative consequences that our actions can have on others, not to care for the good. It also allows our emotions to be much more easily manipulated. Those in power use enormous amounts of monies to manipulate our emotions through the media and advertisement. Unless we are consciously aware of our emotions, unless we realize that to act contrary to our emotions is as much a violation of ourselves as acting contrary to our reason, we will continue to be manipulated and used.

Emotions and Emoting: A Latina Perspective!

Emotions, then, are part of the workings of the mind. Emotions are "vital signs or signals from myself to myself" that contain information, shape how I process that information, contribute to shape what I think, and contribute to how I will respond in the future.[64] I know what I think by putting thoughts into words. But more than that, there is ample evidence that without words the process of thinking is severely impaired or simply impossible. I want to claim the same for emotions. Without emoting emotions are severely impaired or simply impossible. How we show our emotions is very much determined by culture. The issue here is not the "how" but the very fact that expressing emotions is an internal element of emotions, just as are the other elements discussed above. Emotions are harshly limited if they are not expressed, limited not only as to their effects on cognition, beliefs, values, motivations, actions. Their very existence is severely limited. It is a fact that unless we emote, unless our behavior is what we believe is appropriate given the emotions we are experiencing, we question if we are feeling the emotion or just thinking about it. An example here is helpful.

My oldest brother died quite suddenly when my father was 89 years old and beginning to be senile. At my brother's funeral my father was extremely concerned about not being able to cry. I tried to comfort him by telling him we all knew how much he loved my brother, that we all were aware of how sad he was that his oldest son had died. But he knew, and so did I, that something was amiss. In reality I believe that his senility did not allow him to grasp fully the tragedy of his son's early death. His lack of tears was in direct proportion to his lack of emotion about the event, lack of emotion related to the fact that his mind could not comprehend fully what was going on. What a difference in my father from the way he was forty years ago! In 1961 I watched him help fragile old nuns who had to abandon Cuba against their will. My father did not know the elderly nuns. We just happened to be at the airport when they got off the plane. I remember tears streaming down his face as he helped carry them down the stairs of the plane.

Lack of emotional response certainly can lead—does lead— persons to be morally impaired. A person without emotional response "cannot really feel the moral imperative or oughtness of the rules as part of their own reactions. They do not feel the emotional 'mustness' or demand of conscience, nor do they feel anxiety or fear over possible transgressions."[65] It is important to point out that here when I am talking about emotional response and reaction, I am referring to showing emotions, to outwardly expressing what we know inside in other ways than through reason, for the outward expression is part of the emotional way of knowing and the emotional way of being. Again, how the emotions are expressed is culturally bound. But we cannot claim that emoting, in and of itself, is socially constructed, for emoting is an internal element of the emotion. Not to show emotions is to deny the emotions—and this means cutting ourselves off from a way of knowing, from a form of cognition.

Expressing emotions and the emotions themselves are two sides of one and the same coin. Emotions are not like ideas that one can have even if one does not express them. To have emotions is to express them. How are we friends with someone who is profoundly in love, or with someone who has suffered a great loss? With the person in love, well, we have to listen to the many stories about the beloved that she never tires of telling. The fact is that expressing how much she loves the beloved is part of the loving. That is why the person in love delights in talking about her beloved. And the friends that listen often feel the love—they understand it in ways they would not be able to do if, let's say, they would just observe it. The emoting present in the telling is part of the loving and, therefore, the friends can apprehend the love present in the emoting. The same thing is true about being friends with someone who is sad. Her expressions of sadness make the sadness concrete, communicate the sadness because they are part of the sadness. We know that we have to allow ourselves and others to express sadness. It certainly is not good to wallow in sadness—to continue to cry endlessly. But to be sad is to talk about the sadness, about the reason for the sadness. When we talk about sadness or hear others talk about their sadness, we experience the sadness, because the expression of the sadness in words, tears, quietness, or some other culturally bound way, is part of the sadness itself. These two examples clarify what we know well, that the expression of the emotions is internal to the emotion, that the emotion does not exist unless it is somehow expressed.

Why are do some people simply not allow themselves to express their emotions? Why are there circumstances in which people who usually emote freely will not do so? I believe the repression of expressing emotions is tied to the fact that the objects of our emotions, what is valuable and important to us in such a way that we have tied it to our personal fulfillment—to the fullness of our lives—are beyond our control and this makes us vulnerable. This is why, at least in many of the Western cultures, little boys are taught not to cry. As future men they have to learn that they have to be in control of themselves and the situations in which they are involved and, therefore, they cannot allow emotions to be so, therefore, they are taught not to emote. This is the same in situations of negotiation where the person with most power, because he or she has the means to impose the decision taken, often seems the most calm, the coolest, the one most in control of her/himself and the situation, showing no emotions, which is the same as having no emotions (though in reality it might be nothing but a pretense). The powerful person cannot allow herself or himself to emote for that would show lack of control, vulnerability.

Emotions and Justice

What can we say about the relationship between emotions and justice? The old portrait of justice, a blindfolded woman holding a scale, says it all. Justice has been made to depend on objectivity, on being apart from any individual point of view, from any particular way of understanding, or specific situations. Justice has been conceptualized as applying the same rule to all precisely because it is beyond any given situation. It is commonly thought that justice needs to be impartial if it is to be universal—in the sense of being above or beyond any specific circumstance. Objectivity, impartiality and universality have been married to rationality—rationality depending on the use of the intellect apart from any affective function of reason. "The impartial reasoner is detached: reason abstracts from the particular experiences and histories that constitute a situation. The impartial reasoner must also be dispassionate, abstracting from feelings, desires, interests, and commitments that he or she may have regarding the situation, or that others may have."[66] Following this way of thinking, those who seek justice are called to set aside passions, feelings, desires and personal interests. Those who theorize about justice have insisted on reasoning apart from any particular consideration precisely so that the moral subject can come to know the universal principles and be guided by them. "This requires abstracting from the particularity of bodily being, its needs and inclinations, and from the feelings that attach to the experienced particularity of things and events. Normative reason is defined as impartial, and reason defines the unity of the moral subject, both in the sense that it knows the universal principles of morality and in the sense that it is what all moral subjects have in common in the same way. This understanding of reason thus stands opposed to desire and affectivity as to what differentiates and particularizes persons."[67]

This understanding of objectivity, impartiality and normative reason in reality masks issues of power, control and domination. In *mujerista* theology we have repeatedly pointed out how so-called objectivity is nothing but the subjectivity of those who have the power to impose their own point of view on others. The understanding of objectivity that is commonly used makes it impossible to pay attention and value the experiences—the subjectivity—of those who are marginal in society, who have little or no power. In *mujerista* theology we understand objectivity as the need to disclose our subjectivity, to make known our motives, our prejudices, the worldview that colors our way of acting. In *mujerista* theology we have insisted on partiality instead of impartiality and, together with other liberation theologies, we have privileged the poor and the oppressed, valuing their way of dealing with reality as important for all those who seek justice. In our work, we have questioned normativity time and again, for it is the apparatus that maintains the status quo in which Latinas and other marginalized people are kept oppressed. We recognize that groups, families, communities, societies—they all need norms but we contend that we need to keep in mind at all times that norms are socially constructed and that they need to be flexible. Norms have to be always under revision, balancing the wisdom we receive from the past with the challenges that those who are excluded present to us.

In re-working these understandings we have had to pay attention to emotions, to how we feel when our point of view is considered subjective and the one of the dominant group is the one proclaimed objective. It is precisely the experience of being ignored and not valued that makes us rebel against this way of thinking. It is the sense of commitment to and love for the poor and the oppressed that leads us to privilege their viewpoint. We do so not because they are morally better but because being excluded they have little or nothing to protect in the present situation and can see options for a just future that those who need to protect privileges and riches cannot see. Finally, to allow—desire—flexibility when it comes to norms, we have had to be aware of how frightening changes are, of how we prefer what we know—because we think we have some control over it—to what we do not know. To see norms as changing and evolving we have to take hold of our fears, including the fear of risking the unknown so justice may flourish, instead of continuing to claim that change is not reasonable.

For Latinas the way we express our emotions almost always works against us in the USA. As mentioned earlier, our passionate way of communicating is considered irrational because what is reasonable is considered to be "cool"—emotionless. This ignores the fact that though there is a difference "between what a discourse says, its substantive content or message, and how it says it . . . no discourse lacks emotional tone; 'dispassionate' discourses carry an emotional tone of calm and distance."[68] Furthermore, the substantive content or message does not remain the same regardless of how it is said. At times we have to "translate" for grassroot Latinas what they hear not because they do not know the meaning of the words used to communicate the message but because the way it has been said is foreign to them or, from their point of view, does not go hand in hand with the content being expressed. The meaning of a discourse, "its pragmatic operation in a situation of communicative interaction, depends as much on its rhetorical as its assertoric aspects."[69] This is why we struggle to elaborate our own ethical-theological discourse and to express in our own way who God is and how we relate to the divine. To include emotions in the way we explain ourselves and our beliefs about the divine, is not irrelevant to the content we wish to communicate in *mujerista* theology.

Conclusion

Our emotions play a leading role in our moral lives, attaching us to what is good and causing aversion for what is wrong. If it is true that reason judges and tutors emotions, it is also true that emotions need to test and tutor reason. This leads to a moral life in which emotions, thoughts and decisions are integrated into a whole. We have paid little attention to the role of emotions in ethics and morality to the detriment of our integration as full human beings. Many times our struggles for justice have fallen short precisely because we have not paid attention to the emotions that can motivate and maintain them despite obstacles. We have not paid enough attention to the emotional attachments that can help us on a daily basis choose once again to carry on in spite of so many obstacles. We have to understand the need we have to "be emotional" in order to be able to imagine changes and to proceed to bring them about. It is much more comfortable to stay with what is known, to allow ourselves to fear the unknown, than to stir ourselves to risk change. Without expressed emotions—and there are no other kind—we will not be able to move ahead beyond what is. Emotions are very necessary to move us "to spark moral indignation . . . [and] new moral visions of liberation."[70]

Those of us who risk expressed emotions in order to have them play a greater role in our lives will be rewarded with a rich life, not free of difficulties and dangers, but at least, I believe, with greater possibility of contributing to the struggle for justice. Miguel de Unamuno, the Spanish philosopher, pointed out that "one has to live in the midst of a continuous vertigo of passions because only those who are passionate accomplish truly lasting and life-giving deeds."[71] It is important, therefore, to give ourselves over to loving, to living in the most passionate way possible, without setting up frontiers to hold passion at bay. As Julia de Burgos says in her poem *Momentos*

Yo, universal,	*Me, universal,*
bebiéndome la vida	*drinking life*
en cada estrella desorbitada,	*in each out of orbit star,*
en cada grito estéril,	*in each sterile scream,*
en cada sentimiento sin orillas.	*in each sentiment without shores.*

Notes

[1] Margaret Farley, *Personal Commitments — Beginning, Keeping, Changing* (San Francisco: Harper & Row Publishers, 1986), 9.

[2] Ibid.

[3] Ibid., 6.

[4] Ibid., 58–60.

[5] Ibid., 54.

[6] Ibid.

[7] Ibid., 61.

[8] Ibid.

[9] I remember years ago at a presentation I made, a very quiet, almost somber, woman sitting in the first row, who smiled when I said this. After the presentation, she waited until the end of the line and then came to tell me she was Cuban and she was quiet and reserved and timid. "But I always tell them that I am the exception that proves the rule, that Cubans are loud and flamboyant about showing their emotions."

[10] Farley, 30.

[11] I am sure that those who know me will laugh when they read this. I continue to be loud and quite expressive by the standards of this society. I laugh to myself thinking, if only I would really let loose!

[12] Charles Curran, *Directions in Fundamental Moral Theology* (Notre Dame: University of Notre Dame Press, 1985), 63–97.

[13] Farley, 26–27.

[14] Sidney Callahan, *In Good Conscience: Reason and Emotion in Moral Decision Making* (San Francisco: Harper Collins Publishers, 1991), 95.

[15] Ibid., 99.

[16] I thank my dearest friend Nina Torres-Vidal, professor of literature at the Universidad del Sagrado Corazón in Puerto Rico, for introducing me to Julia's poetry.

[17] María Solá, "La Poesía de Julia de Burgos: Mujer de Humana Lucha," in *Julia de Burgos, Yo Misma Fui Mi Ruta*, ed. María Solá (Río Piedras, Puerto Rico, 1986), 9. This and all the other translations from Spanish texts, except Julia's poems, are my own.

[18] Ibid., 10–11.

[19] Ibid., 11.

[20] Ibid., 12.

[21] Ibid., 19.

[22] This short biographical sketch is based on the chronology found in Solá's book. I also gathered some details from Ana L. Duran, "Julia de Burgos existencial," in *Actas del Congreso Internacional Julia de Burgos*, ed. Edgard Martínez Masdeu (San Juan: Ateneo Puertorriqueño, 1993), 165–194.

[23] Solá, "La Poesía de Julia de Burgos: Mujer de Humana Lucha," 7.

[24] Ibid., 20.

[25] I am confident that though some scholars of Julia's poetry might disagree with my emphasis on the role of emotions in her work, none would deny that emotions do play a very important role in it.

[26] Jack Agüeros, trans., *Song of the Simple Truth: The Complete Poems of Julia de Burgos* (Willimantic, Conn.: Curbstone Press, 1997), 3. Throughout this paper I have changed some of the translation provided by Agüeros.

[27] Mercedes S. Julián, "La que se alza en mis versos," in *Julia de Burgos*, cited in Silvia Sauter, "Julia de Burgos, poeta consciente de su auto-fragmentación," in *Actas del Congreso Internacional Julia de Burgos*, 339.

[28] All of the verses in Spanish from Julia's poems are taken from Agüeros' book.

[29] Sauter, "Julia de Burgos, poeta consciente de su auto-fragmentación," 382.

[30] María Monserrate Matos, "Notas de un trabajo inconcluso de José Emilio González (A Julia de Burgos)," in *Actas del Congreso Internacional Julia de Burgos*, 37.

[31] Belén Román Morales, *La Poesía de Julia de Burgos: Ícono de la Nueva Mujer Puertorriqueña* (privately printed, 1999), 12.

[32] Matos, "Notas de un trabajo inconcluso de José Emilio González," 39.

[33] Román Morales, *La Poesía de Julia de Burgos*, 12.

[34] In the next section of this paper I explain that "to feel" and "feelings" are often used as a synonym of experiencing an emotion or an emotion itself.

[35] Sauter, "Julia de Burgos, poeta consciente de su auto-fragmentación," 388–389.

[36] María Arrillaga, "La ruta de Julia de Burgos," in *Actas del Congreso Internacional Julia de Burgos*, 411.

[37] Sauter, "Julia de Burgos, poeta consciente de su auto-fragmentación," 386–387.

[38] Ibid., 391.

[39] Agüeros, *Song of the Simple Truth*, 289.

[40] See pages 209ff. above, "Emotions and Emoting: A Latina Perspective!"

[41] Iris Zavala Martínez, "Aspectos psicohistóricos en la subjetividad de Julia de Burgos. La poesía como praxis," in *Actas del Congreso Internacional Julia de Burgos*, 293–295.

[42] Agüeros, *Song of the Simple Truth*, 151.

[43] Román Morales, *La Poesía de Julia de Burgos*, 53–54.

[44] Ibid., 72.

[45] Doel López Velásquez, "El erotismo en la poesía de Julia de Burgos," in *Actas del Congreso Internacional Julia de Burgos*, 50.

[46] Ibid., 51.

[47] Helmut Hazfeld, *Estudios sobre la mística española*, cited in Reynaldo Marcos Padua, "Misticismo y panteísmo en la poesía de Julia de Burgos," in *Actas del Congreso Internacional Julia de Burgos*, 250.

[48] Mayuli Morales Faedo, "Julia de Burgos: la poesía como autoreflexión," in *Actas del Congreso Internacional Julia de Burgos*, 219.

[49] Emilio Orozco, *Poesía y mística. Introducción a la lírica de San Juan de la Cruz*, cited in Marcos Papua, *Actas del Congreso Internacional Julia de Burgos*, 256.

[50] Román Morales, *La Poesía de Julia de Burgos*, 43.

[51] Delmira Agustini, "Lo Inefable," in *Literatura Hispanoamericana: Antología e introducción histórica*, ed. Enrique Anderson Imbert and Eugenio Florit (New York: Holt, Rinehart and Winston, Inc., 1960), 578.

[52] Farley, *Personal Commitments*, 30–32.

[53] Martha C. Nussbaum, *Upheavals of Thought: The Intelligence of Emotions* (Cambridge: Cambridge University Press, 2001), 60. Here I follow the study of emotions by Nussbaum because of its completeness,

and because it weaves philosophical and psychological views of emotions with ethical and moral perspectives.

54 Ibid., 23.

55 Ibid., 24–25.

56 Ibid., 25.

57 Ibid., 27.

58 Ibid., 29–30.

59 Ibid., 30.

60 Ibid., 30–31.

61 Ibid., 31. Nussbaum makes an important distinction when she comes to the role emotions play in one's goals and ends. She uses the Greek word *eudaimonistic* instead of its English spelling "eudaemonistic," for the Greek word is not limited to happiness or pleasure as the supreme good. This notion of human flourishing, of fullness of life, is inclusive of all to which the person imparts intrinsic value in her life and which are "not all valued simply on account of some instrumental relation they bear to the agent's satisfaction. This is a mistake commonly made about such theories, under the influence of Utilitarianism and the misleading use of 'happiness' . . ." as the only supreme good. See Nussbaum, p. 31, footnote 23 and p. 32.

62 Ibid., 48.

63 Ibid., 1.

64 Callahan, *In Good Conscience*, 103–105. The work of Sydney Callahan here cited provides the basis for much of what follows.

65 Ibid., 107.

66 Iris Marion Young, *Justice and the Politics of Difference* (Princeton: Princeton University Press, 1990), 100.

67 Ibid.

68 Iris Marion Young, *Inclusion and Democracy* (Oxford: Oxford University Press, 2000), 64–65.

69 Ibid., 67–68.

70 Callahan, *In Good Conscience*, 132.

71 Miguel de Unamuno, *Historia de la literatura española*, cited in López Velásquez, in *Actas del Congreso Internacional Julia de Burgos*, 51–52.

11

Reconciliation

An Intrinsic Element of Justice

"That they all may be one so that the world may believe" are words placed on the lips of Jesus by John the evangelist (John 17:21). The context of these words is important: Jesus wants the world to believe that he is one with God and that God has sent him. Jesus knows that his mission, to reveal and begin to establish the kin-dom[1] of God, will be fruitful only if the world believes in him. Furthermore, Jesus knows that whether the world does or does not believe in him and his mission depends on his followers living according to what he has taught them. The world will not believe unless his followers live according to the truths Jesus has taught: unless Christians are indeed one in body and soul, in mind and heart. Matthew 25:31–46 has the clearest explanation of what Jesus meant by being "one." In this parable one finds a stark picture of reality: some are hungry, some have food; some are homeless while others have shelter; some are naked, some have clothing; some are prisoners while others are free; some are sick and others are healthy. There is a rift between different groups in the community. The teaching of the parable is that the rift has to be healed and that only those who work to heal it will belong to the family of God. The healing of what splits humanity, of what separates one from the other, is the true meaning of reconciliation. If what separates us is not bridged, justice will not be able to triumph and the kin-dom of God will not become a reality in our midst.

At the beginning of the twenty-first century the many divisions that exist in our world make it obvious that a central element of the Christian understanding of justice and of work on behalf of justice is reconciliation. Justice is not only "a constitutive dimension of the preaching of the Gospel,"[2] but it is essential to the meaning and mission of the church today. The Bible, as well as a great variety of documents produced by different Christian churches in the last forty years, makes it clear that the work of justice is a religious practice. By extension then, since reconciliation is an element of justice, the work of reconciliation is a religious obligation for all Christians: "All Christians can agree in saying that reconciliation is an essential mission of the Church, that is, that one cannot be a true Christian if one is not motivated permanently by a preoccupation for reconciliation."[3]

Very simply said, it is not possible to conceptualize reconciliation apart from justice, and one cannot be a justice-seeking person without an ongoing practice of reconciliation. This is the belief and understanding on which this article is built. In it I seek to articulate an understanding of reconciliation as a social, political and theological virtue within the parameters of justice. My intention is to present a theo-ethics of reconciliation that will contribute to make justice a reality, since without justice the kin-dom of God cannot flourish; there can be no fullness of life, no peace.[4]

Reconciliation as an Element of Justice

The mode of divine revelation set forth in the Bible provides the basis for understanding justice as a process. The Bible does not set definitions. It does not offer theories but presents rich narratives about the lived-experiences of its people. It is in the midst of their lives that God's revelation happens, that the people of Israel and the followers of Jesus come to understand who God is and the demands God makes on humans. Following this biblical tradition, many systems of Christian ethics and moral theologies today eschew a theoretical approach to justice that focuses on universals apart from any social context or on rational reflections that attempt to demonstrate their validity by being self-enclosed systems. Instead justice is embraced as a process that starts with the experience of those who suffer injustice and who, therefore, seek to change present oppressive structures. As a process justice does not avoid rationality but rather proposes normative reflections that are historic and contextual. To understand justice as a process is to embrace the fact that all "normative reflection must begin from historically specific circumstances because there is nothing but what is, the given, the situated interest in justice from which to start."[5]

Acknowledging justice as a process, however, does not mean that it is only a matter of describing what is. Justice aims to evaluate the actual experience of people as well as their hopes and expectations. This evaluation is also "rooted in experience of and reflection on that very society."[6] It is not a matter of importing from other societies and cultures ideas of "the good" and "the just" to evaluate what is. It is a matter, rather, of listening to the cries of the poor and the oppressed in our midst so as to discover how individually and as a society we fail to make it possible for all to become the persons God created us to be. The norms and ideals used to evaluate the presence of justice in any given situation arise, then, from the yearnings of those who suffer oppression and poverty. They arise from those with whom individually and as a community we have not established right-relationships. The desire for right-relationships is not a foreign or an imposed idea but rather arises out of the desire of the people to have in their lives that love of neighbor that the Gospel of Jesus turned into a commandment for Christians. This understanding of the basis for and meaning of justice makes it clear that different elements of justice will need to be emphasized at different times. However, no matter what element of justice is being discussed, justice, like any other norm or principle, requires exploration of its various meanings and implications.

In the twenty-first century our considerations about justice have to start with the fact that two-thirds of the world lives in poverty and/or is oppressed, lacking what is needed to develop fully. In examining oppression and poverty one discovers some fundamental reasons for these adversities: personal and systemic violence, exploitation, powerlessness, marginalization and prejudice. These are not only causes but also mechanisms that operate at many different levels in our world. As mechanisms they are interconnected and create personal and societal modes of being and doing that maintain a *status quo* where less than one-third of the world controls, consumes and enjoys most of the natural and humanly developed resources of our world. Justice requires an in-depth examination of the various causes of oppression so that effective strategies can be developed. One of the main reasons for the few positive results of the struggles for justice, despite the good will and untiring commitment of many around the world, has been the lack of serious analysis of the causes of oppression and poverty.

How is power understood and used? Who has it and whom does it benefit? An analysis of power is urgently needed if we are to understand the dynamics of oppression in our world. A second area that needs thorough examination is the distribution of goods, both material goods and other goods such as rights, opportunities, self-respect, participation in decision-making and the power to "define" the symbols, images, meanings, behaviors and myths that give character to the different societies. A third area in which much work is needed concerns our notions of diversity and differences. It is precisely our present understanding of differences as what separates, excludes and places persons in opposition to each other that is at the core of all modes of oppression,[7] causing divisions and brokenness. Such an understanding leads to conceptualizing those who are different as outsiders, with those who have power deciding what is normative, themselves, and what is deviant, others. As long as this is the prevalent understanding there is no possibility of having right-relationships, and it will be impossible to create just societal structures that are inclusive instead of exclusive.

Identifying similarity and difference seems to be one way people make sense of their "perceptions, experiences, identities, and human obligations."[8] However, this does not necessarily have to lead one to assign consequences to differences and to positioning one group in relation to another. In other words, most of the time the way differences are understood and dealt with includes making moral judgments about them, deciding without much reflection that because some are different they are better or worse, never just different. Society has capitalized on "categories of difference that manifest social prejudice and misunderstanding"[9] and has ignored ongoing relationships among people that are based on similarities. Society understands boundaries as keeping people away from each other instead of highlighting that "the whole concept of a boundary depends on relationships: relationships between the two sides drawn by the boundary, and relationships among the people who recognize and affirm the boundary."[10] This means that because boundaries do not exist outside connections among people, if we are to bring about a paradigm shift in how we understand differences, we need to emphasize the role of differences in relationships rather than relating them only to what separates.

How can this be done and, more importantly, why should it be done? The fact is that unless one recognizes differences and deals with them in a way contrary to the present mode, there is no possibility to heal the rifts that exist—there is no real possibility of solidarity among people. True solidarity insists on genuine mutuality which can be reached only by recognizing the common interests that bind humanity. Unless we embrace differences and diversity as constituents of relationships instead of seeing them as separating and opposing elements, we will not be able to heal what divides us. We will not be able to be reconcilers. In other words, the work of reconciliation is intrinsic to changing the paradigms that have governed the understanding of differences. The work of reconciliation is a key process in the struggle to create communities of solidarity committed to building a future together. Therefore, reconciliation and solidarity are key elements in our work for justice, for a just future, one where no one is excluded.

Reconciliation as a Moral Choice

The work of reconciliation is a humble process, a road to be traveled together, one step at a time, by those seeking to be reconciled. Reconciliation does not consist in unveiling pre-conceived answers to a given situation. Instead, the work of reconciliation projects itself into the future, opening up and concentrating on possibilities. It is not a matter of repeating or of limiting oneself to the past. Reconciliation understands that there is a plurality of truths and that this plurality is precisely what creates possibilities, what roots human freedom and makes choices possible. These rich possibilities propose and demand options that make reconciliation a moral virtue, a way of being and acting that requires responsible choice. Responsible choice is not about working to control situations. It is not a matter of being absolutely certain, before any steps are taken, that what one chooses is the most effective possible choice or one that guarantees success. Responsible choice recognizes that what one chooses is but one way to proceed, that it is the best possible way to proceed given the present situation and the understanding one has.

Reconciliation makes it all the more obvious that moral responsibility has to focus on responding to others and establishing and maintaining mutuality and that this in turn re-defines the concepts of autonomy, self-reliance, and self-definition. The work of reconciliation focuses on responsibility as "participation in a communal work, laying the groundwork for the creative response of people in the present and the future. Responsible action means changing what can be altered in the present even though a problem is not completely resolved. Responsible action focuses on and respects partial resolutions and the inspiration and conditions for further partial resolutions . . . [by ourselves] and by others."[11] The work of reconciliation has to recognize that those who have been apart and opposed to each other need to move together, one step at a time, willing to accept that risk, ambiguity and uncertainty are part of the process. The work of reconciliation asks above all for a commitment to mutuality, to opening possibilities together even if one might never see them become a reality—this over and above a desire for tangible changes. Reconciliation has to be guided by a sense that the results of much work and commitment may be only a list of shared desires and possibilities, but even such a minimal outcome is the result of mature ethical commitment and work that allows and obliges one to sustain a reconciling attitude and behavior.

Reconciliation is a moral choice because it makes one remember that all persons have themselves been, at some point in their lives, oppressors and exploiters. This makes one understand that good intentions are not enough. Moral action requires the risk of taking steps together, of being accountable to each other, of participating in a process that concentrates on the future precisely by working to alter the present. Reconciliation as moral action makes it clear that healing the rifts that divide people cannot be incidental to one's life. Reconciliation is essential to being a human being, a responsible person, a person fully alive.

Reconciliation for any community that is divided—and as long as there is injustice divisions among people will exist—is the only just way to proceed. It is the only way to embrace the responsibility we all have for our communities and for the country in which we live. The only way to participate effectively, to contribute effectively to the future of our world, is to be reconciling people willing to suggest and explore possibilities together with those we have oppressed or who have oppressed us. Reconciliation is the only way to proceed with all sides recognizing that reality always transcends what is and that the future cannot be a slavish repetition of the present or of the past. Reconciliation is the only way we will all come together to create possibilities for a common, inclusive future that is life-giving for all. Such is the moral responsibility of all those who call themselves Christians. Such is our vocation as a religious people who, while acknowledging our potential for self-deception,[12] believe in eternal possibilities because we believe in an ever-abiding divine presence among us.

Reconciliation: The Biblical Basis

The way reconciliation is understood is greatly influenced by the process and elements the churches have historically considered necessary for what some earlier called "the sacrament of penance" or "confession," and now called "the sacrament of reconciliation." For many, from a religious perspective, reconciliation requires interior repentance, an attitude that rejects wrongs freely done in the past and at the same time accepts responsibility for them. Interior repentance also requires a firm purpose of amendment: in other words, a staunch resolution not to repeat the errors of the past. The sacrament of reconciliation also entails confessing one's sins to God or to a priest as well as offering satisfaction or reparation for the wrong done. This satisfaction or reparation is not made only to God, whom the sinner has offended, but also to the persons who have been "injured by sin, for example, as reparation for injured love, for damage to reputation or property. . . ."[13] Only once all these requirements are fulfilled is forgiveness granted.[14]

If we begin to conceive reconciliation, however, as an intrinsic element of justice and ground it in the biblical understanding of the absolute need to heal divisions as described in the parable in Matthew 25, reconciliation becomes different from how it has been traditionally conceived. Reconciliation as an element of justice is an essential way of knowing and healing brokenness in the world. Three requisites need to be fulfilled before one can come to know the reality of brokenness. First, to know brokenness one has to be in the midst of brokenness, one has to be touched by it and have one's life impacted by it; second, one has to take responsibility for it, understanding one's role in it; third, one has to do something to heal it.[15] To heal brokenness— the work of reconciliation—starts happening the minute one enters into this threefold process of knowing its reality. To take responsibility for and start to work to heal the divisions that exist in any given situation is already becoming involved in the process of reconciliation. We simply cannot defer healing. Reconciliation begins to unfold even though only one side is willing to start working to make it happen. Reconciliation cannot be postponed until those on the other side of the rift are willing to enter into this process. Reconciliation cannot be postponed until reparation and restitution are made. Reconciliation should not be withheld or postponed for any reason whatsoever.

Perhaps this is nowhere clearer than in the early church's understanding of reconciliation reflected in the epistles of Colossians, in 2 Corinthians and in 1 John. The early followers of Jesus understood God's love and reconciliation to be something freely given, something that invited them to respond but was not conditioned by or dependent upon an expected response. The author of 1 John says it succinctly: "We are to love then because God loved us first" (1 John 4:19). God loves first and unconditionally and we should respond by loving others in the same manner and not setting conditions to our love. In Colossians the author talks about Christ's reconciling act which does not depend on who is being reconciled or does not demand reparations but which indeed calls for a response. Reconciliation is presented as a one-sided process on God's part. God knows the reality of brokenness because the rift between God and those created to share in the divine "affects" God, if in no other way than by disrupting God's plans. In 2 Corinthians two ideas about reconciliation become all the more clear. First, "it is all God's work" (2 Corinthians 5:18). Second, reconciliation happens because God does not hold the faults of humanity against us (v. 19). Nowhere in this text does it say that humanity has to change for reconciliation to happen. It says precisely the contrary: humanity changes because of the reconciliation God freely bestows.

Reconciliation was for the early church an intrinsic part of its mission, and mission was considered a constitutive element of the church. The church was to appeal to all to be reconciled to God but this reconciliation was only a second step. The first step has already been given by God: God already has carried out the work of reconciliation. God's love comes first. The church knew that it could not preach what it did not live so it had to be a reconciling church, offering reconciliation freely, placing no conditions on it. The church knew that God appealed to all through the church's preaching and, particularly, through its behavior. That appeal was precisely an appeal to reconciliation (2 Corinthians 5:20).

Based on these gleanings from Scripture, reconciliation has to be considered an element in the justice-seeking process that focuses on the future—a future that starts with the present and takes into consideration the past. In this sense reconciliation is a prophetic action: it has to do with healing people who suffer brokenness and divisions, and it looks for ways to make their hopes and expectations a reality in our world. Reconciliation is a prophetic action because it is about a preferred future of justice for all.

Reconciliation as a Religious, Social, and Civic Virtue

From an ethical perspective reconciliation is a virtue. As such, reconciliation is not only a value but also a praxis: a way of acting in a conscious and reflective way. One has to work at it in order to become a good practitioner of reconciliation. Virtues are not themes to be elaborated in eloquent speeches but rather a way of living. To be good at the virtue of reconciliation one has not only to understand what it is but also to practice it. Virtues involve the disposition and actual competence to accomplish moral good: the virtue of reconciliation leads to actual reconciling behavior. From an ethical perspective, to practice the virtue of reconciliation one has to work in a concrete and effective way to build bridges over the rifts created by prejudices or by diversity of experiences, worldviews or values. The virtue of reconciliation, like any other virtue, requires working at it so it can become a habit, the regular way of relating to others. In turn, because reconciliation becomes a regular way of relating, it also becomes a stable disposition of the person. This means that one cannot say one is in favor of reconciliation and at the same time believe it is enough to work at developing formulas for reconciliation so complex that they are not achievable, or think, for whatever reason, of whole groups of people that are to be excluded from the process of reconciliation. One has to find effective ways of working at reconciliation even if the results are only limited, even if it involves only a few people, even if all it accomplishes is to strengthen one's resolve and provide new perspectives regarding the work of reconciliation. It is obvious, then, that reconciliation does not exist unless one is in the process of reconciling oneself to others, unless one is working to reconcile oneself and others with those from whom we are estranged.

Reconciliation is a religious virtue because, for Christians, the main motive for it is precisely the Gospel message. It is a religious virtue because Christians believe that this is the kind of behavior that Jesus demands from his followers. The biblical passages presented above make it clear that reconciliation is an important element in the manner the God of Jesus "behaves," a behavior self-communicated by God in a way that makes it possible for human beings to embrace it. As a religious virtue, then, reconciliation is a specific form of love. It is a specific form of grace. This means that reconciliation is one of the means God uses to enable human beings not only to relate to the God-self but to participate in divine nature itself.[16] Finally, from a religious perspective, reconciliation, as mentioned above, is not only a matter of personal behavior but is a matter of the mission and very nature of the church.[17]

Reconciliation is also a social virtue. Human beings are social beings called to be in relationship and called to live as members of various communities—family, workplace, neighborhood—that come together to form societies. Unfortunately, if it is true that human beings are social beings, it is also true that we fail repeatedly to be in right-relationships, that mistakes are made, that enmities are created. In this sense human beings live in tension between depending on others and being responsible to them while at the same time wanting to be self-sufficient even to the point of becoming selfish and turning against others. Reconciliation as a social virtue imposes the duty to overcome what separates human beings, what turns one against another, in order to be able to live the sociability that is an intrinsic characteristic of humanity. Not to do so, not to work at overcoming what creates rifts among human beings, is a betrayal of what is a fundamental human characteristic. To create or maintain divisions among persons and peoples is detrimental to all of humanity. This is precisely why reconciliation is a much-needed social virtue.

Finally, in the specific case of the USA at the beginning of the twenty-first century, when this country has waged wars or armed conflict as the aggressor, reconciliation is a civic virtue. It is a disposition and a practice that committed and faithful citizens of the USA have to embrace if they believe in the absolute need there is for justice in order for this country to flourish. A true commitment to reconciliation will bring about a revival or the creation of a moral commitment on the part of this country to respect differences. The "American way of life"—that is, the way the USA is politically, economically, and socially organized, its mores and core values, both secular and religious that constitute the organizing principle of the nation—may be the preferred way for the USA but it is not the only way of life that is good. It is not, therefore, the way of life that has to be chosen by other nations and other peoples in our world. Reconciliation as a civic virtue in the USA at the beginning of the twenty-first century must necessarily start with sobering humility. The USA has to recognize that it needs the rest of the world. It has to search its soul and candidly disclose that it needs others, that it must build common interests with nations and peoples around the world. This country must recognize that without authentic mutual solidarity with other nations the "American way of life" is condemned to disappear. Reconciliation as a civic virtue obliges the people of the USA to recognize that the richness and privileges they enjoy have been obtained and are maintained, to a great extent, at the expense of others. The exploitation that makes possible the richness and privileges enjoyed in the USA is what has created the rift between the USA and other countries and peoples. The need to heal that rift for the sake of the future of the world— that is what reconciliation as a civic virtue aims to accomplish.

Reconciliation: Building a Common Future for All

Reconciliation necessitates that people come together and agree on the future of our world. True reconciliation necessarily will arouse shared feelings and lead to joint action. Reconciliation involves building a common programmatic vision about our world, and this cannot be done outside a process of dialogue. In authentic dialogue the parties involved seek not to convince one another or to move the other to one's own perspective. They seek instead to move all those involved to a point of view and a program of action that has been forged together. For the kind of dialogue needed for reconciliation to happen, we have to embrace a way of understanding differences, as explained above, that does not focus on what separates, excludes and sets us in opposition, but rather recognizes that differences presume boundaries that enable people to make connections and come together. Dialogue cannot happen unless we recognize differences and diversity not necessarily as what separates us but as what we each bring to the table, as the resources from which each of us involved in the process of reconciliation can draw to conceptualize the future and begin to create it.

Such an understanding raises a question: what about our values? A call to true dialogue and reconciliation is not a call to betray one's values. However, all those who dialogue need to understand there are different values and/or that the same values can be actualized differently in diverse circumstances. Sometimes through the process of dialogue one comes to know that what originally were thought to be values contrary to ours are simply values different from ours, not necessarily values opposed to ours. It often happens that personal insecurity makes us incapable of seeing what we could well consider positive in the values held by others. Of course there are values and counter-values. Some values directly oppose or work to diminish the ones we hold. This is important and should not be minimized. However, there are more areas of similarities than of dissimilarities among the values that people hold. Commitment to dialogue makes us become experts in finding these similarities, these areas of agreement, joint understandings, common visions about the future of our world, our future as a people and a nation.

Understanding, appreciating and learning from realities, experiences and worldviews of people who might be quite different from us is essential to the process of dialogue and reconciliation. We are linked to others no matter how dissimilar we might be, for in our world today no country can consider itself isolated, apart from others, not interconnected with others. Common interests exist in our world. We do not need to invent them. We do need, however, to consciously recognize those common interests, to embrace the infinite number of ways in which we are interconnected with people who live far away as much as with people who are nearby.

The first realization in this part of dialogue is indeed the acceptance that we all, out of our experiences, have something to contribute to a common future. Secondly, we are called to learn to see reality from the point of view of others. We are called to de-centralize ourselves and not only to understand the perspective of others but also to learn to see what is positive in their understandings, how their understandings can enrich us. Of course this is not an easy process. We are talking about building a programmatic worldview that uses a shared understanding of history, the experiences of everyday life of people who live in very different circumstances, and our own dreams and expectations about our world. A programmatic worldview has to remain open to developments because it is not about an absolute future but about a historical future. It has to remain open to developments for it must not impose an ideology but rather must respond to the needs of the people and be intentional about being open to different possibilities.[18] Therefore no matter where we live, we need to realize that getting to know each other and learning about the many interconnections that exist among people all over the world is a viable and important first step in the process of reconciliation. We are all the poorer when we forget how we need each other, how we are related to each other. When we do not understand that who we are and what we are about is closely linked to the rest of the world, we are dehumanized because life becomes poorer when it is deprived of what gives all human beings meaning: friendship, love, relationships.[19] Without a strong sense of interdependence we lose in part what is precisely characteristic of the human species: sociability.

This will not happen easily. Often it seems almost impossible even to get those with whom we seek to be reconciled to come to the table. And, though the gratuitousness of God's reconciliation demands of us to be reconciling persons, the process of reconciliation involves more than one party. This means that those with whom we are trying to be reconciled have to recognize that reconciliation is needed. Perhaps the key is to make those we need to be reconciled with understand that what one seeks is not to convince them that they are wrong or to win them to one's side. What we seek is true dialogue that will move us jointly to a place we have created together. What all involve need to understand is that reconciliation is a process and that the dialogue that is central to this process has to start as soon as possible, at whatever level is possible, in whatever circumstances exist. Dialogue in this situation becomes a practice of reconciliation which needs to be sustained and enriched by the common experiences of coming together, of getting to know each other and understanding each other for the sake of a common future.

Reconciliation: Dealing with the Past, Rooted in the Present, in View of the Future

The process of becoming acquainted in new and better ways and of building together a programmatic worldview is but one of the elements of reconciliation. Undoubtedly and necessarily we also have to deal with the wrongs that have been committed on all sides causing pain and suffering to many. This makes the process of reconciliation all the more taxing and difficult, all the more demanding and urgent. Suffering is not the prerogative of any one side. There has been and there is suffering on all sides. There is no easy way through this rough and dangerous part of the path to reconciliation. However, even when it comes to wrongs committed and suffering inflicted we have to keep in mind that reconciliation is first of all about the future, and not about the past. We always have to keep in mind, when looking at the past, that the passing of time makes retrieving it impossible, that who we are today is different from who we were in the past, who we were even in the recent past, even yesterday. This is why "any return is not a return: it is coming into a new place."[20] This is why looking at the past only makes sense if it is part of constructing the future.

The second thing to keep in mind is that in the process of reconciliation dealing with the past, dealing with the wrongs we have done and the pain we have caused each other, cannot be in any way related to a sense of revenge.[21] Revenge is a destructive force that becomes a never-ending and widening spiral of violence. Revenge is a stagnating force that makes future-oriented movement impossible. Revenge is antithetical to reconciliation because it capitalizes on what separates us; it insists on payment for what simply cannot be paid for.[22] Revenge refuses to recognize that wrongs have been committed and suffering has been caused on all sides. Revenge does not make right what was wrong or restore the value of what was lost. Most often revenge stems from attempts to assuage guilt for what we did or allowed to happen, guilt we feel but will not admit. Revenge promotes a self-centeredness that makes any attempt to build common interests and actions impossible.[23]

In dealing with the past we often talk about restitution and retribution. When we claim retribution for those who suffered and are no longer with us, is it not our own needs and expectations that motivate us? Just as we say that the dead demand restitution and retribution, we could say that they pardon those who harmed them and that their memory pleads for reconciliation. Those of us living now are the ones who decide how to appropriate and use what has happened in the past. We do indeed choose how to read into the present and future the sufferings of the past. Those who are alive today, not those who have died, are the ones who will benefit from any restitution and retribution. Therefore, those who are alive today can also move beyond restitution and retribution that focuses on the past and embrace reconciliation with their eyes fixed on the future.[24]

What can we say about those who are still alive who have been personally wronged, who have endured pain and suffering, who can point to specific individuals who have exploited and abused them? This is a most delicate and personal matter but not a private one. Personal forgiveness or non-forgiveness is something in which we all are involved. Any attempt to hide or to ignore the pain and suffering inflicted on some will be devastating for the creation of a common future. But how we deal with that pain and suffering cannot be left in the hands of individuals, for what they do becomes part of how we all make possible or impede reconciliation. Though we need to acknowledge and give a public hearing to the voices of those who have suffered, reconciliation must prevail instead of the demand for retribution or the decision not to forgive.[25]

We have to recognize that if we do not make public the memories of those who suffered personally, individual and national healing will not be possible. However, we also have to embrace the fact that without reconciliation we cannot move on to build the future together.[26] As a people we have to understand that those who have suffered need to tell their stories, to have others witness to the horror that has been inflicted on them, in order to have their memories respected, to find a way of dealing with what they have endured, to regain their dignity and wholeness as human beings. Unless those who have suffered can be healed, the nation will suffer by not being able to benefit from what they can contribute to the building of our common future. Yet the process of personal healing has to happen within the national process of reconciliation and in no way can it militate against it.[27] Those who for many reasons find it difficult to embrace reconciliation, given what they have personally suffered, might do well to take seriously the many who have been at each other's throats, who have been enemies, and yet have chosen to struggle to live together in peace.[28]

A Spirituality, a Culture, a Mystique of Reconciliation

At the beginning of the twenty-first century I believe the future of the USA as a nation and of the whole world depends on our ability to develop a spirituality, a culture, and a mystique of reconciliation that will make it possible for us to practice reconciliation as a religious, social and civic virtue. To embrace a spirituality of reconciliation is to understand that for Christians there can be no possibility of relating to God unless we have a reconciling attitude and a reconciling practice towards each other. Because our relationship with God is intrinsically linked to the way we relate to each other, a reconciling God cannot but ask of those who believe to have a reconciling attitude towards each other. To relate to God is not something apart from how we live our daily lives. Therefore, our response to a reconciling God has to be a reconciling day-to-day living without exception and without conditions.

Culture includes all that we humans have cultivated and dreamed, all that we have created to deal with the world: tools, customs, societal structures, ideas about reality, and representations of ideas. A culture of reconciliation, therefore, requires us not only to counter in every way possible enmity, opposition and alienation, but actually to nurture and foster openness, dialogue and a dynamic understanding of differences not based on exclusion and confrontation. A culture of reconciliation is key in this whole process because all nations have a cultural origin before they have a political one. A culture of reconciliation is important for the USA because the way it has dealt and still deals with many nations and peoples around the globe has resulted in deep-seated mistrust, enmity, war. Given the primacy of culture in all national identification, reconciliation has to be an option that those of us who live in the USA make for ourselves, a practice that we implement in every aspect of our lives.

Finally, we need a mystique of reconciliation. A mystique is an intangible force that enables those who embrace it to face all reality. It refers to an understanding that provides a social cohesion, enabling participants to do what they have not been able to do alone but what becomes possible when one participates in a shared experience.[29] A mystique of reconciliation, therefore, makes possible for us, even in the most adverse of circumstances, to practice the virtue of reconciliation as a way—the most needed way—to be truly Christian, to be truly patriotic. A mystique of reconciliation provides the strength that we might not have individually to struggle against the conviction that we have nothing to repent about, that as a country our motives always are liberty, freedom, and democracy. A mystique of reconciliation will make it possible for us to be open to the dreams and the hopes of people all over the world, particularly the poor and oppressed. It will allow us to welcome other ways of understanding reality and of organizing societies, economies, governments different from those in the USA. Only then will we have a solid base on which to build peace and justice. Only a mystique of reconciliation will help us create a world in which the main preoccupation is how to stand together as one, how to recognize the common interests that bind us, how to be inclusive societies that take into consideration the wellbeing of all peoples.

Notes

[1] The use of kin-dom instead kingdom or reign stems from the desire to use a metaphor that is much more relevant to our world today. From the perspective of *mujerista* theology, the point of reference for kin-dom of God is the concept of family and community that is central to Latina culture. There is also a need to move away from "kingdom" and "reign" because they are sexist and hierarchical metaphors.

[2] 1971 Synod of Bishops, "Justice in the World," in Joseph Gremillion, *The Gospel of Peace and Justice* (Maryknoll, N.Y.: Orbis Books, 1975), 514.

[3] René David Roset, "Para Una Teología y Pastoral de Reconciliación desde Cuba" [unpublished article], November 1981, rev. 1982, 3. René David Roset is an elderly Roman Catholic theologian who has taught for many years at the Catholic seminary in Havana, Cuba, with whom I have visited. Originally he is from Canada.

[4] This echoes the well-known quotation of Martin Luther King,

"Without justice, there can be no peace." See Martin Luther King, Jr., *Stride towards Freedom.* This also echoes the thinking of Pope Paul VI. See Pope Paul VI, "Message of His Holiness Pope Paul VI for the Celebration of the 'World Day of Peace,' January 1, 1972: 'If You Want Peace, Work for Justice.'" http://www.vatican.va/holy_father/paul_vi/messages/peace/documents/hf_p-vi_mes_19711208_v-world-day-for-peace_en.html; accessed July 19, 2004.

[5] Iris Marion Young, *Justice and the Politics of Difference* (Princeton: Princeton University Press, 1990), 5.

[6] Ibid.

[7] Ibid., 169.

[8] Ibid., 7.

[9] Ibid., 9.

[10] Ibid., 10.

[11] Sharon Welch, *A Feminist Ethics of Risk* (Minneapolis: Fortress Press, 1990), 68.

[12] Stanley Hauerwas, *Truthfulness and Tragedy* (Notre Dame: University of Notre Dame Press, 1977), 82–98.

[13] Karl Rahner and Herbert Vorgrimler, "Satisfaction," in *Dictionary of Theology* (New York: Crossroad, 1990), 462. See also articles on "Penance," "Penance, Sacrament of," "Contrition," "Metanoia," and "Penalties of Sin."

[14] The way these different elements are embodied depends on the different church traditions. For example, in the Roman Catholic tradition, confession of one's sins is to a priest while in the Protestant traditions, confession is to God.

[15] I am applying here Ignacio Ellacuría's understanding of the process of knowing reality to knowing the reality of brokenness and the need for reconciliation. There is a fuller explanation of this process in Chapter 6 in this book, "*Lo Cotidiano:* Everyday Struggles in Hispanas/Latinas' Lives." See Ignacio Ellacuría, "Hacia una fundamentación del método teológico latinoamericano," *Estudios centroamericanos* 30:322–323 (agosto-septiembre, 1975), 419.

[16] Though the language I use here is the traditional Roman Catholic theological language, this understanding is also embraced by the Protestant tradition though different terminology is used. See, Rahner and Vorgrimler, "Grace," 196–200.

[17] This point is clear in 2 Corinthians 5:18–20. This is also one of the points René David Roset makes so clear in his 1981 article.

[18] Aloysius Pieris, *An Asian Theology of Liberation* (Maryknoll, N.Y.: Orbis Books, 1988), 24–31.

[19] See Antjie Krog, *Country of My Skull: Guilt, Sorrow and Forgive-*

ness in the New South Africa (South Africa: Random House, 1998), particularly Chapter 10.

[20] Robert J. Schreiter, *Reconciliation: Mission and Ministry in a Changing Social Order* (Maryknoll, N.Y.: Orbis Books, 1992), 11.

[21] The violence between the Israelis and the Palestinians rages on while I write this article. Yesterday a Palestinian woman who lives in a border town in Gaza spoke in her broken English with a USA television reporter. "The people who want revenge have a little heart," she said, gesturing with her hand to show the tiniest of space between her two fingers. Behind her one could see her children playing with their little friends.

[22] The importance of giving up any desire for revenge is striking in the following event. In 1996 the Cuban air force shot down two small civilian airplanes belonging to a Cuban exile group, "Brothers to the Rescue." Though the families of the four men killed have pursued action against the Cuban government in the USA courts, one of the families has taken the position of not asking for nor accepting any monetary compensation for the death of their son. In part their reason might be not to "put a price" on the life of their dead relative. But part has also to do with the desire not to seek revenge.

[23] In the history of my own country, Cuba, there is an important example of the need not to seek revenge. The "*Manifiesto de Montecristi*," Cuba's declaration of independence from Spain, written by José Martí, "the father of the country," on March 25, 1895, twice speaks against vengeance. The document insists that those declaring war have been cleansed of hatred and have a sense of indulgence regarding Cubans who are timid or who are mistaken. It also mentions that during the war and once it is over they will be merciful with those who repent. See Carlos Ripoll, *José Martí: Antología Mayor* (New York: Editorial Dos Ríos, 1995), 59–61.

[24] Desmond Tutu, *No Future without Forgiveness* (New York: Doubleday, 1999), 257–282.

[25] I heard Sister Helen Prejean, a nun who works with persons on death-row and who opposes capital punishment, make this point in a public lecture a few years ago. See Helen Prejean, *Dead Man Walking: An Eyewitness Account of the Death Penalty in the USA* (New York: Random House, Vintage Books, 1994).

[26] This is the understanding of Archbishop Tutu that has become entrenched in large areas of the South African society and that has guided the work of the South African Truth and Reconciliation Commission.

[27] The *Sunday Times* of Capetown, South Africa, December 6, 1998, carried an article entitled, "Forgive the torturer, not the torture," writ-

ten by Wilhelm Verwoerd, lecturer in political philosophy and applied ethics at Stellenbosch University. The article talks about Ashley Forbes, a black South African, tortured by Jeffrey Benzien, who before "The Truth and Reconciliation Commission" of that country had "publicly demonstrated his notorious 'wet-bag' torture technique." The article says that it was "Forbes's choice to put aside legitimate feelings of anger and humiliation and thus, 'get on with the rest of my life.'" The article goes on to say, "Sometimes victims are asked to forgive for the sake of perpetrators, to release the wrongdoers from their burden of guilt. That is an important part of forgiveness, but not the whole story. . . . Forbes shows that forgiveness should be encouraged, perhaps in the first place, as an antidote to the poison of unresolved bitterness and repressed resentment, as a call to those violated to liberate themselves from the prison of victimhood — for the sake of themselves, their children and the rest of society. . . . A powerful emotional reason for resisting forgiveness is because it is seen as diminishing the seriousness of violations. Forgiveness becomes a sign of disrespect to those who have been violated. . . . Archbishop Desmond Tutu . . . is requesting nobody to forgive the gross human-rights violations of the past. It is a call to recognise the humanity of 'perpetrators' even if their humanity is hidden behind a wet-bag. . . . Those who suffered and continue to suffer are given the moral first place they deserve. The truth commission process flows from that commitment."

28 See Antjie Krog, *Country of My Skull*, 23–25.

29 Renny Golden, *The Hour of the Poor, the Hour of the Women* (New York: Crossroad, 1991), 17.

12

Identifícate con Nosotras

A *Mujerista* Christological Understanding

The *Kyrie Eleison*, a well-known prayer heard for centuries in the Roman Catholic Eucharistic liturgy, becomes a very different cry for mercy when it is uttered by those of us who are marginalized by society and suffer discrimination. A petition to an almighty and sovereign God to show mercy and forgive us our sins is transformed, in the *Misa Nicaragüense*, into a cry to Christ Jesus to identify himself with us and to be in solidarity with us instead of with those who destroy us.[1] Vague requests for mercy become concrete: Christ Jesus, acknowledged as Lord but also addressed as a personal God—*Dios mío*—is asked to stand with us, to become one with us.[2] This request for him to join our ranks is not born out of a desire for personal solace and comfort. A private need would not result in a call for solidarity, which usually refers to a public stance taken to identify with and support others. What is at stake in this *Kyrie* is the need of the community for peace, the opposite, in this song, of being "squelched and devoured" by the oppressive class.[3]

Elaborating a *Mujerista* Christology

This prayer, this song, points to the *mujerista* understanding that theology is a praxis—that is, reflection-action that in a spiraling motion integrates the faith of Hispanas/Latinas with the struggle for liberation-fullness of life in which we are engaged in our daily living. Our religious beliefs direct and support action on behalf of liberation for ourselves and our people. Our actions, in turn, lead us to clarify what we believe: what it means for us in our everyday struggles against oppression to believe, for example, in Jesus as the Christ. *Mujerista* theology, recognizing the importance of religious beliefs in the lives of Hispanas/Latinas, seeks to elaborate a theology that does not ignore the political and social realities of our life as a marginalized community within the USA. This reality of being marginalized within the most powerful country in the world nowadays is not simply a matter of location, of our mailing address. The marginalization of Hispanas/Latinas plays a substantial role in our theological-ethical enterprise and provides key elements to our theological praxis. Who is God for us who are pushed to the margins? How do we encounter God at the margins? Who is Christ for us, and how do we present Christ from the margins and to the margins?

What Hispanas/Latinas believe about Christ is not a matter of an applied doctrine, an application of what the churches teach. Our Christology is a praxis: what we believe about Christ comes out of our reality as marginalized Hispanas/Latinas, which is one of struggle for fullness of life. What we believe is, at the same time, a force that sustains this struggle. It is from within this praxis that *mujerista* Christology seeks to answer the question Jesus posed to his disciples, "Who do you say that I am?" (Mark 8:29). Jesus' insistence on a personal answer from his disciples makes clear that what we must elucidate are not christological dogmas but rather the meaning Jesus has for Hispanas/Latinas in our daily lives at the beginning of the twenty-first century. Our Christology, as all Christology whether stated or not, is a historical one. We know Jesus is with us because he joins us in our struggle for liberation-fullness of life.

Our insistence on the historical character of mujerista Christology and on Christology as a praxis, leads to a third understanding: Christology, as is true of all religious beliefs, follows our ethical stance. In other words, human beings, previous to any religious thinking, form ideas about what is right and what is wrong, or, in religious language, what is sin and what is grace. Our consciences begin to be shaped well before the so-called "age of reason," usually set around the age of seven. From a very early age we begin to learn from those around us what is good and what is bad. By the time we begin to include the simplest understanding of Jesus in our thinking, the main patterns by which our consciences judge what we are supposed to do are already formed. These understandings "shape" what we believe about Jesus.[4] In other words, when we begin to explicitly think religiously, we ascribe to Jesus or to God or to whatever concept of the divine we are beginning to form, the ideas we have elaborated about the good. At the personal level answers to questions like, "Who is Jesus?" "What does Jesus want me to do?" "What would Jesus do if he were here?" are not based on our knowledge of Jesus. It is the other way around: the answers we give these questions reveal to us what it is that our consciences are telling us. In this sense, what we believe about Jesus is a mirror for our consciences. For Christians this translates into the claim that, regardless of our protests to the contrary, belief follows practice, belief follows the patterns of goodness that have been deeply sown in our hearts and minds and that guide our daily lives.

A fourth understanding of *mujerista* theology is made explicit by the old custom of melding "Jesus" and "Christ" into one word: *Jesucristo*. The traditional understanding among theologians, although not among the common folk, is that "Jesus" refers to the historical person and "Christ" to what the church has taught us to believe about that Jesus. I propose that we take seriously the fusion of the two "names" and that we abandon the thought that we can find in the past what we need to know and believe today about Jesus and about Christ. In *mujerista* Christology we try to move away from the naïve understanding that we can historically reconstruct who Jesus was, how he understood himself, and what he did. We also try to move away from making normative those christological formulae from the past so heavily laden with historical and cultural understandings. We are indeed respectful of church teaching about Christ, but that is not our emphasis. The custom of folding into one word the name Jesus and the title Christ—*Jesucristo*—provides *mujerista* theology with the creative space needed to elaborate a Christology that responds to what Hispanas/Latinas believe about the message of

Jesus of Nazareth. It does so precisely because it sustains and motivates us in our everyday struggles against what limits liberation-fullness of life and for all that promotes justice and peace.

In this we follow the established tradition of the Gospel writers who created narratives about Jesus that responded to the questions and issues that were alive in the communities for which they wrote. Our attempt to elaborate a *mujerista* Christology is part of our work to provide Hispanas/Latinas with a religious narrative that can help us not only to understand our Christian faith but also to deal with the struggle for liberation-fullness of life that we face everyday. This struggle calls us to be creative, to offer explanations of who *Jesucristo* is for us in ways that have a certain logical flow and coherence. We have always refused to spend time deconstructing theological approaches or church teachings. The precariousness of our communities is such that we feel an urgency to create understandings that are useful in the work of liberation rather than thinking about what was conceptualized in the past. *Mujerista* Christology listens carefully to the voices of grassroot Hispanas/Latinas knowing that they are admirably capable of reflecting on what they believe and of explaining it in ways that contribute to liberation-fullness of life.

Our Christology revolves around three key elements that emerge from the daily praxis of Hispanas/Latinas in the USA, that is, they are rooted in the way Hispanas/Latinas face everyday struggles for their fullness of life. First, Hispanas/Latinas hunger for deep, personal relationships to sustain us in our daily struggles. Second, we need God to help us take care of our people, not expecting God to solve our problems but rather asking God to be our faithful companion in our struggles. Finally, we know that only in so far as we become part of God's family can we really say that we believe in *Jesucristo*.

Familia de Dios—The Kin-dom of God

The concept of the kingdom of God has undergone many transformations since it was first conceived by the Jewish people. Initially it was a concept based on the kingships that had enslaved them, Egypt and Babylon. It was the Iranian influence that provided "a transcendent feel, with the introduction of the end time, the idea of justice, and right living, which would bring about the security of the nation [Israel]."[5] Originally this understanding of transcendence did not project the "kingdom"—a new world order—into a different-world reality. "However, by the end of the first century C.E., a clear distinction emerged between this world, its end, and the setting in place of a new world order. For many people things that were believed to be possible in this world became transposed onto another place and time that were eternal and unchanging."[6] This change in the way the kingdom of God was understood actually added to the despair about its realization in this world that followed the destruction of the Temple in Jerusalem in 70 C.E. Furthermore, projection of the realization of the kingdom of God into the next world allowed it to be conceived of as achievable only by God and achievable once and for all. "The psychic landscape changed significantly from a circle of hope, committed action, change, and back to hope for divine intervention and unchanging absolutes."[7] As a result, from then on, the kingdom of God became an excuse for "nonengagement with the real stuff of life."[8]

Unfortunately the split this created between this-world reality and the kingdom of God (kidnapped from this world and taken to a world yet to come) became useful for those in charge of the newly developing church. They determined the meaning and correct interpretation of all that was "Christian." When in 313 C.E. the Edict of Milan legalized Christianity, the new religion began to gain political and economic power in addition to the religious and moral power over consciences it already held. The church became the only access to the kingdom of God in the world to come and its most powerful symbol in this world. Placing itself above the reality of this world and insulating itself against the vast majority of its members, the church came to link its life with the life of the established order, which it grew to resemble. Though it repeatedly claimed that its role was only religious, the church throughout its history has legitimized and supported those who have social, economic and political power. Historically it has become more and more a tool in the hands of the dominant groups in society. And the image and understanding of Christ have been affected sadly in the same way. Historically the image of Christ proclaimed by the church has seemed to float above human reality, nullifying the most precious meaning of the incarnation of God in Jesus of Nazareth. Christ little by little came to resemble monarchs and pontiffs with absolute power to whom the people only had access on bended knees. This Almighty Lord Jesus Christ was more like a feared judge demanding ever more from the people than he was like a loving mother welcoming and nurturing her children. It was only with the Second Vatican Council in the second half of the twentieth century that one finds meaningful movement in redrawing the meaning of the church and of the kingdom of God, with its great implications for Christology. The most relevant statement from the Second Vatican Council in reference to the relationship between the natural order and the supernatural order where the "kingdom of God" had been ensconced is found in *Gaudium et Spes*, no. 39. The text does not go far enough in relating the growth of the kingdom of God to temporal progress but, at least, the conciliar document affirms "a close relationship between temporal progress and the growth of the Kingdom. . . . Those engaged in the latter not only cannot be indifferent to the former; they must show a genuine interest in and value it."[9] This step taken by Vatican II opened the door for considering theologically "temporal progress as a continuation of the work of creation" and, therefore, for seeing temporal progress as linked to the redemptive act of the life and mission of Jesus of Nazareth.[10]

The theological understanding that "the human work, the transformation of nature, continues creation only if it is a human act, that is to say, if it is not alienated by unjust socio-economic structures,"[11] developed by Latin American liberation theology, opens the possibility for rescuing the "kingdom of God" from the supernatural order. Various liberation theologies elaborated in the second half of the twentieth century make it clear that "kingdom of God" was the expression that Jesus used as the central metaphor for talking about his mission, for which he died on the cross. Every aspect of the life of Jesus related by the Gospels, every word ascribed to Jesus by the Gospels gyrates around the kingdom of God. In what he did and in what he said Jesus was always announcing the kingdom of God or denouncing the anti-kingdom, that is to say, the conditions that not only could not be present in the kingdom of God but that make the realization or coming of the kingdom of God impossible. Liberation Christologies, on the whole, tend to make of Jesus the "definitive mediator of the Reign of God," claiming that he was "the person who proclaims the Reign, who posits signs of its reality and points to its totality."[12] To claim that Jesus was the definitive mediator, they have to posit that who Jesus was and what Jesus said and did are central to the kingdom of God. But much more, it is not only a matter of Jesus and his life being central but also that they are essential. The claim is often made that only Jesus could grasp and live to the fullest what it means to be human. His role as definitive mediator, then, is not outside the realm of what is human but rather is "the fullness of the human."[13] And this is precisely what we mean when we say that Jesus is Christ: that he lived to the fullest his humanity and the mission that it entailed. Because what Jesus did in reference to the kingdom of God is within the human realm, other persons can also be mediators, can also be Christs. As a matter of fact, to understand what Jesus meant by the kingdom of God and how he worked to make it a tangible reality, we have to understand that he stood in line with many other mediators of the kingdom, from Adam and Eve to his own mother, Mary of Nazareth. Furthermore, to understand Jesus and the kingdom of God he proclaimed with his life and deeds, we have to look carefully at the mediators of the kingdom that have lived since Jesus, who have committed themselves irrevocably to the kingdom of God, from the early men and women who were deacons, martyrs and confessors, to contemporary witnesses of the faith martyred or still alive.

All who commit themselves to proclaim with their lives and deeds the kingdom of God are mediators of the kingdom. Each and every one of us has the capacity and possibility of being another Christ, an *alter Christus*. Whether we are mediators of the kingdom of God does not have to do with our capacity to be mediators but rather with the choices we make in our lives, with our commitments, and also with the circumstances in which we live. Our mediation of the kingdom of God is related to the fact that understanding reality always includes dealing with reality. The kingdom of God does not exist apart from us who believe in it, nor does it "pass" through us without being affected by us and affecting us as well. All reality that we come into contact with is changed in some way by how we deal with it or ignore it because all that we do helps "to sustain a conception of the world or to modify it."[14] And the same is true of the kingdom of God.

How does *mujerista* theology deal with the understanding that Jesus was the definitive mediator of the kingdom of God? If this claim indicates that no one can do it as he did it, then we can only agree, for no one can be someone else or do what others do the way they do it. But we can likewise claim that no one else, including Jesus, can do what each of us can do in mediating the kingdom of God. In this sense each of us is unique, as Jesus was. Each of us also mediates the kingdom of God in an essential way and in a way that would not happen without us. This is so because each and every one of us is an image of God, an *imago dei:* each and every one of us carries seeds of divinity that make who we are capable of being and what we are capable of doing essential to the unfolding of the kingdom of God. This is precisely one of the key reasons why we can rescue the kingdom from the other world and incarnate it once again in our midst. This is one of the most important reasons why we see our struggles in this world as part of the overall work of God's creation. It continues in us and with us.

In the first-century Jewish world the metaphor of kingdom was the best way Jesus and his early followers found to indicate how people could encounter a benevolent God, one who would rule in their favor and for their sake. Kingdom was the best way in which they could talk about what values were determinant factors in the life of Jesus' followers. But in today's world the metaphor of the kingdom has become irrelevant because the reality that grounds the metaphor, actual kingdoms, rarely exists any more. Thus, the reference point of the metaphor is foreign to the experience of vast numbers of persons. For this reason alone church officials and theologians should use a different expression to signify the purpose of Jesus' life and mission. However, there is more. The metaphor of kingdom is not only irrelevant; as it has traveled through time, it has lost much of the meaning it had for Jesus and his early followers, often providing room for anti-kingdom values. In *mujerista* theology we believe that the metaphor of kingdom is not appropriate since obviously it refers only to male sovereigns and reinforces once more the male image of God, still the most prevalent one in the church. In *mujerista* theology we believe kingdom is an ineffective and dangerous metaphor for it suggests an elitist, hierarchical, patriarchal structure that makes possible and supports all sorts of systemic oppressions. Given this reality, one of our tasks is to suggest other metaphors that speak cogently and effectively to twenty-first century persons.

To change root metaphors, one has to go into the content of the original one: what were the values ensconced in the metaphor kingdom of God when Jesus and his early followers used it? It was Jesus' way of speaking about *shalom*, about fullness of life. *Shalom* was not a private reality that each individual had to find or construct. Rather, *shalom* was a reality for which people needed to work together. Therefore Jesus made love of neighbor central to life in the kingdom of God. Love is communal, the task of a people and not solely of individuals. *Shalom*—fullness of life—then, is the value at the heart of the metaphor that Jesus used and therefore has to be the central value in any metaphor we use to talk about Jesus' understanding of his life and mission. Today, in *mujerista* theology, *shalom* goes by the name of liberation—a holistic liberation that happens at all levels of life: socially, politically, personally, spiritually.[15]

In *mujerista* theology we suggest replacing "kingdom" with "kin-dom." We suggest moving from a political metaphor to which we have hardly any way of relating to a more personal metaphor that lies at the core of our daily lives. The idea of kin-dom of God, of the family of God, we suggest, is a much more relevant and effective metaphor today to communicate what Jesus lived and died for. This suggestion of the kin-dom of God is in many ways a response to the ongoing concern for the loss of family values and the loss even of a true sense of family in present-day society. Kin-dom of God as the core metaphor for the goal of Jesus' life will help us to reconstitute our sense of family. Moreover, the picture of kin-dom of God that Jesus gives us is a broad one that has to do not exclusively with blood-relatives but also with those who are united by bonds of friendship, of love and care, of community. *Mujerista* theologians bemoan the loss of family but we do not bemoan the loss of what has been called the traditional nuclear family. This so-called traditional nuclear family represents a very private and individualized group more set on defining and protecting its boundaries than in relating and welcoming all those that make life possible and pleasant for its members. The traditional nuclear family is a patriarchal setting where the man is considered the head, the one (perhaps the only one) most capable of representing and defending the family, of guiding and deciding for the family. This is why it is so difficult for society to imagine a family without a man or without a woman to complement the man. This is why we seem incapable of imagining same-sex parents or other than a biological parent carrying out the responsibilities of parenting. The traditional nuclear family in this highly technological industrial period in the USA in the first years of the twenty-first century is a family where relationships are less important than production and accumulation of capital and where if children are not better off economically than their parents, it is presumed that the family has failed. In *mujerista* theology we do not bemoan the disappearance of the traditional nuclear family.

The sense of *familia* that we have in mind when we talk about God's family, the kin-dom, is one in which a true sense of home exists, a sense of belonging and being safe to be and become fully oneself. *Familia* provides for us a sense of unity and cohesiveness that promotes a healthy sense of self-identity and self-worth so important for the development of the person. *Familia* for us "is the central and most important institution in life."[16] Whether personally *familia* is a life-giving structure for us, or unfortunately not a valuable one for whatever reason, *familia* is one of the key markers of our Latina communities. *Familia* is a marker not only of our position in life but also provides a clear indication of how we face life. *Familia* for us is a duty but also, for most of us, it is a never-failing support system. From a very young age, Latinas begin to understand that because of our families we do not have to face the world alone. We are also taught that precisely because the *familia* stands with us, we have a moral responsibility to each of its members who have invested so much in us by claiming us as their own. Who we are and what we do have personal repercussions for them. It is in the midst of *familia*

and because of *familia* that at a very young age we are introduced to the ethical world of responsibilities and obligations, a
world where one is because one is in relationship to others. In
our families we learn that persons are more important than ideas
and that, therefore, we have to take time and care to cultivate
relationships.

Hispanas/Latinas' sense of *familia* is an expansive and broad
one, extending into the community in a formal way. Through
the institution of *compadrazgo* and *comadrazgo* a system of relationships is established between godparents and their godchildren and the parents of their godchildren. But this system reaches
beyond religious occasions, such as baptisms and confirmations,
to secular activities and enterprises. Sponsors of dances, businesses, and sports teams are called *madrinas* (godmothers)
and/or *padrinos* (godfathers) for they not only provide monetary support but also supply vital connections with others to protect and promote the wellbeing of the organizations they sponsor.
Compadrazgo and *comadrazgo* create and sustain an effective
infrastructure of interdependence that has the family at the center and extends family values such as unity, welfare and honor in
all directions into the community.

Familia relies on interdependence, not subsuming the person
but making one realize that the members of our families enable
us to be who we are. *Familia* provides the security needed to
extend ourselves into the community and form the kind of personal relationships that are vital to us without losing our sense
of self. In our families we learn that "as in a prism, . . . reflection
is also a refraction . . . [and that] the identity of the 'we' does
not extinguish the 'I'; the Spanish world for 'we' is *'nosotros,'*
which literally means 'we others,' a community of *otros* [and
otras], or others."[17]

It is true that Latina families are not perfect and that some of
its characteristics are misguided and can cause damage to its
members. We are not setting up Latina families and their relationships as the criteria for the biblical *shalom*. We are simply
insisting on the need to change the metaphor traditionally used
to refer to what Jesus' life and mission was all about. Kin-dom
of God points to what many would say is the central institution
of all societies. Kin-dom embraces understandings and values that

are intrinsic to liberation-fullness of life. To create and sustain an institution where we can be ourselves in a safe way, where our wellbeing is of primordial importance, where a new order of relationships excludes all exploitation and abuse—this is indeed the kind of family all persons would welcome, and relate to goodness, to blessedness, to God.

To the question "Who do you say that I am?" Hispanas/Latinas answer Jesus, "You are my brother, my sister, my mother and my father, my grandmother, aunt, uncle, *comadre* and *compadre*, who stands with me and who struggles with me. You are amazingly special to me because I am amazingly special to you. You are my big brother protecting me, and you are my little sister whom I protect. You are my husband, my wife, my partner, my significant other for whom I am precious and who loves me unconditionally. You and I are family, Jesus. What more can you be for me? What more do you want me to be for you?"

Jesucristo Me Acompaña Siempre— Jesus Christ as Faithful Companion

In the kin-dom of God faith in *Jesucristo* rests squarely on the belief that, supported and encouraged within *familia*, Hispanas/Latinas can begin to live in a different manner, in a just and loving way. Such a *familia* is open and welcoming of all, even though some may choose to exclude themselves. *Jesucristo* and the other Christs of the family are committed to live into the future reality: we are willing to work as hard as we can to establish a way of life which does not erase differences but considers them enrichments so that all can be part of the kin-dom of God. This preferred way of life is not a preconceived notion but rather a path that we create as we travel together. Cutting this path through the intricacies of life, both at the personal and at the sociopolitical level, struggling for justice and liberation in every aspect of our lives, so that everyone can live fully—that is what salvation is all about. What we learn from *Jesucristo*, our oldest sister and little brother, is that salvation is the responsibility of this whole family. Yes, if we truly believe that the purpose of Jesus' life and mission was to begin to create the kin-dom of God, then we can embrace the notion that salvation is not the exclusive task of *Jesucristo*. It is the task of all of us who have Christ as our last name. Allow me to give you an example from the world of Hispanas/Latinas' popular culture of what salvation looks like, of what belonging to and extending the kin-dom of God is all about.

One of the central characters of a soap opera called *Bendita Mentira* (Blessed Lie), televised in the USA a few years ago, was Esperanza—the typical long-suffering mother who sacrifices everything for her children.[18] What is important to note was the interpretation Esperanza herself gave to her actions.[19] She never talked about sacrificing herself for her children but rather always saw what she was doing as loving her children. She saw sacrifice as merely a side effect of what she did, something indeed present but not necessarily valuable. She continually talked about love and allowed her children to live their lives, regardless of all the trouble they got into, standing with them through thick and thin. Two things about Esperanza started me thinking about her as a splash of paint that we can use in our understanding of what it means to embrace the mission that Jesus died for. First, Esperanza confessed to killing the lover of her daughter, a crime she did not actually commit, because she wanted to spare her daughter, whom she thought guilty of the crime. "Greater love has no man [sic] than this, that a man lay down his life for his friends."[20] A famous lawyer defended Esperanza at her trial. He said to the judge that Esperanza's love for her daughter "*me reconcilió con la humanidad*"—"reconciled me with humanity." Is this not what salvation is about, about being reconciled with humanity? What else does it mean to be part of the *familia* of God? "Therefore, if anyone is in Christ, he is a new creation; the old has passed away, behold, the new has come. All this is from God, who through Christ reconciled us to himself and gave us the ministry of reconciliation; that is, in Christ God was reconciling the world to himself [sic], not counting their trespasses against them, and entrusting to us the message of reconciliation."[21]

In another episode of the *novela*, Esperanza's daughter talks with a friend. This daughter, for whom Esperanza had sacrificed so much, used to "hate her mother" but later realized all that her mother had done for her and came to love her. The friend asks Esperanza's daughter what made her change her attitude toward her mother. The daughter answered, *"Yo no sabía querer y ella me enseñó"*— "I did not know how to love and she taught me." The daughter then explained that Esperanza had taught her how to love by what she did, not by what she said. Is this not what salvation is about? Isn't salvation about loving neighbor without measure, loving neighbor not in word but in deed? "Jesus . . . having loved his own who were in the world, he loved them to the end. . . . By this all men [*sic*] will know that you are my disciples, if you have love for one another."[22] Didn't Esperanza behave like a most worthy member of the Christ family?

Is it heretical to say that salvation is not exclusively the task of Jesus? I do not think so. This understanding of being co-redeemers with Jesus is what "the following of Jesus" or "discipleship" means. In the context of the kin-dom of God, what does it mean to be disciples of Jesus? First of all, in *mujerista* theology we try to take seriously the intrinsic link that exists between what has traditionally been called the "object" of our faith and the "act of faith." As Christian believers we do not create the "object" of our faith but believe that the object of our faith is a gratuitous "self-bestowal on us" made by God. This gift of self made by God, however, remains inoperative or ineffectual unless it occasions an act of faith. Therefore, the fact that we believe, which itself depends on God's self-bestowal, "testifies to a reality believed in and is an existential help to understanding what the concrete content of this reality [in which we believe] is."[23] To understand God we need to believe. To be able to know enough about ourselves as members of the *familia* of God we need to be specific about what it means to believe.

Belonging to the *familia* of God, like belonging to any family, means being committed to the values and understandings specific to that family. This is why loyalty becomes such an important virtue in maintaining and enriching the links among family members. But family values are more than the mere transmission of what has been. Values exist principally as virtues; that is to say, values do not exist as abstractions but rather as practices. Without ignoring or denying totally what the values of the *familia* of God have been in the past and what these values are today, we believe that how they are effectively practiced is always in the process of being defined. This, of course, is rooted in our claim that all theology is historical. This claim that values are always in the process of being defined follows a central consideration of pastoral theology: the present situation has to be taken into account. The difference is that in *mujerista* theology we make concerns of the present operative not only at the level of pastoral care, at the level of implementation, but also at the level of understanding who God is and what God is about, that is, at the level of theology. In other words, our understanding of the practice of discipleship—what it actually means to say we are followers of Christ—informs our theology. How we live our faith is intrinsic to our Christian faith.

When one talks about a Christology that emerges from the practice of faith and the personal experience of being a disciple of Jesus, one may be accused of embracing a free-for-all and an everything-goes attitude. This criticism sets relativity over against what is absolutely right. However, in *mujerista* theology we do not understand relativity as non-commitment to what is right but rather as recognizing the centrality of struggling for liberation-fullness of life, in which faith and religion play a vital role in the theological enterprise. The kind of relativity we have adopted is a "responsible relativity,"[24] a way of dealing with reality that takes seriously everyday experience. For us Hispanas/Latinas being a disciple of Jesus means precisely to struggle to live each day in a way that promotes liberation-fullness of life and to become worthy members of the *familia* of God. This is why we insist on the fact that Christology follows ethics, that what we believe about Jesus follows how we conduct our lives. This is why when it comes to being followers of Christ, what we have in mind above all is the right way of acting and being instead of right belief. Again, it is not that belief is not important; it is rather that what we believe about Christ follows our practice of discipleship.

Responsible relativity then allows us to free ourselves from objective universals about the meaning of Christ that often have undergirded structures of oppression. It is precisely because responsible relativity recognizes the presence of subjectivity in all human thinking and knowing that we insist on the historicity of our christological understandings, unmasking so-called

objective understandings as being mere subjective pronounce-
ments of those who have the power to impose them as normative. Responsible relativity helps us to see that what we insist is
"the" truth is only one of the possible explanations of reality and
that the different explanations are not necessarily exclusive of
each other but often, on the contrary, agree with each other, at
least partially. This is why our christological understandings do
not necessarily eradicate traditional ones or those elaborated by
other communities. Responsible relativity also makes us be clear
about the fact that endorsing a certain version of Christology
demands accountability in specific and concrete ways for such a
version and the consequences it brings. Lastly, when it comes to
Christology, responsible relativity encourages the development
of understandings and beliefs that are not offensive to other communities. This makes it possible to have a common point of
reference that allows Hispanas/Latinas to join with other communities in the struggle for liberation. One thing is certain: our
stance regarding responsible relativity in Christology insists on
beliefs about Christ, salvation, the kin-dom of God, and discipleship that do not promote the liberation of some at the expense
of others.

Discipleship for us Hispanas/Latinas is a practice of faith
related to living as a worthy member of the kin-dom of God.
Discipleship has to do with belonging, and belonging is not a
static condition but rather an engagement in creating and sustaining relationships. Being family requires a certain way of being
and doing. From a *mujerista* perspective, the "how" of this being
and doing emerges from what it means to be a member of the
family of God as well as from what we have to contribute to this
family. In other words, it is in being family that we come to
understand what family is. We cannot know the *familia de Dios*
unless we throw ourselves wholeheartedly into being active members of the kin-dom of God. Christology deals with what it
means that *Jesucristo* is our sister and our brother; discipleship
deals with what it means that I am a sister or a brother of *Jesucristo*. It is only in our efforts to be in a sisterly or brotherly relationship with *Jesucristo* that this meaning takes flesh. "In other
words, it is in praxis, and not in the pure concept that the existence and reality" of the kin-dom of God appears and is known.[25]

What does discipleship consist of? What does being a member of the *familia de Dios* look like? It means being committed to liberation-fullness of life. It means insisting on non-objectifying relationships. It means being adamant about including others instead of seeking to exclude them. It means being *familia* first and foremost with the poor and the oppressed. If you are oppressed, what does it mean to be part of the *familia* of God? It means keeping hope alive—hope in the possibility of justice, hope in being able to be the agent of one's life, in being able to contribute to one's own fullness of life and the fullness of life of others in our *familia*.[26] But hope has to be grounded in actual possibilities or it becomes a destructive illusion. Often the poor and the oppressed have no way of making hope operative in their lives for there is no material reality in which to anchor it, no material reality that can sustain their hope and nourish it. For the poor and oppressed to be part of the *familia* of God means insisting at all times on their right to hope, to have others join with them in bringing about at least the most basic material conditions they need to be able to move from despair to hope. The poor and the oppressed contribute to making present the kindom of God in our world by insisting on the need to change radically oppressive structures instead of seeking to participate in them. And for the oppressors? What do the oppressors (and here we do well to remember that the vast majority of us are oppressors in some way or other) need to do to become worthy members of the *familia* of God? Radical conversion is what is called for. Today another word for radical conversion is solidarity with the poor and the oppressed. To be *familia* of God the oppressors have to come to understand that their privileges and well-being depend almost always on the misery and anguish of the vast majority of people in our world. To denounce such a stance and move away from it, oppressors have to realize the interconnections that exist among all human beings, and between human beings and the animal world and the biosphere that sustains us. Once this interconnection is understood, the hope of the poor and the oppressed becomes the hope of the oppressors: fullness of life for oppressors will not happen unless there is also fullness of life for the oppressed.

What role does *Jesucristo* play in all of this? *Jesucristo* together with the other members of the *familia* of God struggles to sustain the poor and the oppressed, to give them a reason to hope by working to create the material conditions they need to begin to move ahead in their lives. *Jesucristo* together with the other members of the *familia* of God struggle to make the oppressors among the family members and beyond understand that they are a threat to their own liberation; that no one will be able to experience fullness of life unless all are given what they need. *Jesucristo*, as other big sisters and little brothers do, cajoles, begs, encourages, demands, and cheers us on in our daily struggles for liberation. One of the most luminous understandings among Hispanas/Latinas about who *Jesucristo* is and what role he plays is that *Jesucristo* simply is with us in the midst of the ordinariness of life, that he simply walks with us. This is why among grassroot Hispanas/Latinas one rarely senses a crisis of faith, despite all the suffering and ills present in their personal lives and in our communities. *Jesucristo* is not thought of as a magician who solves or should solve all the problems we face and free us from all of our troubles. Repeatedly we hear from our *abuelitas*— grandmothers—and other older Hispanas/Latinas that what we need is not to be freed from the struggle but to be given the strength to face the harsh reality of our world. As long as we have the strength to struggle, *Jesucristo* is with us. What is primordial about our Christology is the kind of following of *Jesucristo* that is nothing else but walking with him because he walks with us. *Jesucristo* always accompanies us, and that is why he is the redeemer, the savior, the messiah, the Christ. And how do we know that he always accompanies us? Because we know he is *familia*. We are not alone. He is never alone.

Jesús Mío—Personal Relationship with the Divine

We were sitting in a big circle with grassroot Hispanas/Latinas discussing embodiment and sexuality. All of a sudden, Lola, one of the quiet ones in the group, spoke out of turn. In a hardly audible voice she told us a little about her intimate relations with the man who had been her common-law husband for many years. With her face wrinkled by pain and folding her body as if to protect herself, she finished by saying, *"Nunca tuvo para mí un gesto o una palabra de ternura"*—"he never had for me a tender gesture or a tender word." As she finished talking she lowered her eyes and folded her arms over her chest as if signaling her unwillingness to let anyone else ever hurt her again. She had been wounded to the core of her being by being denied tenderness, that mode of love that can only happen at the most intimate levels of relationship.

Last December I arrived early at my small church, which sits in the midst of a housing project in East Harlem. Originally it was an almost exclusively Puerto Rican community, but more and more Mexicans have been moving into "El Barrio," as this area is called. The priest had agreed to celebrate the feast of Our Lady of Guadalupe, the invocation used in Mexico for Mary, the Mother of Jesus. Mexicans consider themselves daughters or sons of Guadalupe, so it is very important for the community here in New York City to celebrate her day. For Guadalupe's feast, the smell and sight of red roses filled the church. I sat where I could watch the people going up to the side altar where a picture of Our Lady of Guadalupe had been placed. A continuous procession of people made their way up to the altar, knelt, and lifted their eyes to the image of the Virgin. Anyone could see the love for Guadalupe that was reflected in their gestures, in the respect of their demeanor, in the tenderness with which they gazed at Guadalupe's picture. I closed my eyes and tried to understand why Guadalupe is so important in the lives of these people who approached her that day to renew their love for her, their commitment to her as her children. All of a sudden it came to me. Guadalupe is an image of the divine that looks like the Mexican people: her features are those of the Mexican indigenous population. That divinity resembles them means that the divine is not so far removed from them, yes? Gradually I came to understand something very important that I confirmed later on with my friends in the church. Women are used to loving others, to caring for others. So, in many ways, this side of the relationship with Guadalupe was not exceptional. But, as I looked at a middle-aged woman holding on to three little ones while lifting her eyes to Guadalupe, I realized that the difference in this relationship from other relationships is that the people believe that Guadalupe does care for them. She loves them back with the tender love of a mother. These people might not be important to others but they know they are important to her. In our Latina culture, personal relationships are at the center of our lives, at the center of the institutions and organizations—like *familia*, for example—that we create and use in our daily lives. No matter what problem we have and despite the fact that in our highly industrialized society benefits depend on the bureaucracy, Hispanas/Latinas believe that the best way to proceed always is by contacting someone who has personal connections and can vouch for them. Hispanas/Latinas depend on relationships and thirst for deep connections with others not only because we need them as intercessors but also because we need them to be fully ourselves.

It is unthinkable for us Hispanas/Latinas to conceive God in any other way than as a person with whom we have or can have a deep, intimate relationship. Thinking of God as a force of nature or as an energy or power in the universe is not understandable to us and certainly leaves us cold. The divine for us is personal; the divine is incarnated time and again in Jesus, in Mary his mother, in the holy people of past generations that the church has proclaimed saints, in our ancestors, in the people who during their lives have worked for the benefit of that community. The divine is not far from us in the churches where we worship. The divine is with us at all times. This is why we wear medals with images of the divine, why we have images of the divine hanging from the rearview mirrors in our cars, why we have home altars crowded with statues of Jesus, Mary, the saints, and pictures of all those who have done good and, therefore, are connected to the divine. When asked, Hispanas/Latinas answer that, "of course," their dead *abuelitas* are not God, Our Lady of Guadalupe is not God, St. Martin de Porres is not God, St. Barbara is not God. But Hispanas/Latinas know and say that all of these people have access to the divine; that they share in the divine as *alteri Christi*—other Christs.

A few stories illustrate how these *alteri Christi* function for us. In a workshop with a group of Mexican and Mexican-American women in El Paso, I asked the women to whom they prayed in times of trouble. One of the *abuelitas* in the group blurted out, "To Guadalupe." When I asked her how come she did not pray to God, she said to me, "He is a man and he does not understand what happens to us women." Years later when I asked another group of women the same question in Bay City, Michigan, one of them assured the group that she prayed to God. Later that night she came to my room. "Earlier today I told you I prayed to God in times of trouble because I thought that was the right answer. But now I cannot fall asleep without coming to tell you that the truth is that I pray to Guadalupe." And she proceeded to tell me that when her family had a car accident on a slippery highway, as the car was about to hit a cement wall on the side of the road, she screamed, "*Virgen de Guadalupe*, protect my children." Then I think about my own prayers when I am in really difficult circumstances. I pray to my *abuelita*. Knowing how much she loved me and cared for me when she lived with me on this earth, I have no doubt that she helps me in countless ways from wherever she is with God.

The divine is with us and among us but it is so important to notice who is the divine for Hispanas/Latinas. The God whom the churches have proclaimed is an ominous God whose majesty and power confine Him [*sic*] to a pedestal. He is a God to whom adoration is due but from whom one can expect nothing but what is due to us because of our sinfulness. He is a God that demands like a stern parent. This God is in many ways controlled by the church, for the church insists that it alone can tell us who God is and what God is like.

In contrast to this far-removed God, Hispanas/Latinas find nothing but love and welcoming and help from our *abuelitas* and the saints. What about Jesus? Jesus is often seen only as God and, therefore, not too accessible to us. But Jesus is also the very human *Jesucristo* suffering on the cross who touches our hearts and who understands our suffering because he too has suffered. And this is the *Jesucristo* we turn to, the *Jesucristo* who walks with us. Often theologians chide us Hispanas/Latinas—and our Latin American sisters and brothers—for concentrating so much on the Jesus hanging on the cross. Pointing to our lack of understanding of the importance of the resurrection of Jesus, these theologians fail to understand the importance of the personal in the lives of Hispanas/Latinas. They fail to see that for a true relationship with Jesus or with anyone there has to be mutuality—and mutuality needs commonality to exist. It is precisely the Jesus who suffers as we suffer, who is vulnerable as we are vulnerable—that is the *Jesucristo* to whom we can relate.

In my church, on the right-hand-side wall toward the front, there is a huge cross on which hangs a bloody body of Jesus crowned with thorns. I have noticed how some people always get on the right-hand-side line for communion and simply stay there no matter how long that line is. I watch how each time they receive communion and, on the way back to their pews, they stop by the crucifix. Placing their hands on the nailed feet, they lift their faces to *Jesucristo*. *"Lo trato de consolar"*—"I try to comfort him"—one of the women said to me one day. She did not say much more, but I realized the importance for her of being able to do something for *Jesucristo*, the importance of being able to feel that she could take care of this *Jesucristo* who is her very own, her *"Jesús mío."*

Can we humans have true relationship with God? To do so we have to be able to be much closer to God than common church practice and theological explanations allow. The divine has to be much more approachable, and we have to struggle to be real members of the *familia* of God if we want to come close to the divine. And here is where the work for justice comes into play, starting for us at home. Hispanas/Latinas struggle for their families, to make life possible for their children, to take care of the elderly in their communities, and to find at least a tiny space for themselves to flourish. They believe themselves to be good in so far as they do this; they are good precisely in so far they take care of others.[27] This doing for others, being good, and being in a relationship with *Jesucristo* are very much intertwined. Though indeed the majority of Hispanas/Latinas would not express it this way, their relationship with *Jesucristo* and the other *alteri Christi* grounds their lives. Talking particularly to older Hispanas/Latinas, one senses this: how a profound relationship with the divine has transformed them, allowing them to see beyond what is observable, to counsel and comfort beyond their natural ability and expertise. Some of this has to do, undoubtedly, with the wisdom that experience brings, but I believe that much of this depends on their relationship with the divine.

Often objectified by society, often considered by exploitative husbands as cogs in a machine used to produce care and satisfaction for them, often not appreciated by their children who demand from them the material goods so valued by society, Hispanas/Latinas long for deep personal relationships. Often they have nowhere to turn but to the various expressions of the divine that have become so important in their lives. This relationship with the divine, which in turn makes it possible for them to be in relationship with themselves, is what gives Hispanas/Latinas the strength to struggle for justice for themselves and others; it is what gives them the wisdom to survive.

Hispanas/Latinas are very emotional. We feel deeply, and in our culture we are not required to hide our feelings. We are taught, by example more than by anything else, to honor our feelings, for we grasp intuitively early in life that feelings are "a source of imaginative insight" and a motivation for our daily struggles.[28] Emoting, expressing how we feel, is indeed central to the way we relate, for it is in feeling and in allowing ourselves to feel that we come to know more deeply than is possible with only our minds.[29] But if feelings are to carry us beyond what we can grasp intellectually, they have to be intense and passionate; and for passion to exist, one's emotions have to have resonance. Mutuality is an absolutely essential element of a true relationship. Outside the mutuality of true relationships passionate emotions can consume us and destroy us. Often, then, Hispanas/Latinas seek with the divine the passionate relationships they do not find with partners because we know that if we do not feel deeply, we are not living fully. In such relationships mutuality is essential, so it is not surprising that we conceptualize the divine in a way that allows for true mutuality to exist. "*Jesucristo* needs me," we Hispanas/Latinas tell ourselves. "He needs me to comfort him in his sufferings, he needs me to help him bring people to the *familia de Dios*. God knows I need him! I need *Jesucristo*, for I know that I am precious for him."

This is Hispanas/Latinas' way of admitting and insisting on the centrality of relationships, on the need we have for mutuality. The divine has to be accessible to us, *Jesucristo* has to understand us, and we have to be able to contribute to the understanding of who *Jesucristo* is in our world today. We turn to *Jesucristo* whom we love passionately for our salvation, to *Jesucristo* as "the source of creative, relational energy."[30] And frequently he is the only one with whom we can establish a true relationship in which we are not exploited but valued for who we are, a relationship that nourishes us, that saves us in a very personal and holistic way.

Living *Mujerista* Christology

That many questions in life go unanswered is one of the most important things I have learned from grassroot Hispanas/Latinas. Many questions are nothing more than dilemmas, inexorable conundrums, and illogical realities. We can only accept them as part of our daily lives, for we do not have the means to deal effectively with them. For us Hispanas/Latinas, *Jesucristo* is not the one who gives us answers but the one who sustains us when there are no answers. Perhaps *Jesucristo* is actually more present to us in the questions, for they often keep us reaching further, stretching our understandings, enabling us to hope and to commit ourselves more and more to liberation-fullness of life for ourselves and for those for whom we are responsible.

As a consequence of this way of looking at life and because of what *Jesucristo* means for Hispanas/Latinas, *mujerista* theology does not seek to provide answers but rather to help us to go deeper in our questions about God and the divine presence in our lives. There is no single answer to Jesus' question, "Who do you say that I am?" What we Hispanas/Latinas have and, therefore, what *mujerista* theology can offer, is some hint of who *Jesucristo* is, some markers along the way for those who are open to seeing them, markers that show us where and how *Jesucristo* is present to us and with us in our daily lives. Sometimes the only way to understand who *Jesucristo* is for us and how he is present in our lives is through stories. Three stories come to mind.

The story of Helen Prejean, a Roman Catholic nun who has spent a large part of her life ministering in the USA to prisoners on death row, is told in the book *Dead Man Walking*. She describes the day she was accompanying Pat Sonnier, a man in Angola Prison, thirty-six hours away from being executed, hoping for a stay. After praying with him, Helen said to Pat, "If you die, I want to be with you." He answered, "No. I don't want you to see it." Then she said to Pat, "I can't bear the thought that you would die without seeing one loving face. I will be the face of Christ for you. Just look at me."

Ivone Gebara, a leading Latin American ecofeminist theologian, told me this story. One evening, when Ivone was returning to her house in a poor neighborhood in Brazil, a woman who lived near and whose son was very sick stopped her and excitedly told her, "God visited me today." Ivone was surprised and started talking to the woman trying to find out what had happened. A neighbor had turned over to the woman the money she had earned that day so she could buy medicine for her sick son. For Ivone's friend this neighbor had become God, had become Christ. This generous neighbor did not merely "represent" Christ but was indeed Christ made present in a poor neighborhood of Brazil in our own days.

Not long ago in New York City, where I live, a mother, helped by the grandmother, poisoned her daughter and simply disposed of the little body in a garbage can. They did it, they said, because the little girl was possessed by evil spirits. While the city authorities looked for the girl's body in the city's garbage dump, I was having a profound crisis of faith. "Where is *Jesucristo*?" I kept asking myself. "Why did God abandon this innocent little girl?" Then I realized it: that little girl was *Jesucristo* nailed on the cross. In her murder, as in the murder of Jesus of Nazareth, "there is salvation and there is light."[31] That little nameless girl was indeed *Jesucristo*!

Notes

[1] The *Kyrie* is part of the section of the Mass that deals with confession and forgiveness.

[2] Carlos Mejía Godoy y el Taller de Sonido Popular, "Kyrie," in *Misa Campesina*.

[3] The words of the song are as follows: "Christ, Christ Jesus, identify yourself with us. Lord, Lord, my God, identify yourself with us. Christ, Christ Jesus, be in solidarity with us, not with the oppressive class that squelches and devours the community, but with the oppressed, with my people who thirst for peace."

[4] Tom Driver, *Christ in a Changing World* (New York: Crossroad, 1981), 21–24.

[5] Lisa Isherwood, *Liberating Christ* (Cleveland: Pilgrim Press, 1999), 133.

[6] Ibid.

[7] Ibid.

8 Ibid.

9 Gustavo Gutiérrez, *A Theology o f Liberation*, 2nd ed. (Maryknoll, N.Y.: Orbis Books, 1988), 99.

10 Ibid., 100–101.

11 Ibid., 101.

12 Jon Sobrino, "Systematic Christology: Jesus Christ, the Absolute Mediator," in *Mysterium Liberationis: Fundamental Concepts of Liberation Theology*, ed. Ignacio Ellacuría and Jon Sobrino (Maryknoll, N.Y.: Orbis Books, 1993), 441.

13 Ibid., 442.

14 Antonio Gramsci, *Prison Notebooks*, ed. and trans. Quintin Hoare and Geoffrey Nowell Smith (New York: International Publishers, 1975), 9.

15 I am always apprehensive when any list is drawn, for lists are almost always read as if the elements in them could be isolated one from the other. I want to insist on the fact that the struggle for liberation is a holistic struggle, that we cannot be liberated socially, for example, without being liberated personally—within ourselves (psychologically) as well as socially (in our personal relationships). I want to insist especially on the fact that "spiritually" is not a category set apart—that spiritual is intrinsic to the category marked "personally." Here by spiritual I mean simply that the struggle for liberation also has to do with how we relate to God, a God that lives and moves and is among us, in us, a God that is in the social, in the political as well as in the personal.

16 Roberto R. Álvarez, Jr., "The Family," in *The Hispanic American Almanac*, ed. Nicolas Kanellas (Washington, D.C.: Gale Research, 1993), 155. The claims Hispanas/Latinas make regarding family are in no way unique but that they are not unique does not mean that they are not specifically ours.

17 Roberto Goizueta, "*Nosotros:* Toward a U.S. Hispanic Anthropology," *Listening—Journal of Religion and Culture* 27:1(Winter 1992): 57.

18 "Soap opera" is the name given in the USA to theatrical plays televised Monday through Friday for several months. Women are the target audience for these *novelas*—novels—as they are called in Spanish. It is important to notice that because the target audience of the *novelas* in Spanish television are working-class Hispanas/Latinas—the most numerous group in the Latino population—Spanish *novelas* play at night instead of in the afternoon, when American soap-operas, geared to middle-class women who work in their homes, can watch.

19 I hope the "religious" tone of the title of the *novela* and of the name of the mother—Esperanza means hope—are not lost on the reader.

20 John 15:13, RSV.

21 2 Corinthians 5:18–19, RSV.

[22] John 13:1, 35, RSV.

[23] Sobrino, "Systematic Christology," 448.

[24] What I call "responsible relativism" is an adaptation of the ideas of feminist philosopher Lorraine Code. She does not use this phrase, but the treatment of this term presented here is influenced by Code's work. See Lorraine Code, *Rhetorical Spaces: Essays on Gendered Locations* (New York: Routledge, 1995), 185–207.

[25] Jon Sobrino, "Central Position of the Reign of God in Liberation Theology," in *Mysterium Liberationis*, 379.

[26] See Sobrino, "Systematic Christology," 461, n. 10.

[27] Ada María Isasi-Díaz and Yolanda Tarango, *Hispanic Women: Prophetic Voice in the Church*, 2nd ed. (Minneapolis: Fortress Press, 1992), 80–91.

[28] Ibid., 79. See Dorothy Emmet, *The Moral Prism* (New York: St. Martin's Press, 1979), 11.

[29] Mary Grey, *Redeeming the Dream* (London: SPCK, 1989), 87.

[30] Ibid., 97.

[31] Ibid., 375. "Then the poor can be theologized, posited as a *locus theologicus*, recognized as constituting a world in which the signs of the times occur. Now, one can even accept Isaiah's scandalous thesis: in the poor, in the crucified Servant, there is salvation and there is light."

Index

Of Related Interest

Orlando O. Espín and Miguel H. Díaz, editors
From the Heart of Our People
*Latino/a Explorations in Catholic Systematic
Theology*
ISBN 1-57075-131-5

"A must, not only in terms of the ongoing development
of U.S. Hispanic American theological thinking but also
in terms of the future direction of theological discourse
in general."—*Fernando F. Segovia*

Miguel H. Díaz
On Being Human
U.S. Hispanic and Rahnerian Perspectives
ISBN 1-57075-402-0

HISPANIC THEOLOGICAL INITIATIVE BOOK AWARD
WINNER

"A masterful presentation of U.S. Latino/a theologians'
contributions to anthropology." —*Orlando O. Espín*

"Our understanding of the human person, sin,
grace, and salvation will not be the same after
On Being Human."—*Peter C. Phan*

Please support your local bookstore, or call 1-800-258-5838.
For a free catalogue, please write us at

Orbis Books, Box 308
Maryknoll NY 10545-0308

or visit our website at www.orbisbooks.com

Thank you for reading *La Lucha Continues*.
We hope you profited from it.